Drug Abuse

Drug Abuse

A Special Interest Resource Guide in Education

Compiled by Sara Lake,
San Mateo Educational Resources Center

ORYX PRESS

Copyright © 1980 by The Oryx Press
2214 North Central at Encanto
Phoenix, AZ 85004

Published simultaneously in Canada

Printed and Bound in the United States of America

Library of Congress Cataloging in Publication Data

Lake, Sara.
   Drug abuse, a special interest resource guide.

   Includes index.
   1. Youth—United States—Drug use—Bibliography.
2. Youth—United States—Alcohol use—Bibliography.
3. Drug abuse—United States—Bibliography.
4. Alcoholism—United States—Bibliography. I. Title.
Z7164.N17L34   [HV5824.Y68]   016.3622'9   80-22516
ISBN 0-912700-72-6

Contents

Introduction

Although the flower children of the 1960s are no longer much in evidence, the problem of drug abuse has not gone away. Concern has shifted somewhat since that era: marihuana is seemingly more acceptable, while the harmful effects of "legal" drugs (alcohol, tobacco, prescription medication) are coming into focus and awareness is growing of the very dangerous new drug, angel dust. But drug abuse among school children is still a strong cause of anxiety among parents and a serious problem for the schools.

This resource guide attempts to survey the literature on drug abuse as a problem of the 1970s. It is limited to literature dated January 1975 through April 1980. It considers all types of products identified in the literature as drugs or abused substances: narcotics, alcohol, marihuana, tobacco, solvents, etc. It is focused on elementary and secondary age youth. Drug use by college students, a voluminous topic in itself, is mentioned only peripherally. Drug and alcohol abuse by two other groups, parents and educators, is covered, however, because of the impact it has on children.

The guide is divided into two major sections. The first part considers drug use/abuse as a social concern, although still with a focus on school age youth. The second part deals with drugs as a school concern, with particular attention to methods and materials for drug education. The following is a brief synopsis of individual chapters.

"Drug Usage Reports" cites local and national studies of drug usage patterns and trends, drug preferences, and attitudes toward drugs. It also presents some correlations of drug usage to other delinquent behaviors, and basic information on some abused substances: cocaine, angel dust, and solvents.

"Drug Usage in Special Populations" highlights use studies and abuse problems in specific groups—minorities, women, parents, and educators—as well as presenting some cross-cultural comparisons of drug-abuse patterns in different ethnic populations.

"Personal, Attitudinal, and Social Correlates to Drug Use" presents literature on the question, "What factors lead to, or contribute to, drug abuse?" Included here are (1) general social factors, such as television, life-style, crime, and society's attitudes and practices concerning cigarettes, alcohol, and drugs; (2) factors in the drug user's immediate environment, including community attitudes, religion, and,

particularly, the relative importance of parent and peer influence in encouraging or inhibiting drug abuse; and (3) personal factors such as self-concept, mental health, values, and personality traits.

"Medical Research on Drug Effects" deals with recent findings on such issues as alcohol, marihuana, and memory; the fetal alcohol syndrome; effects of parent's smoking on children's breathing; drugs and driving ability; and drug toxicity.

"Drug Rehabilitation Methods" contains citations on therapy techniques for adolescent drug abusers, including family therapy; treatment for children of alcoholics, who are themselves a high-risk group for alcohol abuse; and the controversy between abstinence or moderate drinking as the desirable outcome of alcoholism treatment.

"Drug Legislation" highlights some state and federal legislative issues, such as raising the legal drinking age and decriminalizing possession of marihuana. Also included are some impact studies from states which have either intensified or moderated drug-use penalties.

"Drugs and the Schools: Administrative Concerns" includes these topics: identification of student and faculty drug abusers; creation and enforcement of school drug policy; cooperation with community agencies and the law; and methods for evaluating drug programs, which include tests and scales.

"Drug Education: Perspectives and Approaches" contains examinations and critiques of various approaches to drug education, including scare tactics, knowledge transmission, values clarification, and the development of decision-making skills; and general views on the role and purpose of school drug education. Of particular interest is research on the long-standing concern that drug education may promote, rather than reduce, drug use.

"Drug Education: Inservice Training" describes programs and materials for the training of drug educators, both teachers and community workers, and presents studies on the efficacy of such training in altering teachers' knowledge of and attitudes toward drugs.

"Drug Education: Program Descriptions and Evaluations" cites actual programs, both within the schools and in cooperation with the community. Audiovisual instruction and peer teaching/counseling are two of the program types considered.

"Drug Education: Instructional Materials" includes information on courses, curriculum guides, media, and texts for drug education, both K–12 and for parent/community groups.

Throughout these chapters, bibliographies and resource lists are cited for further exploration of various topics.

Citations in this guide were selected through computer searches of 11 data bases: ERIC; Comprehensive Dissertation Index; National Technical Information Service (NTIS); Psychological Abstracts; Sociological Abstracts; Exceptional Child Education Resources; Child Abuse and Neglect; Social SciSearch; Public Affairs Information Service (PAIS); Magazine Index; and Excerpta Medica; as well as through manual searches of Education Index and the extensive library and information files of the San Mateo Educational Resources Center (SMERC).

Within each chapter, citations are arranged by document format: journal articles, microfiche documents, and books. Notation is made on those citations known to be available for purchase from a standard source. On selected journal articles, an order number prefaced with the letters "EJ" plus the notation "Reprint: UMI" indicates that a photocopy of the article may be purchased from:

Article Copy Service—CIJE
University Microfilms International
300 North Zeeb Road
Ann Arbor, Michigan 48106
(800) 521-3042

All cited microfiche documents have order codes and source acronyms, indicating their availability from one of four ordering sources, as listed below:

DC   University Microfilms
Dissertation Copies
P.O. Box 1764
Ann Arbor, Michigan 48106
(800) 521-3042

EDRS   ERIC Document Reproduction Service
P.O. Box 190
Arlington, Virginia 22210
(703) 841-1212

NTIS   National Technical Information Service
5285 Port Royal Road
Springfield, Virginia 22151
(703) 557-4650

SMERC San Mateo Educational Resources Center
333 Main Street
Redwood City, California 94063
(415) 364-5600 ext. 4403

Note: The preferred ERIC spelling "marihuana" has been used throughout the text of this book. However, in entry titles the original spelling ("marijuana" or "marihuana") has been preserved.

DRUGS AND SOCIETY

Drug Usage Reports

JOURNAL ARTICLES

1. **Alcohol Intoxication and Drug Use among Teen-Agers.** Wechsler, Henry. *Journal of Studies on Alcohol*. v37, n11, p1672–77, Nov 1976.

   A survey of 1,715 junior and senior high school students found that students who reported being intoxicated during the school year were more likely to report using marihuana, amphetamines, LSD, and other drugs than those who did not report being intoxicated.

2. **Angel Death.** Koper, Peter. *New Times*. v10, p46,48–52, Mar 20, 1978.

   This article discusses the effects and dangers of phencyclidine (PCP), its marketing and use as a street drug, and the lack of medical knowledge about it.

3. **Angel Dust: An Overview of Abuse Patterns and Prevention Strategies.** Petsonk, Carol A.; McAlister, Alfred L. *Journal of School Health*. v49, n10, p565–68, Dec 1979.

   Phencyclidine (angel dust, PCP) abuse has increased dramatically over the past several years. School officials are urged to become aware of the signs and symptoms of PCP intoxication. Prevention programs which address the actual situations of adolescents should be targeted at junior high school students. Honest appraisals of the hazards of the drug, when delivered by trusted peer leaders, can help students resist pressures to use hard drugs and may prove more effective than traditional drug education programs.

4. **Angel Dust—Not Heaven Sent.** Vourakis, Christine; Bennett, Gerald. *American Journal of Nursing*. v79, n4, p649–53, Apr 1979.

   Discusses the history and pharmacology of phencyclidine hydrochloride—angel dust—as well as use patterns; profiles of PCP users; and methods of primary, secondary, and tertiary prevention.

5. **Bibliography of the Solvent Abuse Literature.** Barnes, Gordon E.; Vulcano, Brent A. *International Journal of the Addictions*. v14, n3, p401–21, 1979.

   This unannotated, multilingual bibliography includes references from previous bibliographies prepared in this area, as well as recent references obtained primarily from *Index Medicus* and *Psychological Abstracts* through April 1978.

6. **Cocaine: Old Drug, New Problem.** Kegley, Charles F.; Thomas, John A. *Journal of School Health*. v47, n10, p600–02, Dec 1977 (EJ 176 525; Reprint: UMI).

   Legitimate medicinal uses of cocaine are listed, its potential and realized abuse noted, and its psychic dependence effects described.

7. **College Students and Alcohol: An Exploration of Observations and Opinions.** Scheller-Gilkey, Geraldine et al. *Journal of Alcohol and Drug Education*. v24, n3, p30–41, Spr 1979 (EJ 211 813; Reprint: UMI).

   Comparison is made between drinking patterns and opinions on alcohol consumption and family and social backgrounds of college students.

8. **A Comparison of Attitudes and Behavior of High School Athletes and Non-Athletes with Respect to Alcohol Use and Abuse.** Hayes, Robert Wayne; Tevis, Betty W. *Journal of Alcohol and Drug Education*. v23, n1, p20–28, Fall 1977 (EJ 174 598; Reprint: UMI).

   Analysis of a survey of senior high school students revealed significant differences between males and females, and between athletes and nonathletes in their attitudes and behaviors toward alcohol and drinking behavior.

9. **Drug and Alcohol Use, Delinquency, and Vandalism among Upper Middle Class Pre- and Post-Adolescents.** Levine, Edward M.; Kozak, Conrad. *Journal of Youth and Adolescence*. v8, n1, p91–101, Mar 1979.

   Survey findings indicated the use of alcohol and drugs among prepubertal and teenage students, and the involvement of both groups in theft and vandalism. The view advanced by the study was that deficient socialization and inadequate parenting, as well as peer group pressures and psychogenic factors, influenced these behavioral problems.

10. **The Drug Scene: A Student Survey.** Bachman, Jerald G. et al. *Science Teacher*. v45, n6, p27–31, Sep 1978. (EJ 191 229; Reprint: UMI).

    Recent surveys of drug use in the secondary schools indicate cigarettes, marihuana, and alcohol as being the three drugs most frequently used by male and female high school seniors in the class of 1977.

11. **Drug Use and Delinquent Behavior of Small Town and Rural Youth.** Forslund, Morris A. *Journal of Drug Education.* v7, n3, p219–24, 1977.

Findings are based on responses to a self-report type questionnaire administered to ninth- through twelfth-grade students at two high schools in Fremont County, Wyoming. Data indicate there is a significant relationship between drug use and commission of other forms of delinquent behavior for male and female students studied.

12. **Drug Use, Misuse, and Abuse Incidents among Elementary School Children.** Cohen, Stuart J. *Journal of Drug Education.* v6, n3, p247–53, 1976.

The purpose of this paper was to review recent drug use, misuse, and abuse incidents among elementary school children in order to emphasize the fact that the drug problem in society has spread rapidly.

13. **Drug Use Variations between Delinquent and Non-Delinquent Youth.** Ziomkowski, Laurence et al. *Intellect.* v104, n2367, p36–38, Jul-Aug 1975.

Thie report examines drug knowledge, help for drug problems, and the response of a sample of youths to a questionnaire on personal drug use.

14. **A Grand Jury Looks at Drug-Abuse among School Age Children.** *Contemporary Drug Problems.* v8, n1, p31–72, Spr 1979.

This article is the full text of a Presentment of the Sixth Essex County Grand Jury (1978 term), which was convened under the auspieces of the Superior Court of New Jersey to investigate drug use among school age children in Essex County. Included is testimony from school administrators, former students, and others, on the extent of drug activity at the schools; type of drugs used; marihuana as the most abused drug; and the impact of parent example, law enforcement, the media, and drug education on drug abuse. The report ends with the grand jury's recommendations for drug education and law enforcement.

15. **Growing Acceptance of Marijuana.** *USA Today.* v107, n2405, p5–6, Feb 1979 (EJ 207 616; Reprint: UMI).

Summarizes the latest report from an ongoing University of Michigan study of 17,000 high school seniors, "Drug Use among American High School Students, 1975–1977." Statistics on usage of and attitudes toward marihuana are presented, as are usage figures on other drugs, alcohol, and cigarettes.

16. **High School Pot Use Declines.** *Science News.* v117, n8, p121, Feb 23, 1980.

For the first time in more than a decade, marihuana use among US high school students appears to be falling off, according to a study by the University of Michigan's Institute for Social Research. From 1975 through 1978, regular marihuana use had risen from 6 percent to 11 percent. In 1979, however, this increase abruptly halted—a change the researchers attribute to increased public awareness of the potential hazards of daily or near-daily use.

17. **Illicit Drug-Use among Urban Adolescents—Decade in Retrospect.** Hein, Karen et al. *American Journal of Diseases of Children.* v133, n1, p38–40, Jan 1979.

Over the past decade (1967 to 1977), 76,000 adolescents were screened for a history and somatic signs of illicit drug use at a detention center for juveniles and at an adolescent inpatient unit of a university-affiliated hospital. Dramatic changes in the patterns of drug abuse are reported. Opiate use was prominent in the first half of the decade, with a peak in 1970 to 1971, and marihuana use was more prominent in the last five years. Inhalant abuse as represented by glue and halogenated cleaning fluids was documented only early in the decade, while the existence of stimulant and depressant abuse follows still other patterns over the decade. Hospital admissions for serious somatic complications of illicit drug use, namely, overdose, drug-related death, hepatic coma, detoxification, and viral hepatitis, were correlated only with trends in the use of opiates.

18. **Measuring Consequences of Drug and Alcohol Abuse among Junior High School Students.** Babst, Dean V. et al. *Journal of Alcohol and Drug Education.* v25, n1, p11–19, Fall 1979.

The present study attempted to determine the consequences of drug and alcohol abuse for junior high school students in one large New York City school. Students were asked whether they had missed school, had an accident, got shakes or depressed, or got in trouble with family or friends due to alcohol or drug use. Seven percent of all students had experienced at least one of these problems in the last six months. As expected, the more involved students were in alcohol and drug use, the more problems they experienced.

19. **Multiple-Drug Use among High-School Students.** Eisterhold, Martha J. et al. *Psychological Reports.* v44, n3, p1099–106, Jun 1979.

A survey of tobacco, alcohol, and marihuana use was completed by 309 high school students in a rural midwestern county. Frequencies of use of these drugs were similar to data obtained in urban coastal populations. Significant multi-drug-use patterns were identified. Most drug use began at ages 14 or 15 and occurred in social situations implicating social factors as primary determinants of adolescents' drug use.

20. **Multiple Drug-Use Patterns among a Group of High School Students: Regular Users vs. Nonusers of Specific Drug Types.** Seffrin, John R.; Seehafer, Roger W. *Journal of School Health.* v46, n7, p413–16, Sep 1976.

Although no cause-effect relationship can be shown, regular drug use seems to predispose one to further drug experimentation and use, while nonuse of a particular drug seems to predispose one to nonuse of other drugs. Use patterns of alcohol definitely appear to be different from all the other drugs investigated. It is the most widely used, yet the least related to the other drug-use patterns.

21. **National Survey of Marijuana Use and Attitudes.** *Journal of School Health.* v45, n9, p544–46, Nov 1975.

This 1974 survey, conducted by the independent Drug Abuse Council, indicates that 18 percent of Americans 18 and over have tried marihuana, and 8 percent are current users. Among teenagers, age 12–17, 14 percent have tried marihuana, and 5 percent are current users. The adult public is about evenly divided (39 percent to 40 percent) between desiring reduced criminal penalties for marihuana use and wanting marihuana laws made tougher.

22. **The Nature and Extent of Drug Use among Students at a Comprehensive Suburban High School.** Willson, John Paul. *Journal of Drug Education*. v9, n1, p11–20, 1979.

Offers a method of determining appropriate grade level placement of drug education in the school curriculum; describes the nature and extent of drug use among high school students and identifies variables which predict drug use. Freshman use was lowest; sophomore use increased by 72 percent in this sample of students. Upperclassmen changed in mode, but not amount, of use.

23. **New Look at Marijuana.** Gelman, David. *Newsweek*. v95, p42–46, Jan 7, 1980.

This article reviews data on the growing acceptance and use of marihuana by teenagers and even younger children; discusses the new antimarihuana crusade and the decriminalization debate; and summarizes research on the medical effects of marihuana.

24. **Patterns of Tobacco Use among Undergraduates at Harvard and Radcliffe Colleges.** Gould, Nadja Burns; King, Stanley H. *Journal of the American College Health Association*. v26, n5, p239–42, Apr 1978 (EJ 187 746; Reprint: UMI).

Data are presented from the classes of 1964 and 1965 at Harvard College and 1977 and 1981 at Harvard/Radcliffe and show a striking decline in the proportion of freshman students who smoke, from 22 percent smokers in the class of 1964 to 5 percent smokers in the freshman class of 1981. There is every reason to believe that this group of adolescents is responding to information about the dangers of tobacco smoking.

25. **Perceptions of the Use of Drugs—A Cross-Sectional Analysis.** Calhoun, James F. *Adolescence*. v11, n41, p143–52, Spr 1976.

Intensively surveys samples of specific groups (both students and adults) on their differential perceptions of the use of specific drugs or drug types by their own group and the other groups.

26. **A Perspective on Drinking among Teenagers with Special Reference to New York State Studies.** Barnes, Grace M. *Journal of School Health*. v45, n7, p386–89, Sep 1975.

The author reviews several nonstandardized, longitudinal studies and finds no evidence that the prevalence of alcohol use, intoxication, or problems associated with use is on the rise. Because findings indicate that most teenagers who drink do so occasionally and responsibly, she suggests that efforts be concentrated on the minority who are at risk of alcoholism.

27. **Prevalence, Sources and Uses of Tranquilizers among College Students.** Kleinknecht, Ronald A.; Smith-Scott, Janet. *Journal of Drug Education*. v7, n3, p249–47, 1977.

A survey of 344 college students revealed 36.71 percent reported having used minor tranquilizers. While some acquired tranquilizers by their own prescription, the vast majority used them from others' prescriptions or black market sources and used them for pleasure.

28. **Profile of Solvent Abuse in School Children.** O'Connor, Dennis J. *Journal of Child Psychology and Psychiatry*. v20, n4, p365–68, Oct 1979.

The author presents an overview on solvent abuse, commonly called "glue sniffing," among children and adolescents. He discusses types of solvents abused, possible motives for this practice, medical effects, and signs and behaviors which might indicate that a youngster is involved in solvent abuse.

29. **Propoxyphene and Phencyclidine (PCP) Use in Adolescents.** Schuckit, Marc A.; Morrissey, Elizabeth R. *Journal of Clinical Psychiatry*. v39, n1, p7–13, Jan 1978.

Trained interviewers utilized a structured research instrument to analyze drug-use patterns, personal and familial psychiatric problems, and social backgrounds of a consecutive series of 355 adolescents referred by courts to alcohol counselling and education centers in King County, Washington. Within this sample, 4 percent of the subjects used propoxyphene (Darvon) alone, 16 percent reported use of phencyclidine (PCP) alone, and 6 percent reported abuse of both substances. The data consistently reveal that the use of one of these more unusual substances is likely to occur in people with more antisocial, drug, and alcohol problems. Use of both drugs was associated with the most pervasive antisocial history, with over one-third of these subjects fulfilling strict criteria for the antisocial personality. The treatment and prognostic implications of these findings are discussed.

30. **A Six-Year Analysis of Patterns in Non-Medical Drug Use Behavior.** Toohey, Jack V.; Dezelsky, Thomas L. *Journal of School Health*. v48, n1, p672–79, Jan 1978 (EJ 176 588; Reprint: UMI).

The report presents a descriptive analysis of nonmedical drug use over a six-year period (1970–76) among college students enrolled in selected health science classes at five American universities. Information is provided on patterns of marihuana use; social values and marihuana; and patterns of amphetamine, alcohol, barbiturate, cocaine, LSD, and narcotics use.

31. **So Much for Cocaine and LSD—Angel Dust is America's Most Dangerous New Drug.** *People*. v10, p46, Sept 4, 1978.

In this interview, drug expert Steven Lerner answers basic questions about phencyclidine (PCP, angel dust) abuse: What it is and the seriousness of its effects.

32. **Teen Drinking Not on Upswing, Experts Say.** *Jet*. v56, p42, May 3, 1979.

Contrary to popular opinion, teenage alcohol use is not increasing, experts say. Dr. Morris E. Chafetz, president of the Health Education Foundation, and Dr. Howard T. Blane of the

University of Pittsburgh, report analysis of teen drinking surveys between 1941 and 1975 indicates drinking rose steadily from World War II to the mid-1960s, but remained fairly stable thereafter.

33. Teenage Alcoholism. *Forecast for Home Economics.* v25, n6, p42–43, Feb 1980.

This article provides a brief overview on the incidence of teenage drinking and drunkenness, with attention to relationships between alcohol and (1) driving, (2) medication, and (3) pregnancy. A number of resource agencies and educational materials are listed.

34. Three Year Follow-Up Drug Survey of High School Youth in a Typical Georgia School. Arthur, Gary L. et al. *Journal of Drug Education.* v7, n1, p43–52, 1977.

This is the third survey undertaken to assess changes in knowledge and attitudes concerning drugs among students from Georgia high schools. Results revealed 56 percent of the students possessed knowledge of the drug culture and 3 percent had tried hard drugs, with none being regular users.

35. Usage Patterns of Nondrug Alternatives in Adolescence. Barnes, Caroline Purcell; Olson, James N. *Journal of Drug Education.* v7, n4, p359–68, 1977.

This study identifies specific nondrug alternatives most used to achieve a specific mood or state of consciousness alteration. Analysis showed social, physical, and risk-taking activities were used most frequently to achieve positive states and distracting activity, discussion with friend, and personal contemplation were used most frequently to reduce negative states.

MICROFICHE

36. Adolescent Drinking in Two Rural Areas of Mississippi: 1964 and 1975. Hampe, Gary D. Aug 1976, 33p; Paper presented at the Annual Meeting of the Rural Sociological Society (New York, August 26–29, 1976) (ED 127 083; Reprint: EDRS).

The study examined the increase of drinking from 1964 to 1975 among teenagers enrolled in two high schools in different socio-cultural rural areas of Mississippi. The sample was composed of students in two high schools located in a "wet" county and a "dry" county. A questionnaire was administered to 525 students in 1964 and 793 in 1975. Both years, participation was voluntary and respondents completed the questionnaire in small groups of 25 to 40. The dependent variable, "drinker," was considered to be a regular user of alcoholic beverages. Three types of independent variables were used to measure the amount of change by social categories of adolescent drinkers: sociodemographic factors (sex, race, age, and socioeconomic status); religiosity; and parental and peer influences. Findings included: 60 percent of the respondents in 1975 were classified as drinkers compared to 37.5 percent in 1964, an increase of 22.5 percent; increase in the proportion of drinkers occurred by sex, race, age, socioeconomic status, religious behavior, parental attitudes, and peer influences; the largest increases were for Whites, males, and those in the youngest age group; and religious attitudes and peer influence remained very good predictors of adolescent drinking.

37. Alcohol and Drug Use among Vancouver Secondary School Students: 1970, 1974 and 1978. Hollander, Marcus J.; Macurdy, E. Ann, British Columbia Department of Health, Vancouver, Nov 1978, 290p (ED 178 842; Reprint: EDRS).

In 1970, 1974, and 1978 similar surveys of alcohol and drug use were conducted using 10 percent random samples of Vancouver secondary school students (grades 8–12). The reported use of alcohol increased from 61 percent in 1970 to 71 percent in 1974 and 78 percent in 1978, while the use of cannabis increased from 39 percent in 1970 to 42 percent in 1974 and 47 percent in 1978. The use of tobacco, at 72 percent in 1978, had increased from 64 percent in 1974. Stimulant use was about the same between 1974 and the 1978 rate of 15 percent. The use of hallucinogens, inhalants and heroin remained stable at about 20 percent, 10 percent, and less than 2 percent, respectively, between 1974 and 1978 but the use of depressants decreased slightly. More than 8 percent of the students reported having used cocaine. By 1978, girls had become almost as likely to use alcohol or drugs as boys, while in 1974 they were less likely to do so; drug usage also increased with age. Patterns of multiple-drug use were qualitatively the same between 1974 and 1978. As in 1974, the 1978 sample showed little difference between those who had and had not received drug education in both their knowledge and use of drugs.

38. Alcohol and Drug Use in a Suburban Sample of College and High School Students. Tori, Christopher D. 1978, 25p (ED 169 406; Reprint: EDRS; also available from California School of Professional Psychology, 1900 Addison St., Berkeley, CA 94704).

Alcohol and drug use among high school and college students was investigated in a sample of suburban high school (N=1,274) and college (N=468) students. Alcohol consumption was very high (78 percent), with more than half of those using alcohol doing so on at least a weekly basis. While alcohol use was pronounced, 96 percent of those surveyed reported that alcohol was not a "problem" in their lives. More than half of the total sample reported the use of other drugs such as marihuana, cocaine, and amphetamines.

39. Alcohol and Youth. An Analysis of the Literature—1960–75.† Blane, Howard T.; Hewitt, Linda E., Pittsburgh University, PA; National Institute on Alcohol Abuse and Alcoholism, Rockville, MD, Mar 1977, 590p (PB-268 698/8ST; Reprint: NTIS).

Results of a comprehensive survey of the scientific and professional literature for the period 1960–75 relating to alcohol use and abuse by young people are presented. The review was commissioned by the National Institute on Alcohol Abuse and Alcoholism (NIAAA) to produce information on the relationship of youth and alcohol that could serve as a basis for policy determination and as an aid in the identification of research and social action needs. Following an introductory chapter, 10 chapters systematically summarize pertinent research findings, assess methodological issues, offer recommendations for future research, and describe theoretical positions about alcohol and youth. A final chapter summarizes the key findings of the previous chapters, evaluates methodological strengths and weaknesses of the research literature, makes recommendations about future research strategies, and sets forth policy and program alternatives. An extensive bibliography of the literature on alcohol and youth accompanies the report.

40. **Communications Strategies on Alcohol and Highway Safety. Volume II. High School Youth: Final Report.** Grey Advertising, Inc., New York, Feb 1975, 120p. Sponsoring agency: National Highway Traffic Safety Administration (DOT), Washington, DC; National Institute on Alcohol Abuse and Alcoholism (DHEW/PHS), Rockville, MD (ED 123 336; Reprint: EDRS; also PB-24-259; Reprint: NTIS).

The second part of a two-part, two-volume study deals with high school youth and identifies target populations and communications strategies for encouraging personal action steps to prevent drunk driving. Data, collected from interviews and questionnaires, are summarized and presented in tabular form. One-fourth of high schoolers in a representative sample of 397 taken from 25 locations in the US said they had driven once or twice when they knew they were too drunk to drive. About 32 percent said they rode in cars driven by a heavily drinking driver at least once a month. The young believed their driving skills were relatively unimpaired by alcohol and that serious consequences do not exist for teen drunk drivers. Results were used to construct a personality profile of Alcohol Related Situations (ARS)—Involved Youth. Findings indicate that education programs should be aimed at correcting current misconceptions about drinking and driving and should depict personal action to prevent drunk driving as acceptable, expected behavior in the peer group. A technical appendix contains: schematic flow chart of study operations, sample design and field procedures, sample tolerance, development of personality scores, and a 21-item bibliography. The interview and questionnaire forms are also included.

41. **Drug Abuse in the New York City Schools.** A Report of the Select Committee on Narcotics Abuse and Control, House of Representatives, Ninety-Fifth Congress, Second Session (August 30–September 1, 1978). Congress of the US, Washington, DC, Aug 1978, 22p; best copy available (ED 177 385; Reprint: EDRS).

The January 1977 hearing by the US House Select Committee on Narcotics Abuse and Control mandated three days of further hearings in 1978. The focus was upon New York City schools, but reflected many similar situations in other urban school systems according to the committee's judgement. The committee also found that alcohol and marihuana usage (the "soft drugs") have become a recent trend, while PCP usage also made strong inroads; marihuana decriminalization was misconstrued as legalization; absenteeism was correlated with drug abuse; administrative control and awareness of the extent of absenteeism were lacking although state and federal aid were jeopardized by such absenteeism; reentry of hardcore absentees was not attempted; drug intervention programs lacked standardization; teachers needed drug training; NIDA educational material was considered "virtually useless"; school administrators, drug program directors, and law enforcement officials failed to cooperate; drug activity and violence went unreported to avoid the appearance of poor management; security needed bolstering; no federal aid came directly to the school system for drug programs; the police failed to consider the problem in school serious because of the lack of reporting by the school system. The committee's recommendations are attached.

42. **A Drug Interest Survey of Senior High School Students.** Sutherland, Mary S. 1978, 12p (ED 160 590; Reprint: EDRS).

The purpose of this study is to determine the drug interests of a senior high school population via a question-writing technique. Specific drug interests in the areas of herbal drugs, illicit drugs, over-the-counter drugs, prescription drugs, and commercial drugs were examined by requesting students to write out what questions they felt their peers had about drugs. The 75 students wrote 179 questions; 97 relating to illicit drugs, 36 to commercial drugs, 14 to over-the-counter drugs, 15 to herbal drugs, and 17 to prescription drugs. The students expressed special interest in drug addiction, governmental control of drugs, and the effects of drugs found in caffeine, cola, and marihuana. The questions identified in this survey are intended to be helpful in providing guidelines for drug education programs.

43. **Drug Use among American High School Students 1975–1977.** Johnston, Lloyd D. et al., Michigan University, Ann Arbor, Institute for Social Research, 1978, 261p; for related document see entry 44. Sponsoring agency: National Institute on Drug Abuse (DHEW/PHS), Rockville, MD (ED 169 453; Reprint: EDRS; also available from Superintendent of Documents, US Government Printing Office, Washington, DC 20402, 017-024-00783-8).

This extensive publication is the first in a series entitled "Monitoring the Future: A Continuing Study of the Lifestyles and Values of Youth." This volume presents detailed statistics on the current prevalence of drug use among American high school seniors and on trends since 1975. Information on 11 separate classes of drugs is presented, and the overall results on prevalence and trends in drug use are summarized. Except for the use of alcohol and cigarettes, virtually all of the drug use discussed is illicit. The strong focus is on drug use at the higher frequency levels to differentiate various levels of seriousness, or extent, of drug involvement. In addition to describing prevalence and trends in use, this volume contains an assessment of prevailing attitudes and beliefs among American high school seniors concerning various types of drug use and of the ways that these views have been changing over the last two years. It also considers their view of the availability of drugs to high school age youth.

44. **Highlights from Drug Use among American High School Students 1975–1977.** Johnston, Lloyd D. et al. 1978, 50p; parts marginally legible due to small type; for related document see entry 43. Sponsoring agency: National Institute on Drug Abuse (DHEW/PHS), Rockville, MD (ED 160 969; Reprint: EDRS; also available from Superintendent of Documents, US Government Printing Office, Washington, DC 20402, stock no. 017-024-00716-1).

The current prevalence of drug use among American high school seniors and the trends in use since 1975 are the two major topics treated. Also reported are prevailing attitudes and beliefs among seniors concerning various types of drug use. Eleven separate classes of drugs are distinguished: marihuana (including hashish), inhalants, hallucinogens, cocaine, heroin, natural and synthetic opiates other than heroin, stimulants, sedatives, tranquilizers, alcohol, and cigarettes. Considerable attention is focused on drug use at the higher frequency levels, in order to help differentiate levels of seriousness, or extent of drug involvement. A relatively accurate picture of the drug experiences and attitudes of each high school class in the United States, beginning with the class of 1975 is presented. Accurate changes in usage are monitored from one year to another, for both high school seniors as a whole and for particular subgroups.

45. **International Drug Use; Research Issues 23.** Austin, Gregory A., Ed. et al. Documentation Associates, Los Angeles, 1978, 219p. Sponsoring agency: National Institute on Drug Abuse (DHEW/PHS), Rockville, MD (ED 177 454; Reprint: EDRS; also available from Superintendent of Documents, US Government Printing Office, Washington, DC 20402; stock no. 017-024-00874-5).

This collection of resources contains 95 summaries of research conducted on drug use in countries other than the United States, and is designed to be an introductory set of readings which provide a basic familiarity with drug-use patterns in foreign countries. The first section contains 23 studies on the United Kingdom while the second section contains 72 studies organized by major geographical area and then by individual country. In each section the studies are cited alphabetically; the table of contents provides an overview of the geographic arrangement and the countries and drugs discussed. A wide range of topics is presented including epidemiological issues, law enforcement, personality, marihuana, and cross-cultural aspects of drug use. A supplementary bibliography of additional readings is also included.

46. **An Investigation into the Effects of Alcohol Use in Ontario Schools.** White, James et al., Ontario Department of Education, Toronto, 1978, 242p (ED 166 833; Reprint: EDRS—HC not available; also available from Ontario Government Bookstore, 880 Bay Street, Toronto, Ontario, Canada M7A 1L2).

The purpose of this study was to determine the effects of alcohol use on student behaviors in Ontario schools. The study was designed to investigate the prevalence of alcohol use by students in grades 7–13 and the effects of drinking on classroom and school behaviors by interviewing both students and teachers. The teachers were surveyed to determine their awareness and perceptions of drinking problems at their school. The report presents a short review of the pertinent literature, a description of the research methods, and the findings from both the student and teacher questionnaires. The major findings provide an indication of the extent to which alcohol use causes problems in schools throughout the province; the types of problems drinking creates; the extent and frequency with which students use beer, wine, liquor, and other drugs; the relationship between drinking and the use of other drugs; the effects of drinking on social relationships; and the extent to which grade, grade average, and sex influence alcohol-related student behaviors.

47. **National Institute on Drug Abuse Research Monograph 21. Phencyclidine (PCP Abuse: An Appraisal).**† Petersen, Robert C.; Stillman, Richard C., National Institute on Drug Abuse, Rockville, MD, Division of Research, Aug 1978, 323p (PB-288 472/ 4ST; Reprint: NTIS).

The monograph was derived from a technical review held in response to the recent emergence of phencyclidine abuse as a problem of widespread proportions. The papers are aimed at a professional and scientific audience concerned about how to cope with the problem of PCP abuse. They provide an overview of the present state of knowledge about phencyclidine, clinical reports of reactions to this drug, and suggestions for treatment. In addition, because of the initial underestimation of the seriousness and extent of PCP abuse, this monograph stimulates thinking about better ways to anticipate newly emerging drug problems.

48. **A National Study of Adolescent Drinking Behavior, Attitudes and Correlates. Final Report.** Rachal, J. Valley et al., Research Triangle Institute, Durham NC, Center for the Study of Social Behavior, Apr 1975, 405p. Sponsoring agency: National Institute on Alcohol Abuse and Alcoholism (DHEW/PHS), Rockville, MD (PB-246 002; Reprint: NTIS).

A questionnaire survey was conducted in the spring of 1974 among US high school students concerning drinking practices, drinking attitudes, and problems related to alcohol consumption among American youth. The questionnaires were completed by a total of 13,122 students in grades 7–12 for a nationwide two-stage, stratified sample. This report contains a brief background statement on drinking during adolescence, and sets forth the purpose, methodology, and major findings of the research.

49. **Phencyclidine Use among Youths in Drug Abuse Treatment.** Philadelphia Psychiatric Center, PA, Jan 1978, 25p. Sponsoring agency: National Institute on Drug Abuse (DHEW/PHS), Rockville, MD (ED 154 316; Reprint: EDRS; also available from Superintendent of Documents, US Government Printing Office, Washington, DC 20402, stock no. 017-024-00709-9).

A study was conducted of phencyclidine use by a national sample of 2,750 youthful drug-abuse clients representing 97 drug-abuse treatment programs. Data from this 1976–77 client survey indicated that phencyclidine use is widespread. More than 31 percent of the subjects reported current or past use of phencyclidine, with males and females having similar exposure rates. While the sample cannot be viewed as representative, the data do indicate that phencyclidine is in use in all regions of the country with the highest rates reported in the Great Lakes and Midwest regions. Further examination of the data suggests that phencyclidine subjects tend to be multiple-substance users who, on the average, take twice as many different substances as other youthful drug users. It was also found that more than half the phencyclidine subjects reported using the drug one or more times weekly over the course of a three-month period. Phencyclidine users were more likely than nonusers to report having had difficulties involving toxic reactions, self-destructive acts, and prior treatment episodes.

50. **Polydrug Use: An Annotated Bibliography.** National Clearinghouse for Drug Abuse Information Special Bibliographies, No. 3, June 1973. National Institute on Drug Abuse (DHEW/PHS), Rockville, MD, National Clearinghouse for Drug Abuse Information; Student Association for the Study of Hallucinogens, Biliot, WI, Jun 1975, 40p (ED 120 655; Reprint: EDRS; also available from Superintendent of Documents, US Government Printing Office, Washington, DC 20402).

Although most discussions of mood-altering drugs and patterns of use typically focus on a single drug or particular drug class, it is a widely acknowledged fact that the majority of drug users, from the junior high school experimenter to the hard-core narcotic addict, employ more than one legal or illegal substance to alter their subjective states. Multiple-drug use has been documented by epidemiological investigations among several major population groups including: students, housewives, military personnel, doctors, alcoholics, and narcotic addicts. Patterns of multiple-drug use are invariably complex but can generally be broken down into three major categories: (1) the use of combinations of drugs; (2) the concomitant use of separate drugs; and (3) the consecutive or sequential use of two or more substances in an alternating fashion. Multiple drug-use patterns can be considered in light of the pharmacological classes of the drugs involved. Some users, for example, restrict their drug taking to particular types of substances, such as depressant drugs (alcohol, sedative/hypnotics, minor tranquilizers, and narcotics), or stimulant drugs (amphetamines and cocaine), or hallucinogens (including cannabis, LSD, mescaline, and related substances). Other users mix not only individual drugs but pharmacological classes of drugs as well. Because an overwhelming number of articles written on particular drug-using patterns mention, at least in passing, the predominance of multiple-drug use, items were selected for inclusion in this guide only if they treated the phenomenon of polydrug use exclusively or as a major point of focus.

51. Public Experience with Psychoactive Substances: A Nationwide Study among Adults and Youth. Part 1, Main Findings. Abelson, Herbert I.; Atkinson, Ronald B., Response Analysis Corporation, Princeton, NJ, Aug 1975, 212p; some pages may reproduce poorly. Sponsoring agency: George Washington University, Washington, DC, Social Research Group; National Institute on Drug Abuse (DHEW/PHS), Rockville, MD (ED 117 598; Reprint: EDRS).

This is a study of beliefs, attitudes, and behavior with regard to a wide range of legal and illegal drugs. Included are data about coffee, tea, tobacco, and illicit drugs such as marihuana and heroin. The report covers the current situation and highlights trends from two prior studies on drug abuse conducted for the National Commission on Marihuana and Drug Abuse. The present survey adds considerable new information reflecting current interests and issues. The report includes summary information of recipient experience with the drugs; user patterns and characteristics; medical usage of psychotherapeutic drugs; findings on other substances such as tea, coffee, cigarettes, and alcohol; and beliefs and attitudes related to drugs. There are also extensive appendices. Findings of the survey include the fact that the public has more experience with marihuana than with any other psychoactive drugs studied, with the next highest being over-the-counter psychotherapeutic drugs. There are strong age relationships connected with the use of marihuana; social use of illicit drugs is the most common pattern; nearly half the adult population report some experience with prescribed psychotherapeutic drugs; and, finally, virtually no change has been reported in adult cigarette consumption over the past several years, whereas a marked increase for younger people has been noted.

52. A Review of Drug Abuse and Alcohol Abuse among Children and Youth. Treatment of Delinquency Series, Chapter 7. Lotsof, Antoinette B., Wilkes College, Wilkes-Barre, PA, Educational Development Center, 1975, 67p (ED 170 683; Reprint: EDRS; also available from Educational Development Center, Wilkes College, Wilkes-Barre, PA 18703).

The seventh part of a 10-part series, this report was compiled by the Educational Development Center at Wilkes College. The series deals with various aspects of the treatment of delinquents and is intended as a summary of research findings in each of the areas treated. Each report was prepared by a scholar-practitioner and is presented in a way that will be of value to professionals who deal both directly and indirectly with the treatment of delinquent youth. This part deals with drug and alcohol use and abuse by adolescents. After presenting a learning theory approach to the problem, it discusses how and why drugs tend to be used by youths in American society. It also contains sections of information on marihuana, amphetamines, alcohol, and other commonly abused drugs.

53. Rural-Urban Differences in Drinking Driving Behavior; Attitudes and Perceptions of Kansas Youth. Hartman, John J., Wichita Department of Community Health, KS, Sep 1977, 29p; Paper presented at the Annual Meeting of the Rural Sociological Society (Madison, WI, September 1977). Sponsoring agency: National Highway Traffic Safety Administration (DOT), Washington, DC (ED 142 355; Reprint: EDRS).

The statewide survey examined whether there were differences (1) in the drinking/driving attitudes and self-reported behavior of high school students, (2) between those defined as "alcohol involved" and the "noninvolved," and (3) between the Wichita youth compared to the remainder of the youth from throughout Kansas. Data were collected from 1,676 high school students during the 1974 spring semester. Responses were analyzed for differences between those who had consumed alcohol within the last month (alcohol involved) and those who had never or within the last month consumed alcohol (noninvolved). Data were analyzed using nonparametric statistics; the .05 significance level was used to specify significant statistical findings. The characteristics of sex, age, family income, race, and school class were examined for the Wichita and the state youth, and alcohol involved and noninvolved youth. Findings included: 63 percent of the state sample were alcohol involved as compared to 54 percent of the Wichita sample; although only about 13 percent of each subsample were old enough to legally purchase alcohol, 45 percent of the Wichita sample and 52 percent of the state sample below 18 years of age were alcohol involved; alcohol involvement tended to increase with grade level and family income in both samples; 24 percent of the Kansas sample and 10 percent of the Wichita sample did most of their drinking while driving around; and females in all classifications were more willing to drive after becoming drunk at a party.

54. Summary Report: Surveys of Student Drug Use, San Mateo County, California, 1968–1976. Department of Public Health & Welfare, San Mateo County, CA, 1976, 12p (ID 005 157; Reprint: SMERC—HC not available).

This document is a brief summary report limited to observations on trends relating to the use of drugs, alcohol, and tobacco by San Mateo County junior and senior high school students. With the addition of the 1976 data, the findings support the data from the 1975 summary report that there appears to be a slight decreasing trend in the use of several of these substances.

55. **A Survey of Substance Use among Junior and Senior High School Students in New York State. Report No. 1: Prevalence of Drug and Alcohol Use, Winter 1974/75.** New York State Office of Drug Abuse Services, Albany, Nov 1975, 52p.; for related document see entry 318 (ED 140 173; Reprint: EDRS).

The intent of this survey is to achieve an understanding of the drug-use patterns of youngsters in New York's secondary schools. It was initiated to gather in detail the extent and dimensions of alcohol and drug use among a sample of New York students in grades 7–12. This survey was conceived as a benchmark study—to establish a statistical baseline against which trends could be measured. The report is organized into three parts: (1) sample and methodology, (2) questionnaire construction and application, and (3) findings.

56. **Young Men and Drugs—A Nationwide Survey. National Institute on Drug Abuse Research Monograph Series 5.** O'Donnell, John A. et al., National Institute on Drug Abuse (DHEW/PHS), Rockville, MD, Feb 1976, 166p. Sponsoring agency: Special Action Office for Drug Abuse Prevention, Washington, DC (ED 159 547; Reprint: EDRS; also PB-247-446; Reprint: NTIS).

Results of a national survey of drug use among young males (19–30) are reported. For most drugs, half or more of the users used the drug less than 10 times. The data suggest a possible decline in the use of cigarettes. Several implications of the drug epidemic of the late 1960s are noted. Differences of drug use between Blacks and Whites seem to be diminishing. There is no indication of any decline in annual prevalence of use of any drug except psychedelics. Veterans show no higher rates of current drug use than nonveterans. Less than 3 percent of the sample report treatment for drug use. Other associated variables, i.e., urban density, unemployment, nonconventional attitudes, and lower educational levels are discussed.

Drug Usage in Special Populations

JOURNAL ARTICLES

57. **Adolescent Children of Alcoholic Parents and the Relationship of Alateen to These Children.** Hughes, Judith M. *Journal of Consulting and Clinical Psychology*. v45, n5, p946–47, Oct 1977.

Investigates whether or not children of alcoholic parents suffer adverse emotional consequences and whether or not Alateen is beneficial to such children. Adolescents with an alcoholic parent who were not members of Alateen had significantly higher scores on the negative scales of the Profile of Mood States.

58. **Alcohol Drinking Patterns among Asian and Caucasian Americans.** Sue, Stanley et al. *Journal of Cross-Cultural Psychology*. v10, n1, p41–56, Mar 1979.

Previous studies have attributed low rates of alcoholism and alcohol consumption among Chinese and Japanese to genetic or to cultural factors. The present study examined the responses of 47 Asian and 77 Caucasian American students who completed questionnaires concerning their drinking patterns, their own and their parents' attitudes toward drinking, and the cues they used to control alcohol consumption. Asian students were also administered assimilation measures. Results indicated that (1) Asians reported more moderate drinking, (2) degree of assimilation was positively related to drinking, (3) attitudes toward drinking were related to reported drinking and were more negative in the case of Asians and their parents, and (4) Caucasians reported more extensive use of cues in the regulation of their drinking. The results suggest the importance of cultural factors in drinking patterns.

59. **Alcohol Use among Mexican-American Youth.** Guinn, Robert. *Journal of School Health*. v48, n2, p90–91, Feb 1978 (EJ 180 398; Reprint: UMI).

The author presents findings on alcohol use among Mexican American youth, with selected demographic, attitudinal, and behavioral variables.

60. **The Alcoholic Teacher: A Growing Concern of the Next Deacde.** Zimering, Stanley; McCreery, Marianne. *Journal of Drug Education*. v8, n3, p253–60, 1978.

The early signs and symptoms of alcoholism are not easily observed. An insidious pattern of lateness, family disorders, excuses, frequent visits to the doctor, poor performance on the job, and perhaps job-related accidents, befall this individual.

61. Alcoholism and the Family. A Survey of the Literature. Waititz, Janet C. *Journal of Alcohol and Drug Education*. v23, n2, p18–23, Win 1978.

Reviews studies on the emotional and behavioral difficulties suffered by children living with an alcoholic mother or father.

62. Black-White Adolescent Drinking: The Myth and the Reality. Higgins, Paul C. et al. *Social Problems*. v25, n2, p215–24, Dec 1977 (EJ 172 838; Reprint: UMI).

Analysis of 1970 data from a study or adolescent behavior in Atlanta (N=1,383) shows that Black teenagers are no more likely and often are less likely than White teenagers to be involved in drinking behavior. When Black teenagers do drink, they are more likely than White teenagers to drink within the family. The results imply that among Blacks, adult problem drinking may not be as strongly related as was suspected to those who drink as adolescents and the social contexts in which adolescents learn to drink.

63. The Causes and Consequences of Alcohol Abuse among Black Youth. Brisbane, Frances. *Journal of Afro-American Issues*. v4, n2, p241–54, Spr 1976.

Explores the potential causes of abusive use of alcohol among young Blacks, focusing on the Black family, with emphasis given to the children, their peers, their communities, and the poverty conditions that influence their life-styles and drinking patterns. The data include interviews with 13 males, ages 8–13 years, and 9 females, ages 13–15 years, and questionnaire data from 27 males, ages 16–23 years.

64. Children of Alcoholic Parents: A Neglected Issue. Triplett, June L.; Arneson, Sara W. *Journal of School Health*. v48, n10, p596–99, Dec 1978 (EJ 202 324; Reprint: UMI).

Little attention has been focused on the children of alcoholic families, and the few studies that have been conducted indicate that these children are at grave risk for developing long-lasting psycho-social and educational problems. Their self-esteem suffers as a result of constant conflict, inconsistency, and role confusion in the home, and it is also known that academic performance and the ability to develop positive peer relationships are also greatly affected. In an effort to determine the scope of this problem, 51 Iowa school nurses attending an Annual School Nurse Conference were queried about: (1) their awareness of the problem, (2) who should be responsible for intervening with these children, and (3) what the role of the school nurse is in working with these youngsters. Based on their responses as well as findings in the literature, suggestions regarding appropriate nursing interventions are offered.

65. Children of Alcoholics. Chafetz, Morris E. *New York University Education Quarterly*. v10, n3, p23–29, Spr 1979 (EJ 219 013; Reprint: UMI).

It is estimated that 29 million American children have alcoholic parents. The author documents the unstable environment and psychological consequences suffered by these children, who are at great risk of becoming alcoholics themselves.

66. Drinking Problems of Native American and White Youth. Forslund, Morris A. *Journal of Drug Education*. v9, n1, p21–27, 1979.

Found that American Indian youths tend to experience more serious consequences of drinking than do White youths from the same area with regard to feeling high, getting drunk, passing out, suffering loss of memory, being stopped by police, having automobile accidents, and getting into trouble with parents.

67. Drug-Related Cognitions among Minority Youth. Myers, Vincent. *Journal of Drug Education*. v7, n1, p53–62, 1977.

Interviews with a nationwide sample (N=1,357) of young and low-income Black, Chicano, and Caribbean men and women, as well as with nonminority counterparts, reveal that, although one-half of the respondents have used illicit drugs, the large majority are uninformed about the effects of licit and illicit drugs, and do not know much about a range of other drug-related consequences.

68. Female Adolescent Drinking Behavior; Potential Hazards. Lee, Essie E. *Journal of School Health*. v48, n3, p151–56, Mar 1978 (EJ 184 124; Reprint: UMI).

A review of the literature confirms the apparent increase in drinking by boys and girls. This article reports the increasing use of alcohol by girls and the associated risks. Some predisposing personal and behavioral characteristics are discussed, such as: the particular hazards of fetal syndrome; the significant impact of the physiological and psychological effects of menstruation and other related female phenomena; and the confusion in sex roles (resulting from the inability to freely combine masculine and feminine personality characteristics within oneself in a women's liberation environment) accelerating risk possibilities in girls.

69. Functions of Drinking for Native American and White Youth. Forslund, Morris A. *Journal of Youth and Adolescence*. v7, n3, p327–32, Sep 1978.

A self-report questionnaire study compared Native American Indian and White adolescents in Wyoming separately by sex, with respect to their reasons for drinking. The 30 items were grouped in three categories: positive-social, personal-effect, and experiential reasons. The functions of drinking appear to be quite similar for these Indian and White youths.

70. Inhalant, Marihuana, and Alcohol-Abuse among Barrio Children and Adolescents. Padilla, Eligio et al. *International Journal of the Addictions*. v14, n7, p945–64, 1979.

Prevalence of inhalant, marihuana, and alcohol abuse was studied in a sample of 457 male and female Mexican American children and adolescents between the ages of 9 and 17. Subjects resided in four housing projects in East Los Angeles. All interviews were conducted by local adolescents. Results indicated that, compared to a national sample, Mexican American adolescents were at least 14 times more likely to be currently abusing inhalants. The prevalence rate of marihuana was double the national rate, but the prevalence of alcohol was equal to that found nationally. Reasons for elevated substance-abuse rates are explored.

71. Myths versus Data on American Indian Drug Abuse. Streit, Fred; Nicolich, Mark J. *Journal of Drug Education*. v7, n2, p117–22, 1977.

A drug- and alcohol-use prevalence study was conducted among Montana Indians by Montana Indians. The results raise questions about culture transmission as a drug prevention strategy. Also, there is evidence of a high proportion of youth with deceased fathers. Implications for further prevention needs are presented.

72. Patterns of Alcohol and Multiple Drug-Use among Rural White and American-Indian Adolescents.
Cockerham, William C. *International Journal of the Addictions.* v12, n2–3, p271–85, 1977.

The findings of this study lend general support to the hypothesis of Whitehead et al., that users of any one drug will show increased probability to use another drug when compared to those not using that drug. Additionally, it was found that rural Indian youth are somewhat more likely than rural White youth to be involved with alcohol, marihuana, and hard drugs.

73. Patterns of Drug Use among Mexican-American Potential School Dropouts.
Bruno, James E.; Doscher, Lynn. *Journal of Drug Education.* v9, n1, p1–10, 1979.

Studies a sample of Mexican American students identified as potential dropouts and finds drug use is widespread. Cigarettes, marihuana, and alcohol are used by the majority of students. ''Social'' drugs are used more often. Students do not think that general drug use causes social problems; however, girls' attitudes differ from boys'.

74. Problem Drinking in the Education Profession.
Russell, Robert D. *Phi Delta Kappan.* v60, n7, p506–09, Mar 1979 (EJ 197 906; Reprint: UMI).

Examines some causes of problem drinking, outlines case histories of problem drinkers in education, and examines some responses to the problem drinker.

MICROFICHE

75. Adolescent Life Stress as a Predictor of Alcohol Abuse and/or Runaway Behavior.
van Houten, Therese; Golembiewski, Gary, National Youth Alternatives Project, Inc., Washington, DC, 1978, 123p. Sponsoring agency: National Institute on Alcohol Abuse and Alcoholism (DHEW/PHS), Rockville, MD (ED 173 460; Reprint: EDRS).

The connection between parental alcohol abuse and adolescent life stress, adolescent alcohol abuse and adolescent running away is explored in this study of 907 adolescents ranging in age from 12–17. The purpose of this study is to determine whether or not alcohol abuse and running away can be viewed as a response to, or an escape from stress. It is reported that the majority of runaways say they left home because of family problems, including parental alcohol abuse. A population of two groups, runaway and nonrunaway, was used in this study to test for a correlation between parental alcohol abuse and adolescent running away. A questionnaire was administered to the entire population of 907 adolescents and a Life Events Inventory (LEI) was administered to a subsample of these adolescents. Final analysis of the questionnaire data supported positive correlations between adolescent alcohol abuse, running away, and parental alcohol abuse. The analysis also showed similarities in drinking patterns for runaways and nonrunaways. The results indicated, however, that despite many similar characteristics between

runaways and nonrunaways, differences existed between these two groups. It was found that parental alcohol use/abuse is one of the most significant factors in adolescents' drinking.

76. Alcohol Use among Native Americans: A Selective Annotated Bibliography.
† Street, Pamela B. et al., California University, Berkeley, School of Public Health, May 1976, 123p (PB-268 483/5ST; Reprint: NTIS—HC not available).

This bibliography was initiated as a result of the recognition by the Office of Alcoholism of the state of California that there was a need for the compilation of reference materials dealing with the drinking behavior, problems, treatment, and related issues concerning the Native American population and, in particular, the Native American population of California. To that end, the Office of Alcoholism contracted with the Social Research Group to produce an annotated bibliography in this general subject area.

77. Alcohol Use among the Spanish-Speaking: A Selective Annotated Bibliography.
† Treiman, Beatrice H. et al., California University, Berkeley, School of Public Health, California Office of Alcoholism, Sacramento, May 1976, 55p (PB-268 474/4ST; Reprint: NTIS—HC not available).

This bibliography was initiated as a result of the recognition by the Office of Alcoholism of the state of California that there was a need for a listing of reference material dealing with the drinking patterns, behavior, problems, treatment, and related issues concerning the Spanish-speaking population and, in particular, the Spanish-speaking population of California. To that end, the Office of Alcoholism contracted with the Social Research Group to produce an annotated bibliography in this general subject area.

78. Blacks and Alcohol: A Selective Annotated Bibliography.
† Treiman, Beatrice R. et al., California University, Berkeley, School of Public Health, Jul 1976, 95p (PB-268 447/OST; Reprint: NTIS—HC not available).

This bibliography was initiated as a result of the recognition by the Office of Alcoholism of the state of California that there was a need for the compilation of reference materials dealing with the drinking behavior, alcohol-related problems, treatment, and other alcohol-related issues concerning the Blacks in the United States, and in particular, the Blacks in California. To that end, the Office of Alcoholism contracted with the Social Research Group to produce an annotated bibliography in this general subject area.

79. Chicano Alcohol Abuse and Alcoholism in the Barrio.
Jasso, Ricardo, Aug 1977, 45p (ED 171 436; Reprint: EDRS).

Conducted in January 1977, the community survey examined alcohol abuse and alcoholism among Chicanos in the barrios. Data were obtained from 160 respondents (119 females and 41 males) from three geographic areas in San Antonio: the special impact area of Casa Del Sol (an alcoholism program) and the cities of San Antonio and Alamo Heights. Information was gathered on the sociogeographic characteristics of the drinking places, alcoholism awareness, family attitudes and opinions about alcoholism, the consequences of alcoholism, drinking cultural patterns and values, and familiarity with Casa Del Sol. The findings included: 50 percent of the respondents were familiar with Casa Del Sol; 8.7 percent drank because of peer pressure and expectations, 30 percent because of personal, familial, and economic reasons, 30.6 percent because "les gusta tomar" (they enjoyed drinking), and 5 percent for social reasons; 32 percent had had contact with the jail in an alcohol related issue; 31 percent responded that drinking was done at home after work or during weekends, and 30 percent said drinking took place at "la cantina" (bar); 49 percent said they worried about someone who drank in the family; 34.4 percent defined alcoholism as an "un vicio" (a bad vice). Since the majority of the respondents were females, four questions were analyzed to measure the difference in perception and interpretation between the males and females. The analysis showed no difference between the two groups in their responses at the .05 level of significance.

80. Drugs, Alcohol, and Women's Health: An Alliance of Regional Coalitions. Final Report. Nellis, Muriel et al., Department of Health, Education, and Welfare, Washington, DC, 1978, 119p. Sponsoring agency: National Institute on Drug Abuse (DHEW/PHS), Rockville, MD (ED 172 044; Reprint: EDRS).

The needs of women and the content of existing information programs concerned with drug and alcohol abuse and general health were investigated through a nationwide Alliance of Regional Coalitions on Drugs, Alcohol, and Women's Health sponsored by the National Institute on Drug Abuse. Results indicated that: (1) multisubstance abuse is common, but few programs deal with it; (2) substance-abuse problems among women have not been documented adequately; (3) a federal interdepartmental task force is needed to focus on these problems; and (4) delivery systems for comprehensive and cost-effective health care services are necessary.

81. Drugs and Minorities. Research Issues 21. Austin, Gregory A., Ed. et al., Documentation Associates, Los Angeles, CA, Dec 1977, 229p. Sponsoring agency; National Institute on Drug Abuse (DHEW/PHS), Rockville, MD (ED 167 673; Reprint: EDRS—HC not available).

This volume contains summaries of the latest research focusing on the issue of the extent of drug use and abuse among racial and ethnic minorities and the factors influencing it. Taken into consideration are age and sex differences among users, narcotics addiction, socioeconomic influences, cultural factors, racial factors, demographic factors, criminal activity, institutional use, and social impact. Each summary presents the purpose and scope of the research or study, the methods employed, the results obtained, and the author's conclusions. A guide to the summaries gives the racial/ethnic composition of each study's sample and indicates which of the following factors it deals with: (1) multidrug or opiate drug use; (2) epidemiology; (3) sociocultural factors; (4) psycho-social factors; (5) attitudes; (6) crime and laws; and/or (7) treatment. In addition, an index and a complete list of the studies included in this volume are provided.

82. Educational Variables and Drug Use among Puerto Rican Adolescents. Munoz, Raul A. et al. Mar 1978, 25p; Paper presented at the Annual Convention of the American Personnel and Guidance Association (Washington, DC, March 19–23, 1978); for related document see entry 85. Sponsoring agency: National Institute on Drug Abuse (DHEW/PHS), Rockville, MD (ED 165 030; Reprint: EDRS).

A longitudinal study of educational variables and drug use was conducted by interview with 635 young Puerto Rican adults. Half had been selected as representing a "high risk" population, half a "normal risk" population. Correlational analyses revealed that the use of all drugs was associated with a negative attitude toward school among both sexes. Academic performance was poorer for males who later had greater involvement with all drugs, but this effect was less consistent among the females. Inconsistent results for the two sexes were also observed on the effects of educational and occupational aspirations on drug usage. Discriminant function analyses, aimed at predicting drug preference from academic characteristics, yielded significant functions for males, but not for females. Two significant functions found for males indicated that occupational aspirations were most discriminating among drug usage categories.

83. Endangered Children and the Misuse of Intoxication by Controlling Adults. Walonick, David. 1977, 15p (ED 156 961; Reprint: EDRS).

A review of the academic literature regarding the existence or lack of relationship between chemically dependent adults and neglected or abused children supports the conclusion that alcohol and other drugs are a significant factor in most behavioral patterns associated with endangering children. The author identifies five modes of parent/child interaction relating to child abuse and drug abuse or addiction: neglect, physical abuse, sexual abuse, forced ingestion of drugs, and neonatal drug dependence. Included are data on these forms of abuse.

84. Father's Alcoholism and Children's Outcomes. Robins, Lee N. et al. May 1977, 20p; Paper presented at the Annual Medical-Scientific Meeting of the National Alcoholism Forum (Eighth, San Diego, CA, May 1977). Sponsoring agency: Public Health Service (DHEW), Arlington, VA (ED 152 892; Reprint: EDRS—HC not available).

This paper presents some results from a group of St. Louis born Black males aged 31–36 who were systematically interviewed during the year 1965–66. The sample in this report is deemed a high risk population because the fathers are at very high risk for alcoholism and the children are at high risk for unfavorable school and legal outcomes independently of the father's drinking. The paper presents correlates of alcoholism in the fathers, and the consequences of the father's alcoholism for the school and police records of their children. The study demonstrates a constellation of difficult family settings in which Black city-reared children are likely to find themselves if they have an alcoholic father. They are more likely to be illegitimate, to have a young father and parents who have not finished high school, to live in a broken home, and to have a father who has been arrested. The association between having an alcoholic father and these circumstances can probably be explained both by intoxication's directly reducing the foresight necessary for taking adequate precautions during intercourse and by the fact that alcoholism is particularly common among men who were impulsive and sexually active youth. Each of the aspects of family life predicted by having an alcoholic father was also associated with truancy and dropout rate in the offspring of these fathers.

85. Health Characteristics as Precursors of Substance Abuse in Puerto Rican Adolescents. Haran, Elizabeth M. et al. Mar 1978, 18p; Paper presented at the Annual Convention of the American Personnel and Guidance Association (Washington, DC, March 19–23, 1978); for related document see entry 82 (ED 165 031; Reprint: EDRS).

In a longitudinal study of precursors of drug usage, data collected in 1968 on health variables were related to substance/use patterns obtained in 1975–76. Some 657 young Puerto Ricans were interviewed for this study, drawn from a pool of about 5,000 questionnaired in 1968. The major findings were that the health factors associated with drug involvement were mainly those of habit and fatigability. Other factors which could be used as descriptors of specific substance users included sensory impairment and digestive problems as well as not having psychosomatic or mobility problems. The best predictors were found in the areas of: habits, especially sleeping patterns; facial appearance; sense receptors (eyes, ears); mobility and activity restrictions; heart trouble; nervousness; and the taking of prescription medicines or pills. The highest number of associations as well as the best predictive ability was found in the marihuana and alcohol groups. The least amount of significant relations and predictors was found in the realm of heroin use.

86. Hearing before the Subcommittee on Alcoholism and Drug Abuse of the Committee on Human Resources, United States Senate, Ninety-Fifth Congress, First Session on Examination on the Impact of Alcoholism Abuse on the Family Life. Congress of the US, Washington, DC, Senate Committee on Human Resources, Jun 1977, 120p (ED 155 565; Reprint: EDRS—HC not available).

This Senate subcommittee hearing concentrates on the effects of alcoholism on the family. It states that there are now more than 28 million children of alcoholic parents, including adults who are affected by parental alcoholism. Other research cited indicates that at least half of the total number of juvenile delinquents have family members with excessive drinking problems; almost 50 percent of all divorce cases show excessive use of alcohol as a major causative factor; and a correlation exists between battered wives, child neglect, child abuse, and alcohol abuse. A number of expert witnesses offer testimony concerning the extent and causes of family-related alcohol problems, as well as suggestions for legislative action.

87. Hispanic Drinking Practices: A Comparative Study of Hispanic and Anglo Adolescent Drinking Patterns.* Sanchez-Dirks, Ruth Dolores, New York University, 1978, 224p (7818456; Reprint: DC).

A descriptive study of the drinking behavior of Hispanic students in comparison to Anglo junior and senior high school students. The study sample is a subsample of a larger nationwide survey conducted by the National Institute on Alcohol Abuse and Alcoholism in the Spring of 1974 on the drinking behavior of adolescents.

Little research has been done on the drinking practices of American Hispanics. The study focuses on the differences and similarities of the Hispanic and Anglo students by ethnicity and sex in four areas: sociocultural factors, social integration factors, attitudes toward the use of alcohol, and life expectations.

The Hispanics reported a lower percentage of drinkers than the Anglos and a higher percentage of abstainers. Hispanic males report drinking the most alcohol, and the Hispanic females the least, in comparison to the Anglo males and females. The greatest difference in attitudes between the ethnic groups is their views concerning female use of alcohol. The Hispanics overwhelmingly agreed that it was worse for a woman to drink alcohol than for a man. A majority of the Hispanic females scored low on their tolerance for transgression. Comparison of mean religiosity score and consumption levels indicated that Anglo abstainers are more religious than Hispanic abstainers, but Hispanic drinkers are more religious than Anglo drinkers at all consumption levels.

88. An Investigation of the Relationship between Substance Abuse and Child Abuse and Neglect. Black, Rebecca; Mayer, Joseph, Washingtonian Center for Addictions, Boston, MA, 1979, 101p. Sponsoring agency: National Center on Child Abuse and Neglect (DHEW/OHD), Washington, DC (ED 175 228; Reprint: EDRS).

Research on the role of alcoholism and opiate addiction in child abuse and neglect is reviewed, and a study of the adequacy of child care in families of 200 alcohol or opiate addicted parents is reported. Demographic data are included, and incidence and characteristics of physical and sexual abuse and neglect are reported. Sex of the addicted parent distinguished between families in which there is no maltreatment, as did availability of financial and social supports. Among summary notes listed are the conclusions that most alcoholic or opiate addicated parents did not physically or sexually abuse their children; 42 percent of the addicted parents had been recipients of physical abuse during childhood; children were neglected in all families with addicted parents, although in most instances the neglect was considered mild; and despite differences in demographic and socioeconomic characteristics, children were abused or neglected equally often in families with an alcoholic or opiate addicted parent.

89. Racial Differences in Rural Adolescent Drug Abuse. Staggs, Frank M., Jr.; Nyberg, Kenneth L. Sep 1977, 19p; Paper presented at the Annual Meeting of the Rural Sociological Society (Madison, WI, September 1–4, 1977) (ED 151 107; Reprint: EDRS).

Drug abuse and the differences in drug-use patterns and related behavior between rural Blacks and Whites were examined. Questionnaires were administered to 993 (369 Black and 624 White) rural adolescents in grades 7–12 in randomly selected schools in Texas. The instrument totaled 15 pages containing 65 items which yielded 178 quantifiable variables. Of the 178 variables, 134 directly dealt with various aspects of drug use and yielded six operational categories: respondent's use, peer use, parental use, peer influence, parental influence, and drug acquisition and dealing. The remaining 44 variables centered around measures of the respondents' biography, indicants of parental marital and socioeconomic status, various measures of religious membership and participation, career aspiration, death attitudes, delinquent activities, and television viewing practices. Findings included: Whites reported substantially greater use of liquor than did Blacks; females reported greater use of "uppers" and "downers" than did males; adolescents from single-parent households were more likely to use all drugs than in households where both parents were living; adolescents reporting positive relationships with their mother and father were less likely to use any drugs than those with less favorable relationships; drug use increased with grade level; and while Blacks were found to be less likely to use drugs on the whole, they were found to be more likely to sell drugs for more money than were Whites.

90. Subcultural Differences in Drinking Behavior in U.S. National Surveys and Selected European Studies. Cahalan, Don. Aug 1977, 27p; Paper presented at the Annual Conference on Experimental and Behavioral Approaches to Alcoholism (Os-Bergen, Norway, August 28–September 1, 1977). Sponsoring agency: National Institute on Alcohol Abuse and Alcoholism (DHEW/PHS), Rockville, MD (ED 151 642; Reprint: EDRS).

This paper summarizes ethnic and other subcultural differences in drinking behavior and drinking problems, with primary emphasis upon the series of US national surveys conducted by the author's social research group during the last 15 years. The author discusses comparative findings from surveys conducted by others in several European countries, drawing attention to the need for comparability of methods in any future studies conducted for the purpose of making cross-national or subcultural comparisons.

91. Summary of the Findings from a Study about Cigarette Smoking among Teen-Age Girls and Young Women. Yankelovitch, Skelly and White, Inc., New York, Feb 1976, 18p. Sponsoring agency: American Cancer Society, Inc., New York (ED 127 526; Reprint: EDRS—HC not available).

This paper presents the major results of a study for the American Cancer Society on cigarette smoking among teenage girls and young women and findings relevant to the prevention and quitting of smoking. The four major trends found in this study are: (1) a dramatic increase in cigarette smoking among females; (2) an intellectual awareness of the dangers of smoking; (3) belief in an all-pervasive smoking environment; and (4) growth and acceptance of the "new values" generated by college students of the 1960s. In its efforts to break down the myth of an extensive smoking society and to utilize the positive elements of the "new values," the study presents the following list of findings which can be used in an antismoking campaign: (1) teenage smokers are more sophisticated than nonsmokers; (2) smoking is not identified with rebelliousness; (3) peer relationships are a dominant factor in smoking; (4) antismoking education needs to begin at an earlier grade level than supposed; (5) young women smokers express a high need for independence; (6) working women smoke less than housewives; (7) identification with the women's movement does not encourage smoking; (8) pregnancy only causes a cutback in smoking; (9) children are less militant than formerly in their efforts to curb smoking among their parents; and (10) light smokers can quit more easily than heavy smokers. The study indicates there is a definite

potential for getting females to quit, but more emphasis must be placed on the nonaddictive qualities of smoking in antismoking campaigns.

92. Toward an Understanding of the Mental Health and Substance Abuse Issues of Rural and Migrant Ethnic Minorities: A Search for Common Experiences. Ryan, Robert A.; Trimble, Joseph E. May 1978, 28p; Paper prepared for the National Conference on Minority Group Alcohol, Drug Abuse and Mental Health Issues (Denver, CO, May 22–24, 1978) (ED 174 382; Reprint: EDRS).

The current reversal of the rural to urban migration trend among Blacks, American Indians, and Hispanics will create a myraid of coping and adaptation problems for the urban to rural migrant and the rural nonmigrant as well. It is possible to gain a partial understanding of the likely problems by reviewing studies of the ethnic minorities' rural to urban migration and the coping patterns of rural and migrant communities. New migration patterns will undoubtedly affect mental health and substance abuse, two areas closely tied to coping and adaptation strategies. Studies of the incidence of mental illness among rural and migrant minorities have shown no consistent pattern of failure to adjust. Criticism of these studies focuses on their use of hospital statistics to determine incidences of mental illness and their failure to consider migrant characteristics and circumstances under which a move occurred. The type and extent of substance abuse varies among ethnic groups but is increasing for the rural and migrant ethnic minorities as it is for their urban counterparts. Although studies have identified stresses which affect substance abuse, they have not determined the impact of social mobility and environmental change on substance abuse. Among the many research needs is the need to identify the indigenous mechanisms used to control and prevent emotional problems and abuses of narcotics and alcohol.

93. Training the Human Resources, July, 1977 Bulletin. National Institute on Drug Abuse (DHEW/PHS), Rockville, MD, Jul 1977, 16p (ED 159 505; Reprint: EDRS—HC not available; also available from Superintendent of Documents, US Government Printing Office, Washington, DC, 20402, stock no. 017-024,00619-0).

The Division of Resource Development of the National Institute on Drug Abuse is giving increasing emphasis to the needs and concerns of women, both in treatment and as workers in the field. Recently there has also been increased interest in the problems of the female substance abuser on the part of the Alcohol, Drug Abuse, and Mental Health Administration and the Congressional Oversight Committee. This publication is devoted to topics in the field of substance abuse that concern women. The rising drug use among women and the need for improved services for women are discussed. Three women and their work with substance abuse are briefly described. Another section describes Caritas House, a Cranston, Rhode Island, drug treatment center for adolescent girls. The publication reviews several conferences held in the last year in which the treatment of drug-dependent women was either a central or major concern. Other sections discuss legislation developments, cover some of the treatment programs designed to give women special attention, and review five publications about women.

BOOKS

94. Maternal Drug Dependence Incidence, Drug Use Patterns and Impact on Children. Carr, J. N. New York: Odyssey House, Inc., 1975, 18p.

Discusses the incidence and dangers of maternal drug abuse in all social classes. Poor prenatal nutrition, neglect, and early exposure to drugs are cited as severe threats to young children. Early identification and treatment of drug-abusing mothers are advocated.

95. El Uso de Alcohol; A Resource Book for Spanish Speaking Communities. (The Use of Alcohol). Trotter, Robert T., II, Ed.; Chavira, Juan Antonio, Ed. Atlanta, GA: Southern Area Alcohol and Education Training Program, Inc., 1977, 100p.

This monograph addresses the issue of alcohol use and abuse in Spanish-speaking communities of the United States. Two annotated bibliographies are included. The first covers cross-cultural research about alcohol use and abuse and works specifically relating to Latin America. The second bibliography contains articles on Mexican American, Puerto Rican, and other Spanish-speaking communities in the US. A review of alcohol education and alcohol prevention materials is also provided. Several original articles concerned with the conceptualization, planning, and implementation of alcoholism programs and treatment approaches are also included in this volume. Recommendations for improving efforts in the areas of alcoholism research, prevention, and education relevant to Spanish-speaking communities are made. Brief reports and recommendations of concerned individuals are appended.

Personal, Attitudinal, and Social Correlates to Drug Use

JOURNAL ARTICLES

96. Abusive Alcohol Drinking: A Study of Social Attitudes of Youth in a Military Community. Alsikafi, M. et al. *Drug Forum: The Journal of Human Issues.* v7, n3–4, p317–28, 1978–79.

Examines attitudes toward excessive alcohol drinking among military dependents residing in Europe. Favorable attitudes toward excessive drinking are relatively common in this population. Sociopsychological dimensions as perception of causes leading to alcohol intake, cognitive level of alcohol, and attitudes toward alcohol education are significantly related to attitudes toward excessive drinking.

97. Acquisitional Processes Underlying Illicit Alcohol-Abuse in Underage Children—Observational-Learning Model. Jones, John W. *Psychological Reports.* v45, n3, p735–40, Dec 1979.

This study examined 25 boys and 35 girls in an elementary school and found illicit alcohol use occurred in one out of five. Moreover, the frequency of weekly alcohol consumption among both the students' families and friends, as *observed* by the student, reliably predicted alcohol consumption rates by male students but not females. The obtained pattern of results is discussed in terms of an observational learning model of youths' drinking behavior, and implications of the findings are given.

98. Adolescent Alcohol Abuse: A Review of the Literature. Walker, Betty A. et al. *Journal of Alcohol and Drug Education.* v23, n3, p51–65, Spr 1978 (EJ 189 494; Reprint: UMI).

This review of the literature on adolescent drinking—an increasingly urgent problem among adolescents in the United States today—examines the patterns of alcohol use and abuse among youth. Variables considered are: psychological characteristics, adolescent attitudes toward drinking, parental attitudes toward adolescent drinking, religious influences, and peer pressures. Prevention and treatment attempts are also considered.

99. Adolescent Alcoholism—Motives and Alternatives. Ghadirian, A. M. *Comprehensive Psychiatry.* v20, n5, p469–74, Sep–Oct 1979.

Juvenile Use of alcoholic beverages has reached an alarming point, particularly among female teenagers. Illicit use of drugs by adolescents reflects not only a basic insecurity in their world of transition, but also a search for purpose and identity. The use of alcohol and psychoactive drugs is viewed primarily as a problem of volition and personal choice, rather than an inevitable disease. Thus, prevention is possible in the context of a realistic and healthy system of education and family life.

100. Adolescent Drug Use: The Role of Peer Groups and Parental Example. Annis, Helen M. *Ontario Psychologist*. v7, n4, p7–9, Oct 1975.

Research is reviewed on two opposing theories of the development of adolescent drug use. One emphasizes the impact of parents' drug use, the other the role of peers. It is concluded that parental attitudes are a primary factor in forming adolescent attitudes toward drug use.

101. Age and Drug Use by Rural and Urban Adolescents. McIntosh, William Alex. *Journal of Drug Education*. v9, n2, p129–43, 1979.

Assesses the importance of age in determining the use of conventional and illicit drugs among secondary school students in Texas. Age/drug use relationships were examined in terms of sex, age, and residence of respondents. Rural students' use of deviant drugs exceeded that of urban students. Conventional drug use increases with age, but no such relationship exists for deviant drugs. Patterns of drug use appear to be characteristic of specific sex, racial, and residential subgroups.

102. Alcohol: A Description and Comparison of Recent Scientific vs. Public Knowledge. Buckalew, L. W. *Journal of Clinical Psychology*. v35, n2, p459–63, Apr 1979 (EJ 211 982; Reprint: UMI).

After noting recent research on the nature, effects, and consequences of alcohol use/abuse, this article describes the results of a survey of high school and college students on that issue. Implications of the low overall knowledge level; specific informational deficits; and age, sex, and racial variables in knowledge are discussed.

103. Alienation, Drugs, and Social Class. Nussel, Edward J.; Althoff, Sally A. *Health Education*. v8, n3, p26–28, May–Jun 1977 (EJ 168 689; Reprint: UMI).

The results of this study suggest that discussions about alienated youths retreating to drugs may be oversimplified; it is possible that drugs have become such an acceptable part of the youth culture that alienation has little to do with overall consumption.

104. Angel Dust Use in an Outpatient Setting—Clinical Profile and Implications for Treatment. Goldstein, George et al. *American Journal of Drug and Alcohol Abuse*. v6, n2, p163–72, 1979.

This study identified two populations of 20 young people who were self-reported users of marihuana in one group and angel dust in the other. The two populations were evaluated on a series of demographic and psychological variables in an attempt to discover whether there are significant differences between them and, if so, whether there is in fact a clinical profile which may be descriptive of nonacute reactions to angel dust. Results indicate that there are significant differences on variables that distinguish angel dust users in an outpatient setting.

105. Antecedents of Adolescent Initiation into Stages of Drug Use: A Developmental Analysis. Kandel, Denise B. et al. *Journal of Youth and Adolescence*. v7, n1, p13–40, Mar 1978.

Predictors associated with adolescents' initiation into three cumulative stages of drug use—hard liquor, marihuana, and other illicit drugs—were investigated. The strongest predictors were prior involvement in deviant behavior (hard liquor); peer influence and adolescent beliefs and values (marihuana); and relationship to parents and depression (hard drugs).

106. Attitudes of Middle-Class Heroin Abusers towards Representatives of the Educational System. Rathus, Spencer A. et al. *Adolescence*. v11, n41, p1–6, Spr 1976.

Investigates heroin abusers maintaining themselves in suburban schools, and correlates of heroin abuse, many related to the educational system. Particular attention is given to subjects' attitudes toward school personnel. While no significant differences were found in their attitudes toward teachers and principals, guidance counselors were viewed less favorably.

107. Attitudes toward Alcoholism and Drug Abuse among a Group of High School Students. Hart, Larry. *Journal of Drug Education*. v5, n4, p351–57, 1975.

High school students (N=81) were surveyed regarding their attitudes on nine factors regarding the alcoholic and his/her alcoholism, and the drug abuser and his/her drug abuse. Analysis of the data indicated that on eight of the nine factors the students tended to view the two pathologies in essentially the same way. In general, these high school students possessed ambivalent attitudes regarding the alcoholic and the addict, perhaps related to their lack of knowledge and inability to conceptualize these pathologies.

108. Awareness of Substance Abuse and Other Health-Related Behaviors among Preschool Children. Tennant, Forest S., Jr. *Journal of Drug Education*. v9, n2, p119–28, 1979.

Preschool children were shown eight pictorial representations of substance abuse. All children could identify some of the behaviors and relate some health benefits or hazards of the behavior. Parents and television were the primary sources of knowledge. Preschool children may be a suitable target population for substance abuse and other health-related education.

109. Childhood Onset of Alcohol Abuse. Mitchell, James E. et al. *American Journal of Orthopsychiatry*. v49, n3, p511–13, Jul 1979.

From case studies of eight children, who began to abuse alcohol between ages 8 and 12, this paper draws correlations on parent involvement with alcohol; family environment and drinking practices; and child behavior, interpersonal relationship, and school performance indices which may help identify children at risk of alcohol abuse.

110. The Concept of a Drug in First and Third Grade Children. Korn, James H. *Journal of Drug Education*. v8, n1, p59–67, 1978.

Short interviews were conducted with 48 first-grade and 37 third-grade children. All third-grade children vs. 54 percent of those in first grade had some concept of a drug. Parents were most frequently mentioned as the source of drug knowledge, with television next.

111. Demographic, Value, and Behavior Correlates of Marijuana Use among Middle Class Youths. Dembo, Richard et al. *Journal of Health and Social Behavior.* v17, n2, p176–86, Jun 1976.

This paper examines contrasting views of marihuana use among middle-class youth: (1) the perspective that sees the use of this substance as antisocial and (2) the position that argues that marihuana use is normative in its reflection of a commitment to a peer-oriented, adolescent life-style that values an openness to new experiences. The findings support the prosocial nature of the use of marihuana among the youths who were studied.

112. Dependency Traits among Parents of Drug Abusers. Tennant, Forest S., Jr. *Journal of Drug Education.* v6, n1, p83–88, 1976.

Studies question whether there is a significant association between parents' dependency traits and drug habits in their offspring. Reported here is a survey of 1,091 young males. The reported occurrence of parental alcohol consumption, smoking, use of stimulants and sedatives, and overeating were compared among abusers and nonusers of hashish, amphetamines, and opiates.

113. Drinking Myths: A Guided Tour through Folklore, Fantasy, Humbug & Hogwash. Doland, Joseph S. *Journal of Drug Education.* v5, n1, p45–49, 1975.

The author believes that American society has so many drinking problems because we have so many wrong ideas about drinking. The intention is to dispel these myths.

114. Drug Use and Mental Health among a Representative Sample of Young Adults. Gove, Walter R. et al. *Social Forces.* v58, n2, p572–90, Dec 1979 (EJ 215 299; Reprint: UMI).

Findings in this study on the relationship between drug use and mental health include: (1) users of any one drug have a high probability of using other drugs; (2) drug use is related to psychiatric symptoms; and (3) the more kinds of drugs used, the worse the mental health of the user. It is speculated that drug use may be a coping strategy for persons who experience various forms of psychological distress and who use drugs in an attempt to improve their mental health.

115. Drug Use and School Dropout: A Longitudinal Study. Annis, Helen M.; Watson, Carol. *Canadian Counsellor.* v9; n3–4, p155–62, Jun 1975.

A longitudinal design was employed to study the relationship between drug use and school dropout in a general high school population. The results supported previously reported findings by demonstrating greater use of most licit and illicit drug categories by school dropouts following their withdrawal from school. It was concluded that drug use functions as part of the constellation of contributing factors that precedes dropping out of school, but that dropout status itself may play a causal role in fostering self-identification and/or social group contacts which promote the development of drug abuse patterns.

116. Drugs and the Medicalization of Human Problems. Hills, Stuart L. *Journal of Drug Education.* v7, n4, p317–22, 1977.

The focus in the mass media on illegal drug abuse among the young has obscured an epidemic increase in the misuse of legal psychoactive drugs in America. The threat to society from the widespread use of mood-altering drugs—encouraged by the pharmaceutical industry and medical profession—is explored. The increasing tendency to define unpleasant human feelings and troublesome behavior as a "disease" to be corrected with drugs may serve to (1) diminish pressures to seek more fundamental approaches to the real sources of the drug user's distress, and (2) individualize and depoliticize complex social problems.

117. Effects of Drug Commercials on Young Viewers. Atkin, Charles K. *Journal of Communication.* v28, n4, p71–79, Fall 1978 (EJ 204 406; Reprint: UMI).

Discusses children's television viewing, particularly their exposure to advertisements for proprietary drug products, and relates this to their views of the amount of sickness in society and the reliance on medicine. Although results did not provide clear and consistent patterns, a tentative profile was drawn of the type of preadolescent who tends to be most influenced by over-the-counter drug commercials: a bright, higher status male or female who is usually healthy and whose parents disapprove of medicine use.

118. Factors Affecting the Incidence and Acceptance of Cigarette Smoking among High School Students. Rudolph, Joseph P.; Borland, Barry L. *Adolescence.* v11, n44, p519–25, Win 1976.

This study attempts to determine the extent of smoking in a high school population, to identify the relationship between students' smoking status and conditions contributing to the continuation of smoking among students. Results indicate that, although smoking is regarded as harmful by most students, this recognition seems to have little or no effect on rates of smoking among students. Nor does it affect attitudes toward school smoking rules. The majority of students (61 percent) favored changes in the school code to permit smoking on campus.

119. The Family as a Context for Developing Youthful Drinking Patterns. Fontane, Patrick E.; Layne, Norman R., Jr. *Journal of Alcohol and Drug Education.* v24, n3, p19–29, Spr 1979 (EJ 211 812; Reprint: UMI).

Similarities between drinking behaviors of college undergraduates and their parents indicate that family environment has an impact on the drinking behavior of offspring.

120. Family Socialization and Adolescent Personality and Their Association with Adolescent Use of Marijuana. Brook, Judith S. et al. *Journal of Genetic Psychology.* v133, n2, p261–72, Dec 1978.

This study examines family socialization practices and adolescent personality/attitudinal characteristics, their interrelation, and association with adolescent use of marihuana. Two hundred and eighty-four adolescents and their mothers served as Ss. As hypothesized, parental socialization factors and adolescent personality/attitudinal attributes each had an independent effect on adolescent use of marihuana and each comprised its own set of sufficient conditions for adolescent marihuana use.

121. Father-Distance and Drug Abuse in Young Men.
Schneider, Robert J. et al. *Journal of Nervous and Mental Disease*. v165, n4, p269–74, Oct 1977.

Previous clinical work has indicated that addicted men (both alcoholic and heroin dependent) have a distant or negative relationship to their father. To test this hypothesis and to attempt to quantify the concept of "father-distance," a 16-item questionnaire regarding a young man's relationship to his father was given to three groups: a heroin and alcohol addicted group; a general psychiatric outpatient group; and a control group. The results indicated that only the addicted group had significant elevations of the father-distance score. This appears to substantiate the hypothesis that many drug abusers view their relationship to their father as difficult or distant. Their greater father-distance than the psychiatric outpatient group indicates that the behavior of drug abuse may be different from other emotional problems of young men and is more specifically associated with a disturbed father/son relationship. The implications for treatment are profoundly important. Limited treatment programs which assume the presence of social skills are likely to fail for those identified as father-distant. We suggest that drug addicted young men who have poor social skills need a treatment program which makes use of the developmental factors related to the process of identification. The treatment should therefore be comprehensive, probably residential for a significant period of time, highly structured, supportive, nurturing, and authoritarian.

122. Marijuana and Psychedelic Use: Are They Deviant Responses? Davis, Carl S. *Drug Forum: The Journal of Human Issues*. v6, n4, p315–26, 1977–78.

Focuses on the state of psychological health of young drug users rather than relying on a model of dysfunction to understanding their behavior. There were 81 Ss within the ages of 16 and 23. Each S responded to the Personal Orientation Inventory. There were no significant differences in psychological health.

123. On Variations in Adolescent Subcultures. Kandel, Denise B. *Youth and Society*. v9, n4, p373–84, Jun 1978.

The attributes of adolescents involved in marihuana- and nonmarihuana-using peer groups are described. Adolescent subcultures are highly differentiated and involvement with peers does not necessarily entail rejection and estrangement from parents. The crucial factor in the adolescent's feelings toward adults is not involvement in peer group per se but involvement in a marihuana-using peer group.

124. Psychological Factors and Adolescent Illicit Drug Use: Ethnicity and Sex Differences. Paton, Stephanie M.; Kandel, Denise B. *Adolescence*. v13, n50, p187–200, Sum 1978 (EJ 188 243; Reprint: UMI).

Of four psychological factors examined in a representative sample of New York State secondary school students, only two, depressive mood and normlessness, show a positive relationship with the use of illicit drugs, especially drugs other than marihuana. The association of depressive mood and normlessness with illegal multiple-drug use varies by ethnicity and sex, being consistently stronger among girls and among Whites. In addition, depressive

mood is negatively related to multiple-drug use for Black and Puerto Rican boys. These findings suggest that psychological factors play a different role in adolescent drug involvement within various social and cultural groups.

125. Reentry—Study of Movement of Young Drug-Users toward Mainstream Society. Wallach, Amira. *Psychiatry*. v40, n3, p242–58, Aug 1977.

In studying the permanency of membership in the hippie subculture, the author concentrated on the degree of movement of 105 drug-using subjects back toward mainstream participation. In general, it appears that non-reentry subjects, who usually came to the hippie subculture with deep psychological disturbances, "dropped out" at a younger age and more completely than reentry and semi-reentry subjects. As a result, they were more likely to remain in the drug subculture.

In contrast, subjects who came to the subculture with milder disturbances dropped out temporarily and were more likely to find a marginal mainstream reentry position.

The reentry group came to the subculture for mild experimentation and exploration, associated with attempts to gain greater insight into themselves. Although most had personal problems when they chose the extended psychosocial moratorium of the hippie subculture, their crises seemed to be reactive to their stage of development and life circumstances rather than resulting from deep psychological disturbances. Developmentally, they used this time as an extended postadolescence.

126. The Relationship between Television Advertising and Drug Abuse among Youth: Fancy and Fact. Payne, Donald E. *Journal of Drug Education*. v6, n3, p215–20, 1976.

Television advertising of over-the-counter drugs has been suspected of being a contributing factor in drug abuse among youth. Recent research suggests that these suspicions are ill-founded. What is worse, they focus attention, effort, and resources on a factor which is simply irrelevant to the problem.

127. Relationships between Drug Knowledge and Drug Attitudes for Students in Large, Intermediate, and Small Schools. Whiddon, Thomas; Halpin, Gerald. *Research Quarterly*. v48, n1, p191–95, Mar 1977 (EJ 168 788; Reprint: UMI).

Possession of knowledge does not ensure negative attitudes toward drugs; these attitudes often reflect those of the community.

128. School Adjustment, Drinking, and the Impact of Alcohol Education Programs. Burkett, Steven R.; White, Mervin. *Urban Education*. v11, n1, p79–94, Apr 1976.

Examines various correlates of drinking consistent with the hypothesis that "problem" drinking is frequently tied to withdrawal from the success stream through high school and involvement in patterns of peer rebellion in which physical aggression, immediate gratification, and peer loyalty are strongly emphasized. Both drinking and nondrinking subjects were receptive to school-centered alcohol programs (lectures, films, and guest speakers). Subjects were 545 male and 513 female senior class students in three high schools.

129. Self-Esteem Patterns Distinctive of Groups of Drug Abusing and Other Dysfunctional Adolescents.
Ahlgren, Andrew; Norem-Hebeisen, Ardyth A.
International Journal of the Addictions. v14, n6, p759–77, 1979.

Self-report measures on seven scales representing four broad processes of self-esteem were used to contrast three groups of drug abusers (pretreatment, in-treatment, and posttreatment) with two other groups of institutionalized dysfunctional youth (runaways and learning disabled), and a "normal" public school sample. The patterns of self-esteem differences distinguished the pretreatment and in-treatment drug abusers, suggesting that low self-esteem may not be a consequence of personal dysfunction alone, but may play a causal role in drug abuse.

130. A Sociological Look at Alcohol-Related Problems: A Talk Prepared for High School Students. Roizen, Ron. *Journal of Alcohol and Drug Education.* v24, n1, p31–38, Fall 1978 (EJ 198 800; Reprint: UMI).

The cultural and historical factors that have combined to make alcohol a problematic beverage for Americans are discussed.

131. Some Correlates of Drug Use among High School Youth in a Midwestern Rural Community. Tolone, William L.; Dermott, Diane. *International Journal of the Addictions.* v10, n5, p761–77, 1975.

A disproportionate random sample of 136 high school students from a small town in northern Illinois were surveyed about drug use (marihuana, hallucinogens, speed) and drug education. Results were correlated to students' personal characteristics, family life and structure, and peer group pressure. Peer group pressure was found to be the most influential variable in drug use. Associations were also found with less intact families and parental use of legal drugs.

132. A Study of Smoking Behavior and Smoking Education at Junior High Level. Chen, Ted T. L.; Thompson, Linda. *Health Education.* v11, n3, p7–10, May–Jun 1980.

This study of 414 predominantly White, middle-class, urban ninth-grade students showed that a large proportion smoke cigarettes, especially among the girls. Besides peers, mothers have the strongest influence on youth smoking behavior change. Smokers and nonsmokers differ in their knowledge. Students feel that smoking education should be an integral part of a school health program and that teachers should be better prepared to teach the subject.

133. A Survey of Drug Use Beliefs, Opinions and Behaviors among Junior and Senior High School Students—Part One: Group Data. Seffrin, John R.; Seehafer, Roger W. *Journal of School Health.* v46, n5, p263–68, May 1976.

A study conducted in a school district in the Midwest indicates that the students are basically reflecting the mores of society—permissive about alcohol but not approving of other drugs.

134. Teenage Drunkenness; Warning Signal, Transient Boisterousness, or Symptom of Social Change? Finn, Peter. *Adolescence.* v14, n56, p819–34, Win 1979 (EJ 215 358); Reprint: UMI).

Several current views on the origins and meaning of adolescent intoxication are reviewed and the validity and utility of each perspective discussed. It is concluded that each occurrence of teenage drunkenness should be analyzed individually.

135. Trends in the Use of Alcohol and Other Substances on Television. Greenberg, Bardley S. et al. *Journal of Drug Education.* v9, n3, p243–53, 1979.

Analyzes usage of alcohol, tobacco, and illicit drugs during two recent television seasons. Alcohol predominated, accounting for more than two-thirds of all coded substance acts. More than two acts of alcohol use were found per hour in each season. The middle-class and comic characters did the heavier drinking.

136. TV Drug Advertising and Proprietary and Illicit Drug Use among Teenage Boys. Milavsky, J. Ronald et al. *Public Opinion Quarterly.* v39, n4, p457–81, Win 1975–76.

Revealed a negative relationship to exposure to drug advertising and use of illicit drugs in the sample population.

137. The Utilization of Attitudes and Beliefs as Indicators of Future Smoking Behavior. Downey, Ann Marie; O'Rourke, Thomas W. *Journal of Drug Education.* v6, n4, p283–95, 1976.

This study assesses if initial attitudes and beliefs of a behaviorally homogeneous group (1,228 females and 868 males) can be utilized as indicators of future smoking behavior. Results suggest attitudes and beliefs of initial never smokers may serve as indicators of future behavior.

138. Values and Attitudes of High School Drug Users. Graham, Donovan L.; Cross, William C. *Journal of Drug Education.* v5, n2, p97–107, 1975.

This study seeks to identify personal value orientations, philosophical attitudes, and social attitudes of high school students. Two questionnaires (Philosophical Attitude Description Inventory and Personal Attitude Questionnaire) were administered to 700 eleventh- and twelfth-grade students. Significant differences were demonstrated between drug users' and nonusers' values by discriminant analysis. Drug users were more subjective, unstructured, individual value oriented, and opposed to conservative Christianity.

139. When Do They Learn? A Study of Drug Awareness in Children in a Rural Elementary School. Freeman, Janice K.; Freeman, William H. *Journal of Drug Education.* v7, n2, p133–40, 1977.

"Awareness" of drugs among rural elementary school students (N=53) was studied with a word-association test of drug slang and words with no drug connotations given to students randomly selected from each of the six grades. The study suggests rural students are not immune to influences of the drug culture.

140. Where Have All Flower Children Gone—5-Year Follow-Up of a Natural Group of Drug-Users. Ramos, Manuel; Gould, Leroy C. *Journal of Drug Issues*. v8, n1, p75–84, Win 1978.

Using the senior author's unique access, the fate of 95 predominantly street-oriented, nonpatient, noncriminal, "natural," heavy drug users ("freaks") from the late sixties is documented. It was found that in five short years social networks had disintegrated, 80 percent of the "freaks" had assumed "normal" drug using behavior, 70 percent abandoned deviance as a way of life, and 60 percent escaped the ill consequences of detection by the law. "Street days" variables were analyzed with those from the follow-up period to determine why some went straight and others drifted towards other forms of deviance. Present way of life was more easily understood as a manifestation of their present situation than as vestigial characteristics of their deviant past. Reform occurred not necessarily because of the ever increasing efforts to "stop the drug problem," but rather because of subtler, more natural processes.

141. You Can't Help but Get Stoned: Notes on the Social Organization of Marijuana Smoking. Zimmerman, Don H.; Wieder, D. Lawrence. *Social Problems*. v25, n2, p198–207, Dec 77 (EJ 172 836; Reprint: UMI).

Examines a set of features intimately involved with marihuana use, e.g., the organization of marihuana distribution at the street level and the etiquette of social expectations regulating the use of marihuana on social occasions.

MICROFICHE

142. Alcoholism. Caliguri, Joseph P., Ed., Missouri University, Kansas City, School of Education, 1978, 306p (ED 179 865; Reprint: EDRS).

This extensive annotated bibliography provides a compilation of documents retrieved from a computerized search of the ERIC, Social Science Citation Index, and Med-Line databases on the topic of alcoholism. The materials address the following areas of concern: (1) attitudes toward alcohol users and abusers; (2) characteristics of alcoholics and their families; (3) alcohol and its impact on industry, armed forces, minorities, the community, hospitals, women, and teenagers; (4) the pathology of alcohol use; and (5) legislation on alcohol. Overall, the time period covered is from 1950 to 1978, with the great bulk of the materials coming from the 1966 to 1978 period.

143. Attitudes toward Use of Marijuana of Freshmen and Senior Students in Four Selected Hamilton County High Schools.* Plummer, Portia Flake; Indiana University, 1977, 159p (7813802; Reprint: DC).

The purpose of this investigation was to design and construct a valid and reliable evaluation instrument capable of assessing attitudes toward use of marihuana and to determine whether there were any differences in attitudes with respect to the class, sex, or school attended by the subjects. The study was limited to the freshmen and senior students in four selected Hamilton County Indiana secondary schools.

On the basis of the findings within the limitations of the study, the following conclusions were drawn: (1) the measuring instrument was both valid and reliable; (2) freshmen students do not have the same attitudes regarding use of marihuana as do senior students; (3) female students do not have the same attitudes regarding use of marihuana as male students; and (4) students in the four schools have varying attitudes toward the use of marihuana.

The following recommendations are made as a result of the foregoing study: (1) the results of this study should be regarded as a modest step in collecting reliable data with regard to attitudes in the use of marihuana, not as an end within itself; (2) the instrument should be revised periodically to provide consistency with new developments in respect to attitudes and issues of marihuana usage by high school students; (3) application of the instrument should be undertaken using a large geographical population and/or different demographic variables; (4) a test instrument should be developed to ascertain the extent to which the intersexual difference in attitudes toward use of marihuana is a physiological or psychological characteristic; and (5) the present instrument should be correlated with practice and knowledge inventories.

144. Attitudinal and Normative Factors Associated with Adolescent Cigarette Smoking. Newman, Ian M. et al. Oct 1978, 29p; Paper presented at the Annual Meeting of the American Public Health Association (Los Angeles, October 16, 1978) (ED 166 130; Reprint: EDRS).

This paper describes an attempt to use a model of behavioral intention as a diagnostic tool to provide useful data for the preparation of health education programs for adolescents in the area of cigarette smoking. The theory of this model is that a person's behavior is a function of his/her behavioral intention which, in turn, is a function of his/her attitude towards a behavior and his/her perception of subjective or social norms concerning that behavior. Participants in testing this model were high school students in the upper three grades. Questionnaires were designed to indicate students' attitudes on smoking, reasons for smoking or not smoking, and the extent of the influence of significant others on their decisions. It is stated that use of this model provides a qualitative as well as a quantitative understanding of cigarette smoking by high school students. Included in this document are samples of questionnaires submitted to participants and tabular analysis of results.

145. The Bearing of Certain Aspects of the Mother-Son Relationship upon the Son's Tendency toward Narcotics Addiction.* Tiboni, Vito B. A., Catholic University of America, 1976, 184p (7623206; Reprint: DC).

The purpose of this study was to determine if empirical support exists for theories maintaining that the mother/son relationship is an important factor in drug addiction. More specifically, this study examined four aspects of the mother/son relationship which included overprotection, demanding, dependency, and rejection as measured by the instruments utilized for this purpose. Of particular concern was the drug addicted subjects' perception of the mother in relation to those variables. Mothers' self-evaluations of both groups were also investigated and a correlation was determined between the responses of the mothers and their sons for both instruments. The study was designed in order to determine if the two groups of subjects (addicted and nonaddicted) perceived their mothers in a significantly different manner; if the two groups of mothers perceived themselves in a significantly different manner; and if a significant correlation existed between the sons' perception of their mothers and the mothers' perceptions of themselves for both groups.

The subjects of both the drug addicted and the nondrug addicted groups were selected from male, Viet Nam era veterans at the Brooklyn, New York Veterans Administration Hospital inpatient census. The drug addicted group consisted of 50 subjects randomly selected from 250 drug addicted patients. The comparison (nondrug addicted) group consisted of 50 subjects randomly selected from 450 medical patients who had been admitted for various medical problems, excluding those who have had alcohol addictions or psychiatric histories. A technician, who was unaware of the purpose of this study and the populations from which the subjects were selected, randomly administered the two instruments to the subjects of both groups and their mothers.

Drug addicted and nondrug addicted subjects were asked to evaluate their mothers on the variables of overprotection, demanding, dependency, and rejection by means of the selected subscales of the *Parent-Child Relations Questionnaire II (PCR II)* and the *Adjective Check List (ACL)*. The use of two separate instruments was intended to strengthen the findings by examining separate measures of the same qualities. Using the same instruments, the mothers of both groups were asked to do a self-evaluation on the same variables. Comparisons were made between the perceptions of the two groups of sons toward their mothers and between the self-evaluations of the two groups of mothers.

The results of the data analysis produced evidence that hospitalized addicted sons perceived their mothers as significantly more overprotecting, demanding, creating more dependency, and rejecting than did hospitalized nonaddicted subjects. The data indicated that mothers of addicted subjects also perceived themselves as significantly more overprotecting, demanding, creating more dependency, and rejecting than did mothers of nonaddicted subjects.

The results indicated that rejection may be the most overt and recognized trait among mothers of addicts. Overprotectiveness, fostering dependency, and demanding may be traits that are no less important, but less recognized, and more covertly affecting the sons' behavior and possible predisposition toward drug abuse.

146. Becoming a Marijuana Dealer. Criminal Justice Monograph, Volume VII, No. 3. Milor, Charles A., Sam Houston State University, Huntsville, TX, Institute of Contemporary Corrections and the Behavioral Sciences, 1976, 20p (ED 141 682; Reprint: EDRS).

This study presents an analysis of the process of becoming a marihuana dealer. It is only through an understanding of this process that the problem of marihuana can be completely understood. The process of becoming a dealer is seen as a process consisting of two parts: (1) the development of the external relationships which allow entrance into the marihuana-using groups, and (2) the rationalizing of the internal norms and goals of the larger society to those of a marihuana dealer. The social controls of society that prohibit marihuana use are outlined, and focus of the study is directed at the social processes that take place in the development of a dealer. There could be a predisposition in the personality of the people who become dealers, but unless this potential is subjected to the processes described in this paper, the potential will never be realized.

147. Categorizing Drugs and Drug-Taking: A More Meaningful Approach. Gold, Robert S.; Duncan, David F. 1975, 39p (ED 163 370; Reprint: EDRS).

This document reviews various definitions of the nature and classification of drugs. Difficulties with existing categorizations which use such bases as clinical utility, molecular structure, effects on the central nervous system, legality, and hazard potential are discussed. A more meaningful categorization based on the availability and sources of psychoactive drugs is offered. Categories include herbal, over-the-counter, prescription, unrecognized and illicit drugs, and tobacco and alcohol. Connotative meanings of the drug categories are examined in terms of the semantic differential. College student interests concerning drug categories are reported. Concerns about psychoactive drugs are mentioned. A typology of use patterns associated with motivations includes experimental, social-recreational, circumstantial-situational, intensified, and compulsive drug use. Use patterns are summarized. A traditional evaluation of use patterns reviews drug use, misuse, and abuse definitions. Finally addiction, habituation, and drug dependence are discussed.

148. The Context and Implications of Drinking and Drug Use among High School and College Students.* Kendall, Richard Fenwick, New York University, 1976, 199p (7619514; Reprint: DC).

The present study examined the drinking and drug-use patterns of a national sample of 430 college and 393 high school students in terms of eight "contextual" variables (exposure to drug use, positive attitudes about drugs, moral values, religious involvement, sexual involvement, counter culture identification, radical political beliefs, and parental use of alcohol) and five "implication" variables (delinquent behavior, alienation from school, family estrangement, psychological distress, and scholastic performance).

It was not the purpose of the study to establish causal links between the dependent and independent variables but rather to gain a better understanding of the attitudinal and behavioral contexts in which each occurs in the general student population and of what implications, if any, each behavior has in relation to the student's academic, psychological, social, and familial functioning.

Use of stepwise multiple regression analysis to control for each of the two dependent variables (i.e., drinking and drug use) while examining the context and implications of the other, made it possible to assess the unique qualities of each.

It was found that student drinking and use of illicit drugs take place in highly similar attitudinal and behavioral contexts but that these contexts also differ significantly. Both behaviors are highly related to exposure to the use of illegal drugs by peers. They are also highly related to the student's rejection of many traditional moral norms (e.g., sexual prohibitions) and social institutions (e.g., organized religion). Drug use, however, differs from drinking in that it is also highly related to the student's acceptance of norms and values associated with the so called "counter culture" (e.g., radical political beliefs, rejection of material success, etc.). These differences are discussed in terms of their implications for possible increases in the incidence of heavy alcohol use by high school and college students.

Examination of the implication variables also showed that both behaviors are related to feelings of alienation from school, estrangement from family, and to higher levels of delinquent behavior other than drinking and drug use. These relationships were stronger for drug use than for drinking; also, they were more marked for high school students than for college students. Psychological distress and scholastic performance were not found to be materially related to either drinking or drug use.

The findings are discussed in terms of their relevance for understanding the overall social significance of both student drinking and use of illicit drugs as well as their bearing on the possible increase of drinking among students—particularly in high school.

149. Developmental Dependencies. Hochhauser, Mark. Sep 1979, 31p; Paper presented at the Annual Convention of the American Psychological Association (87th, New York, September 1–5, 1979); best copy available (ED 179 858; Reprint: EDRS).

Researchers have long focused upon the problems of student/adolescent drug use; however, such a limited perspective may actually provide inaccurate information as to the actual nature and extent of total drug use. It may be more appropriate to emphasize a lifespan developmental perspective regarding drug-abuse behaviors, insofar as drug use must be analyzed on a continuum during the lifetime of the individual, rather than as an isolated experience during a particular period of development. Analyzing drug-abuse behaviors from such a developmental perspective includes six periods of development: the fetal period, infancy, childhood, adolescence, adulthood, and old age. Based upon joint considerations of developmental psychopharmacology and the biological boundaries of learning, an hypothesis of "developmental dependencies" may account for some of the interactions between drug abuse and the continually developing organism.

150. Drinking among Rural Youth with Implications for Rural Institutional Development. Lassey, Marie et al. Sep 1977, 51p; Paper presented at the Annual Meeting of the Rural Sociological Society (Madison, WI, September 1977) (ED 144 729; Reprint: EDRS).

During a three-month period ending in January 1977, questionnaires were given to 889 eighth- and twelfth-grade students to determine the extent of drinking among rural teenagers in Idaho and the sociological and psychological factors affecting their drinking habits. At least 16 percent of eighth graders and 34 percent of twelfth graders drink frequently. A much higher proportion of each age level drink occasionally. Both groups tend to have their first drink at home: home is also the most frequent drinking place for eighth graders, and the car is the most common drinking place for twelfth graders. Both groups obtain alcoholic beverages primarily from their friends. Drinking behavior of parents, closeness of relationship with parents, and communication with parents are strongly related to drinking patterns of both groups. An even stronger relationship, particularly for twelfth graders, exists between drinking and friendship patterns. Parents are most influential in determining whether drinking occurs for nondrinkers in both grades. Friends are more influential for frequent drinkers in both grades. Problem drinking is more likely to occur among families without close ties and when problem oriented communication between parents and child is minimal. Nondrinkers in both grades feel that parents are the best source of information about alcohol. The same is true for eighth graders who drink. However, the twelfth-grade drinkers feel the mass media are the most credible. Therefore, any program to discourage alcohol abuse must consider these factors.

151. Drinking Behaviors and Attitudes among Selected Adolescents of a Michigan Secondary School.* Griffin, Patricia Louise, University of Michigan, 1976, 344p (7619146; Reprint: DC).

The study is concerned with the use of alcoholic beverages among adolescents. A comprehensive questionnaire developed by the investigator, and revised after a pilot test, was administered to a random sample of 470 high school students, grades 9–12, of one Michigan suburban public high school. Items in the survey utilized both closed-ended and open-ended questions; the open-ended questions were included to allow students to better express their opinions about adolescent drinking. The survey was designed to provide information concerning: (1) the demographic characteristics of the adolescents and their general drinking behaviors; (2) specific drinking behaviors of the adolescents, their families, and their friends; and (3) the adolescents' feelings about and reasons for their drinking, opinions about drinking by themselves and others, and the extent of their knowledge about the use of alcoholic beverages.

A general conclusion of the study was that the majority of students regularly drink alcoholic beverages to some extent. Among other conclusions are the following: (1) more males than females drink alcohol, drink it more frequently, and in greater amounts; (2) beer is the favored alcoholic beverage, and the majority of students drink it with some degree of regularity; (3) students who drink less frequently display better school-related behaviors than do those who drink more frequently; (4) the drinking history of the majority of students is that of having a drink of beer offered to them at home by age 13; (5) students drink the most amount of alcohol in a party situation in which drinking is taking place; (6) the majority of students who drink report that their parents have knowledge of their drinking; (7) the majority of students who drink do so to some extent because they like the taste and because it makes them feel good, or feel high; (8) the majority of students agree to some extent that excessive use of alcohol can be harmful to a person's health, alcoholism is an illness, there is nothing wrong with the custom of having a couple of drinks to relax, and it is all right to get drunk once in a while if it does not become a habit; (9) the majority of students hold one or more personal opinions that drinking is in some respect all right; and (10) the majority of students feel that using drugs is more harmful to a high school student than drinking alcohol.

Summaries and implications of the statistical and descriptive findings, and recommendations for school counselor involvement with the problem of adolescent consumption of alcoholic beverages, were presented in the study.

152. Drugs and Crime: The Relationship of Drug Use and Concomitant Criminal Behavior. Research Issues 17. Austin, Gregory A., Ed.; Lettieri, Dan J., Ed., Documentation Associates, Los Angeles, Dec 1976, 277p. Sponsoring agency: National Institute on Drug Abuse (DHEW/PHS), Rockville, MD (ED 159 546; Reprint: EDRS; also available from Superintendent of Documents, US Government Printing Office, Washington, DC 20402, stock no. 017-024-00556-8).

This volume of abstracts of a major research and theoretical studies dealing with the relationship between drug use, criminal behavior, and the law, is concerned with criminal acts other than the possession of, or trafficking in, illicit drugs. Included are 107 selected studies categorized into seven major topic areas: reviews and theories, drug use and criminal behavior, addiction and criminal behavior, drugs and delinquency, crime and female drug use, the impact of treatment modalities, and the economics of drugs and crime. Some critical issues explored by the studies are raised in the following questions: (1) What kinds of crimes are committed by what types of drug users? (2) Is crime a necessary corollary to drug use? (3) What impact have changes in drug laws had on criminal behavior? Each abstract includes methodology, results, and conclusions. Materials were identified through a comprehensive literature search of major clearinghouses, databases, library collections, and special bibliographies.

153. Drugs and Personality: Personality Correlates and Predictors of Non-Opiate Drug Use. Research Issues 14. Austin, Gregory A., Ed. et al., Documentation Associates, Los Angeles, CA, Jul 1976, 135p. Sponsoring agency: National Institute on Drug Abuse (DHEW/PHS), Rockville, MD (ED 159 545; Reprint: EDRS; also available from Superintendent of Documents, US Government Printing Office, Washington, DC 20402, stock no. 017-024-00531-2).

This collection of abstracts from current research and theoretical studies explores various aspects of the relationship between nonopiate drug use and personality. The literature covers a period from 1968 through 1975 and focuses on tests that were conducted on adolescents and college students from the United States, Canada, and Sydney, Australia. Each abstract conveys what was done, why it was done, what methodology was employed, what results were found, and what conclusions were derived from the results. As many as 59 different types of testing instruments were used to determine if a subject's personality trait (e.g., sensation-seeking, emotional instability, insufficient ego strengths, etc.) would lead to the use of drugs such as alcohol, LSD, marihuana, and amphetamines. A supplemental bibliography of additional reading is also included in the volume along with several indexes designed to meet the needs and interests of further researchers.

154. Family Socialization and High School Social Climate Effects on Adolescent Alcohol and Marijuana Use.* Willette, JoAnne Lightle, University of Maryland, 1977, 190p (7812895; Reprint: DC).

The variables parent orientation (as measured by the Bowerman and Kinch Parent-Peer Group Orientation Questionnaire, 1959), parents' behavior (alcohol and drug use), and high school social climate were investigated as they relate to adolescent alcohol and marihuana use. The adolescent's attitudes toward alcohol and marihuana were included as intervening variables. A theoretical model was presented which suggests that parent orientation and parents' behavior influence adolescent attitudes and substance use while the high school social climate has a modifying effect on the relationship.

Data from a population of 2,611 ninth- and eleventh-grade students in rural, suburban, and urban schools were used. Measures of parent orientation and the adolescent's attitudes toward and use of alcohol and marihuana were obtained by self-report questionnaire. Parents' behavior was a measure of the parents' frequency of alcohol and drug use as reported by the adolescent. A measure of high school social cimate was devised based on the prevalence of alcohol and marihuana use in the school.

Parent orientation was found to be inversely related to adolescent substance use. Persons with low parent orientation scores were more likely to use alcohol and marihuana than those with high parent orientation scores. Parent orientation was also related to age of the adolescent. As age increased, parent orientation decreased. In addition, it was found that adolescent substance use increased with age.

Parents' behavior was found to be positively related to adolescent substance use. As the parents' alcohol and drug use increased, the adolescent's alcohol and marihuana use increased. However, parents' alcohol use was found to be a stronger predictor of adolescent behavior than parents' drug use, as measured in this study.

An investigation of the relationship between parent orientation and parents' behavior indicated that as parents' drinking increased, parent orientation decreased. It appears that the child may learn from the parents' behavior even in the absence of a strong parent/child affectional bond.

High school social climate was found to have an additional influence on adolescent substance use. Even though parent orientation was found to be a deterrent to adolescent substance use, a high use high school social climate somewhat weakened the strength of this relationship. Furthermore, the data suggested that the high alcohol use climate in the high school is a secondary factor which reinforces the influence of frequent parent alcohol use and counteracts the positive influence of nondrinking parents.

The original theoretical model presented parent orientation and parents' behavior as family socialization variables. High school social climate was the test factor while adolescent attitudes were the intervening variables preceding adolescent substance use. The concluding chapter presents an alternative conceptualization of the relationships among the variables. Here, parents' behavior and high school social climate were seen as two environmental supports influencing adolescent behavior.

155. Growing Up in America: A Background to Contemporary Drug Abuse. Macleod, Anne, Biospherics Inc., Rockville, MD, 1976, 105p. Sponsoring agency: National Institute on Drug Abuse (DHEW/PHS), Rockville, MD (ED 159 536; Reprint: EDRS; also available from Superintendent of Documents, US Government Printing Office, Washington, DC 20402, stock no. 017-024-00290-9).

This book is aimed at helping school personnel and others understand the world as youths experience it and to prepare them to respond to young people's search for philosophical answers. Understanding the life context and viewpoint of young adolescents is assumed to be a prerequisite for understanding drug abuse and for communicating with youngsters about drug abuse. The text is based principally on youngsters' self-reports recorded throughout the literature and on studies of life in inner city and suburban environments. However, many of its findings and the commentary reflect and are applicable to youths and their schools in all types of communities. Also included in this text are literature excerpts and discussions of how schools can attempt to meet the needs of youth from a variety of environments. Annotated bibliographies concerning drug use and the special problems of young adolescents are included for both teachers and students.

156. Handbook on Drug Abuse. Dupont, Robert I. et al., Metrotec Research Associates, Washington, DC, Jan 1979, 439p. Sponsoring agency: National Institute on Drug Abuse (DHEW/PHS), Rockville, MD (ED 176 128; Reprint: EDRS).

A decade of professional research on drug abuse has produced both an abundance of materials and a vocabulary that is not shared by planners, clinicians, and policymakers. This handbook compiles the major developments of the period and their treatment and research implications in a style intended to be understood by all three types of professionals. Over 40 authors surveyed the literature in their own areas of expertise, often including their own viewpoints and recommendations. The nine sections of the book range from the history of the field through treatment modalities, as well as specific methods for specialized needs; specific drugs or classes of drugs; drug use from both a psychosocial and epidemiological perspective; the special issues of management, training, and prevention; and a section on research prospects and an assessment of future direction of the field.

157. Marijuana: College Students' Expectations.
Rumstein, Regina. Mar 1978, 25p; Paper presented at the Annual Meeting of the Eastern Psychological Association (49th, Washington, DC, March 29–April 1, 1978) (ED 165 065; Reprint: EDRS).

College students' expectations regarding the physiological, psychological, and social effects of marihuana were investigated. A sample of 210 undergraduates stated their expectations about the effect of the drug by answering a series of structured-response type questions. Also, Ss provided background information related to their expectations about marihuana. Overall, the data suggest that students' expectations about the effects of marihuana were largely contrary to research findings and tended to discount potentially harmful consequences of the drug. Marihuana use was considered an educational issue, and decriminalization of it was strongly favored. Users, occasional users, and nonusers differed significantly in expectations about marihuana effects which lent support to hypotheses based on the theory of cognitive consistency. Of interest were sex differences on selected background variables. Women as compared to men seemed to hold more disapproving attitudes about the use of marihuana, reported greater difficulties in obtaining the drug, used it less frequently, and knew fewer marihuana smokers. Expectations about marihuana should be taken into account when trying to develop relevant drug education programs.

158. Perceptions of Five and Six-Year-Old Children concerning Cultural Drinking Norms.* Penrose, Gloria Benson, University of California, Berkeley, 1978, 162p (7904574; Reprint: DC).

The purpose of this study was to determine whether awareness of cultural drinking norms and attitudes toward the use of alcoholic beverages are present, if in only rudimentary form, in the young child. The objective of the inquiry was to provide useful data upon which guidelines, based on empirical evidence, can be developed as to the earliest feasible time for parents, teachers, and others, to begin education of young children about alcohol and drinking.

Drinking alcoholic beverages is viewed as learned behavior dependent upon modeling and imitation for the most part. The models are assumed to be the child's parents, especially, the same-sex parent. Attitudes and value formation toward alcohol and drinking are seen as emanating from identificatory processes, including sex typing and role taking.

A parent's questionnaire was devised to yield information on parental drinking practices.

The major hypotheses were that young children are aware of a cultural drinking norm in this country; that they can differentiate between alcoholic and nonalcoholic beverages in that they are able to discriminate as to the appropriate use of either. That is, they recognize that alcoholic beverages may be drunk by adults during festive or nonfestive occasions, but that children generally do not drink alcoholic beverages at either time. Socioeconomic class or sex were not expected to make a difference in the responses.

The task was presented in the form of a guessing game. Ten black and white drawings portraying male and female adults and children engaged in five festive and five nonfestive activities were used with ten prototypes of beverages, in color, five alcoholic and five nonalcoholic. While all of the beverages, both alcoholic and nonalcoholic were exposed to view, the child was asked to guess which beverage each of the individuals in each scene would like to drink.

The sample was comprised of 89 five- and six-year-old children in five kindergarten and five first-grade classes in five public elementary schools. The sexes were approximately even in number.

The findings provide strong support for the major hypotheses. That children five and six years of age are aware of a cultural drinking norm may be seen from the frequency of their alcoholic choices on both festive and nonfestive occasions, and from their alcoholic choices for adults on both festive and nonfestive occasions. Firm evidence that they discriminate between the appropriate use of alcoholic and nonalcoholic beverages and are able to differentiate between them is seen in the frequency of their alcoholic choices for adults versus children on either occasion. As expected, there were no statistically significant differences on these variables according to sex or socioeconomic group membership.

Many of the findings specifically serve to indicate that perceptions about alcohol and drinking are clearly present at this young age but that attitudes are not yet well developed or firmly set and may be most amenable to influence in ways which will prevent later problems with alcohol. A major conclusion is that education about alcohol and drinking could profitably begin at five years of age or at the kindergarten level.

159. Perspectives on the History of Psychoactive Substance Use; Research Issues 24. Austin, Gregory A., Documentation Associates, Los Angeles, CA, 1978, 319p. Sponsoring agency: National Institute on Drug Abuse (DHEW/PHS), Rockville, MD (ED 177 455; Reprint: EDRS; also available from Superintendent of Documents, US Government Printing Office, Washington, DC 20402, stock no. 017-024-00879-6).

This collection of resources contains 34 studies which summarize significant developments within the history of psychoactive substance use in developed countries since the sixteenth century. The primary intent of this volume is to provide a greater awareness of the ubiquity of drug use in the past and of the complex and varied factors which have influenced its spread, society's response to the spread, and the effects of that response. The studies review drug use since the Renaissance in the United States, Europe, and Asia with an emphasis on the following substances: alcohol, coffee, tobacco, ether, cocaine, amphetamines, marihuana, opium, and the opiates. Each section includes an introductory review, chronology, and summaries of previous research.

160. Predicting Adolescent Drug Abuse: A Review of Issues, Methods and Correlates. Research Issues 11. Lettieri, Dan J., Ed., Macro Systems, Inc., Silver Spring, MD; National Institute on Drug Abuse (DHEW/PHS), Rockville, MD, Dec 1975, 370p; a few pages may reproduce poorly in hard copy due to small print of original (ED 119 424; Reprint: EDRS; also available from Superintendent of Documents, US Government Printing Office, Washington, DC 20402, publication no. ADM–76–299).

Presented are 18 papers on predicting adolescent drug abuse. The papers have the following titles: "Current Issues in the Epidemiology of Drug Abuse as Related to Psychosocial Studies of Adolescent Drug Use"; "The Quest for Interpersonal Predictors of Marihuana Abuse in Adolescents"; "Assessing the Interpersonal

Determinants of Adolescent Drug Use''; ''Speculations on Possible Changes in Youthful Lifestyle between the 1960s and 1970s''; ''A Psychological Approach toward the Meanings of Drug Use''; ''An Approach to the Classification of the Lifestyles of Narcotic Abusers''; ''Individualized Prediction as a Strategy for Discovering Demographic and Interpersonal/Psychological Correlates of Drug Resistance and Abuse''; ''A Social Psychological Approach to Substance Abuse Construct Validity—Prediction of Adolescent Drug Use from Independent Data Sources''; ''Computer Interview Questionnaires for Drug Use/Abuse''; ''Personality Factors Related to Drug and Alcohol Use''; ''Self-Esteem as a Predictor of Adolescent Drug Abuse''; ''Ego Mechanisms and Marihuana Usage''; ''Chemical Substance Abuse and Perceived Locus of Control''; ''Behavioral and Demographic Correlates of Drug Use among Students in Grades 7–12''; ''Teenage Drug Use—A Search for Causes and Consequences''; ''Predicting Time of Onset of Marihuana Use—A Developmental Study of High School Youth''; ''Drug Use Research Items Pertaining to Personality and Interpersonal Relations—A Working Paper for Research Investigators''; and ''Some Comments on the Relationship of Selected Criteria Variables to Adolescent Illicit Drug Use.''

161. Psychodynamics of Drug Dependence. NIDA Research Monograph 12. Blaine, Jack D., Ed.; Julius, Demetrios A., Ed., National Institute on Drug Abuse (DHEW/PHS), Rockville, MD, May 77, 154p; pages 36–72 and 82–87 were removed prior to filming due to copyright (ED 151 681; Reprint: EDRS; also available from Superintendent of Documents, US Government Printing Office, Washington, DC 20402, stock no. 017-024-00642-4).

This review includes chapters by several medical and sociological experts, and seeks to identify the key personality traits in drug dependence. It is a study of individual rather than physical and sociological variables. An attempt is made to discover the part played by one's own psychodynamics and their relationship to substance abuse.

162. The Relationship of ''Significant Others'' Attitudes toward Adolescent Drinking and Adolescent Problem Drinking.* Luszczak, Michael Jacob, United States International University, 1979, 97p (8000241; Reprint: DC).

The hypotheses tested were: H_1 There is a significant difference in the degree of problem drinking between those adolescents who are exposed to parents' extreme attitude that alcohol drinking by adolescents is completely unacceptable or completely acceptable and those adolescents who are exposed to parents' moderate attitude that it is acceptable if the adolescent drinks only once in a while or on special occasions. H_2 There is a significant difference in the degree of problem drinking between those adolescents who are exposed to a closest friend's extreme attitude about alcohol drinking and those adolescents who are exposed to closest friend's moderate attitude. H_3 There is a significant difference in the degree of problem drinking between those adolescents who are exposed to closest friend's attitude that alcohol drinking by adolescents is completely acceptable and those adolescents who are exposed to parents' extreme attitude that it is completely unacceptable. The importance of the study is that the findings of this research may be of use in planning of educational program, prevention, and therapy for adolescent problem drinkers.

A descriptive survey was used to obtain the data. The subjects (N=97) were divided into two groups. One group consisted of the adolescents who were exposed to ''significant others'' extreme attitudes, whereas the other group consisted of adolescents who were exposed to ''significant others'' moderate type of attitude. The instrument used was a questionnaire which included an Alcohol Problem Index, which determined the level of the adolescent's problem drinking, and questions which determined the type of ''significant others'' attitude to which the adolescents were exposed. Data were collected from adolescents who voluntarily presented themselves at the youth agencies to obtain help in their personal problems. The data were analyzed using chi square test for statistical significance and Pearson's test for correlation.

Significant difference for H_1 was found in the degree of problem drinking between those adolescents who were exposed to parents' extreme type of attitude and those adolescents that were exposed to parents' moderate type of attitude. The data indicated that parents' extreme attitudes appeared to influence more adolescents who developed low and medium levels of problem drinking than the moderate attitude did. No significant difference for H_2 was found, but the frequencies indicated that the closest friend's extreme attitude appears to influence more adolescents who developed a high level of problem drinking than the moderate attitude did. No significant difference was found for H_3 but the frequencies indicated that the parents' attitude of complete unacceptance kept the number of adolescents that developed a high level of problem drinking to a lower frequency than was found for the closest friends' attitude of complete acceptance.

163. Religious Affiliation, Norm Quality, and Drinking Patterns of Adolescents.* Hogan, Edmond Pascal, Washington State University, 1979, 126p (7923486; Reprint: DC).

This study addresses the question of why some adolescents, in their drinking habits, reflect adherence to the directives of the church to which they are affiliated concerning the appropriate use of alcohol, while others do not.

Two dependent variables are utilized: a quantity-frequency index of alcohol use, and a social effects scale which measures the type and degree of problems which are associated with excessive indulgence in alcohol. The two main independent variables are the strength of bonds to religion and religious affiliation. The latter variable was operationalized according to the attitudes of the religions of interest concerning appropriate use of alcohol. Those religions in which any use of alcohol is regarded as a violation of church norms are classified as ''proscriptive,'' while the religions which set down specific directives concerning the conditions under which drinking is considered appropriate as well as defining the quantity of alcohol to be consumed are categorized as ''prescriptive.'' The population under investigation is comprised of tenth-grade students from public schools in a medium-sized city in the state of Washington.

Four hypotheses were tested and support, in varying degrees, was found for each. In respect to quantity and frequency of alcohol use, the strength of bonds to religion was found to be the best predictor. When the bonds to religion were strong, both the proscriptive and prescriptive groups were found to indulge in alcohol to the degree predicted. That is, the proscriptive group were likely to be abstainers, while the prescriptive group drank in moderation. When the bonds were weak, both groups tended to drink to an excessive degree.

With respect to social effects, the proscriptive subjects who drank experienced more problems with authority as well as more interpersonal and psychological problems. Again, the strength to bonds to religion proved to be the better predictor. Implications for control theory, as well as for future research, are discussed.

164. Reporter's Guide: Drugs, Drug Abuse Issues, Resources. Parachini, Allan. 1975, 87p (ED 146 537; Reprint: EDRS; also available from Drug Abuse Council, 1828 L Street, NW, Washington, DC 20036).

The purposes of this booklet are: (1) to serve as a commentary on the evolution, state, and problems of drug reporting; (2) to make the journalist aware of the prominent issues and some of the major misconceptions common among reporters, readers, and/or listeners; (3) to serve as a guide to the fundamental background literature of the field; (4) to act as a source guide to potential interview or reference persons; and (5) to be a guide to terminology. It focuses primarily on the class of drugs which, for nonmedical use, are and have been illegal. Additionally, it contains research tips on drug reporting, a list of nationally important resource organizations, and lists of resources at both the individual and the state level. Information is extensive and well organized.

165. Research Issues Update, 1978; Research Issues 22. Austin, Gregory A., Ed. et al., Documentation Associates, Los Angeles, 1978, 319p. Sponsoring agency: National Institute on Drug Abuse (DHEW/PHS), Rockville, MD (ED 177 453; Reprint: EDRS; also available from Superintendent of Documents, US Government Printing Office, Washington, DC, stock no. 017-024-00876-1).

This collection of resources contains abstracts of selected research studies and theoretical expositions dealing with psychosocial aspects of drug use, culled from professional literature published between 1974 and 1977. The 13 topics covered in this survey include: sex, pregnancy, attitude change, family/peer influences, employment, crime, criminal justice, cocaine, personality, psychopathology, and driving. Each reference is outlined by a chart in terms of the drug used, sample size and type, age, sex, ethnicity, geographical area, methodology, data collection instrument, dates conducted, and number of bibliographic references. Further details are provided in statements focusing on the purpose, methodology, results, and conclusions of the research.

166. Self-Concept and Drug Involvement among Urban Junior High School Youths. Dembo, Richard et al. Dec 1976, 42p; Paper presented at the Annual Meeting of the American Educational Research Association (New York, April 4–8, 1977) (ED 142 874; Reprint: EDRS—HC not available).

Data from a survey of inner-city junior high school youths examined how their self-images related to their drug use. Boys and girls who were oriented to drug/gang or drug culture values were involved with drugs; those who were educationally oriented were not into substance taking. In finding that the boys and girls related to their environment in a manner that was consistent with their drug taking, the results emphasize the interface of personality and sociocultural perspectives on substance use. Limited insight into the youngsters' drug behavior is provided by focusing on them as

individuals or on prevalent values in their community. Neighborhood values assume importance when they become internalized into the youths' self-perceptions and are reflected in their activities.

167. Smokers vs. Nonsmokers: Toward an Understanding of Their Differences. Buhl, Joanne M.; Bell, Roger A., Louisville University, KY, School of Medicine, Apr 1976, 20p; Paper presented at the Annual Convention of the American Alliance for Health, Physical Education, and Recreation (Milwaukee, WI, April 2, 1976) (ED 123 217; Reprint: EDRS).

This research was conducted to contribute to the general knowledge concerning differences between smokers and nonsmokers. The data were obtained from a major epidemiologic study conducted in 1973 in the southeastern United States. A survey instrument composed of 403 questions and administered to 2,029 randomly selected adults was designed to elicit mental and physical health information as well as sociodemographic and service utilization data. Significant differences have been found between smokers and nonsmokers. The highest percentage of smokers was found among males, those aged 30–44, the less educated, the divorced or separated, the middle socioeconomic class, those experiencing larger numbers of stressful life events, those who did not grow up with both their real parents, and those who had unhappy childhoods. Smokers as a group tended to score higher on psychological scales measuring anxiety and depressive symptomatology. The findings support that smoking is a compensatory form of behavior, a symptom of other problems of emotional health. Until it becomes possible to identify individuals who are biologically cancer prone and to therefore direct educational efforts toward specific target groups who will suffer the most debilitating consequences of smoking, intervention must be persistent, individualized, and socially reinforced. (Charts and graphs are included in the report.)

168. Social Identification and Drugs: An Exploration of the Social Bases of Suburban High School Student Drug-Using Behaviour.* Yangyuoru, Yvon, Loyola University of Chicago, 1975, 163p (7514530; Reprint: DC).

Using the family/school/peer group as a theoretical framework, the present study examines differential student involvement with drugs and its immediate sociocultural context: the interests, activities, and social characteristics differentiating drug users from nonusers within a suburban Catholic, all boys high school in the Midwest.

Methodologically the study combines self-administered questionnaire (involving the entire student community of 1,107 students) and a follow-up interview of a limited number of randomly selected sample of students stratified by year in school and grade point average. The complementary questionnaire and interview data were used to test the hypotheses that student drug-using behaviour is contingent on: (1) nonstable family structure; (2) nonnurturing family relations; (3) parental drug relatedness; (4) parental high socioeconomic status; (5) nonreligious background of students; (6) marginal religiosity of student; (7) association with drug-using friends; (8) high involvement in student organizations; and (9) poor academic performance.

The data suggest that family structure and level of socioeconomic status do not appear to be significantly related with student drug use within this community. The most important distinctions with regard to student drug use occur in terms of four pairs of dichotomies: integration vs. marginality, religiosity vs. nonreligiosity, nurturant vs. nonnurturant family relations, and nondrug-using friends vs. drug-using friends. These are theoretical constructs and not monothetic categories. Within this context, the nondrug-using student could be located on one end of the continuum, the drug-using student at the other extreme. The typical nondrug-using student is most likely to define himself/herself as a "scholar," "jock," "greaser," or "student leader." S/he has good relationship with his/her parents, participates frequently in religious activities, and considers himself/herself a deeply religious person. S/he is well integrated in the school system in that s/he is a high academic achiever (at least a B grade point average) and is more involved in student organizations or activities. Most or all of his/her close friends also abstain from drugs. The typical drug-using student is mose likely to describe himself/herself as a "freak." In terms of family structure, s/he tends to come from a home in which the father figure is absent; his/her relationship with parents is either indifferent or poor. In terms of the school system, s/he is marginal both in academic achievement (C+ or less grade point) and participation in student organizations and activities. His/her interest in religion is defined either as none or, at best, intellectual, and his/her participation in religious activities is marginal. Most or all his/her friends are users of drugs. Differences in drug use correspond to differences in self-conception. What these data add to the findings of previous analysis is information on student's self-conception and how this relates to religiosity, family relations, family structure, academic performance, student organizational participation, types of close friends, and drug-using behaviour.

169. Structural and Symbolic Aspects of Phencyclidine (PCP) Use in Philadelphia: A Case of Rational Drug Use?* Walters, James Michael, Medical College of Pennsylvania, 1979, 162p (7917530; Reprint: DC).

The dissertation challenges the widely held belief that the use of illicit psychoactive drugs by youth in our society is necessarily dysfunctional and/or psychopathologic. It hypothesizes a purposive model of functional drug use. According to this model, the use of drugs—even as potent as phencyclidine—would be functional and rational in adolescent society, if there were: (1) ideological prescriptions for use and proscriptions against misuse, (2) structural/ functional supports for use and penalties for misuse, and (3) a demonstrated history of attempts to manage drug use.

Employing an ethnographic approach, the investigator studied the social structure, lifestyles, and drug use of a network of adolescents in and around Philadelphia. Data were gathered and analyzed by standard ethnographic techniques: (1) participant observations, (2) a demographic and drug history survey of all respondents (N=50), (3) indepth interviews with the PCP users (N=27), and (4) ethnoscientific analysis of the interview and observation data.

Drug use, in this case exemplified by PCP, was found to be a central symbol in an adolescent society. It defines social types, and organizes time and space via the central ritual of social drug use, viz. partying. These strong prescriptions for drug use are balanced by proscriptions against misuse. Chronic overusers, pejoratively labelled "burn-outs," are disrespected and often ostracized. These opposing constraints result in complex folk schemes for assessing a drug's quality, potency, and dosage.

It is concluded that in the adolescent world of a large metropolitan area such as Philadelphia, drug use has become a *social fact*. Drugs, a tolerance of them, a willingness to experience them, are essential functions of mainstream adolescence today.

170. A Study of Significant Knowledge and Attitudes of High School Counselors concerning Students Who Are Involved in the Moderate and Heavy Use of Marihuana.* Gardner, Charles Louis, University of Georgia, 1975, 145p (762229; Reprint: DC).

Much of the literature on drug-abuse counseling refers to the need for high school counselors to improve their knowledge about drug abuse and to develop more open-minded attitudes toward youth who use drugs. The purpose of this study was to identify significant competencies of high school counselors in terms of knowledge and attitude in working with high school students who become involved in the moderate or heavy use of marihuana. High school counselors, high school principals, and counselors in drug day-treatment and mediation centers throughout the state of Georgia were surveyed. The drug day-treatment and mediation center counselor group was used for comparison purposes because it was assumed to be the most competent group. The high school principal group was surveyed because the knowledge and attitudes of high school principals determine the policy structure within which high school counselors must perform. High school counselors were surveyed because their competencies in terms of knowledge and attitudes were of primary interest.

The survey instrument was developed through several procedures. A pool of 140 cognitive items was drawn from reports of empirical and scientific research in the field of drug abuse. These items were analyzed by a panel of experts, and 40 items on which a high degree of agreement was identified were included in the first four subtests. A fifth subtest was composed of attitudinal items which correlated to the Rokeach Dogmatism Scale in a significant range or a range near significance.

Group and age were employed as independent variables. Tests of mean difference (t tests) identified the drug day-treatment and mediation center counselors' group as scoring significantly higher on the cognitive subtests than did the high school counselors' group and the high school principals' group. The t tests identified the high school counselors' group as scoring significantly higher on the cognitive subtests than did the high school principals' group. The high school principals' group was identified as scoring significantly higher on the dogmatism subtest than did the high school counselors' group. The high school counselors' group scored significantly higher on the dogmatism subtest than the drug day-treatment and mediation center counselors' group. The younger high school counselors' subgroup scored significantly lower on the dogmatism subtest than did the older high school counselors' subgroup.

Chi square procedures were employed with individual items to identify patterns of responses which would indicate how the sample groups perceived certain fundamental concepts, procedures, and issues in working in a helping relationship with students who use marihuana on a moderate or heavy basis. The indication was that the younger high school counselors' subgroup and the drug day-treatment and mediation center counselors' group considered psychological factors to be the most prevalent causes of marihuana use as contrasted to the older high school counselors' subgroup and the high school principals' group which considered permissiveness to be the most prevalent cause of marihuana use. The younger high school counselors' subgroup and the drug day-treatment and mediation center counselors' group considered counseling as the most effective approach to helping marihuana using students. The older high school counselors' subgroup and the high school principals' group considered disciplinary approaches to be more effective than counseling with drug-abusing youth.

171. A Survey of Drinking Behavior among Montana State University Students and the Potential for Problems with Alcohol: Implications for Counseling Services, Alcohol Education, and Student Personnel Services.* Fleming, Robert John, Montana State University, 1976, 184p (774972; Reprint: DC).

The purpose of this study was to investigate the role of selected family, peer, and personal factors influencing the use of alcohol by college students. These sociological and psychological factors were conceptually considered in terms of their possible influence on the respondents' observable drinking behaviors and their nonobservable attitudes considered in the context of various components of alienation.

A review of literature revealed that the drinking behaviors of college students were essentially a group phenomenon, that even though virtually all collegians drink they nevertheless did so in moderation, and that their drinking practices mirrored, to some extent, those of their parents. Little literature was found regarding alienation and student drinking. The literature reviewed linked alienation with various personality factors but had little to say about its development and maintenance.

The results of this study indicated that the drinking behaviors of college students were influenced by those of their parents and their friends. This study also indicated that students' drinking practices were influenced by their personal experience of alienation.

Some of the major conclusions reached were that: (1) parents' drinking behaviors were powerful shapers of those of their children; (2) maternal problem drinking was shown to be associated with the alienation component, normlessness; (3) peer drinking behaviors influenced those of the respondent; (4) peers were selected, in part, according to their similarity of values with those of the respondents; (5) selected reference group factors were shown to have associations with the several elements of alienation; and (6) the respondent's level of alienation was shown to have associations with his/her quantity and frequency of drinking, age at onset of drinking, and potential for problems with alcohol.

Some of the recommendations offered were: (1) that alcohol and drug education include sociological and psychological material in addition to physiological and pharmacological information; (2) that future research efforts study the differences between male and female drinking practices; (3) that the effects of parental problem drinking on children be investigated; (4) that the origins, development, maintenance, and effects of alienation be examined in depth as it concerns drinking practices; and (5) that people in the helping professions be given opportunities to learn about problem drinking.

BOOKS

172. The Age of Sensation: A Psychoanalytic Exploration of Youth in the 1970s. Hendin, Herbert. New York: McGraw-Hill, 1977, 354p.

Through interviews with college students and analysis of popular literature, the author has attempted to create a portrait of emotional life in America. Finding an overall feeling of fragmentation, depression, and flight from intimacy and committment in our society, he examines student behaviors in reaction to these negative pressures: drug abuse, sexual problems, and suicide.

173. Alcohol: The Delightful Poison: A History. Fleming, Alice Mulcahey. New York: Delacorte Press, 1975, 138p.

The author reviews the history of alcoholism and drinking customs with special emphasis on America. The myths and mysteries of alcoholism are also considered.

174. Drugs, Society, and Human Behavior. Ray, Oakley. St. Louis, MO: C.V. Mosby Company, 1978, 457p.

The varied aspects of drugs, their source, abuse, chemical composition, and physical, personal, and social effects are explored. Seven units cover the following areas: (1) an overview on drug use, a brief history of drugs, and discussion of social implications; (2) the human nervous system and the actions of drugs; (3) "nondrug drugs" such as alcohol, nicotine, caffeine, and over-the-counter drugs; (4) the use and misuse of psychotherapeutic drugs; (5) the narcotic drugs; (6) the "phantasticants"; and (7) conclusions and discussion of drug use in modern society.

Medical Research on Drug Effects

JOURNAL ARTICLES

175. Alcohol, Marijuana, and Memory. Loftus, Elizabeth F. *Psychology Today.* v13, n10, p42–43, 45–46, 48, 50, 54, 56, 92, Mar 1980.

Presents recent findings on the effects of marijuana and alcohol use on short- and long-term memory. Both social and chronic use are discussed. It is concluded that alcohol and marijuana are similar in that they both appear to impede the process of forming new memories.

176. Alcohol Metabolism: All in the Family. *Science News.* v115, n1, p6, Jan 6, 1979.

Evidence already exists that alcoholism may "run in the family." Recent studies have shown as much as a four-fold increase in alcoholism among children of alcoholics over children of nonalcoholics. Now, University of Washington researchers have conducted experiments which indicate a possible genetic factor—a more intense metabolic reaction to alcohol among relatives of alcoholics.

177. The Diagnosis and Treatment of the PCP Abuse Syndrome. Parts I & II. Smith, David E. et al. *International Drug Report*. v20, n3, p2–3, Mar 1979; *International Drug Report*. v20, n4, p4–5, 15, Apr 1979. (Available from International Narcotic Enforcement Officers Association, Albany, NY.)

From a law enforcement and medical viewpoint, this article describes four behavioral stages of the PCP abuse syndrome: acute PCP toxicity, PCP toxic psychosis, PCP precipitated psychotic episodes, and PCP induced depression. Each stage is outlined and its salient clinical features illustrated through case studies.

178. Educational Implications of Drug Abuse. Hochhauser, Mark. *Journal of Drug Education*. v8, n1, p69–76, 1978.

Observing the steady decrease in SAT scores during the past decade, while noting the steady increase in drug use during the same time period, several implications are considered for the potentially deleterious effects of drugs on emerging adolescent cognitive processes, especially learning and memory.

Possible drug behavior relationships are viewed from a developmental perspective (e.g., sex, age, and maturation rate), insofar as drug effects will be directly related to the level of physiological and psychological maturation achieved by the drug user. Consequently, proposals are made dealing with drug education in the schools.

179. The Fetal Alcohol Syndrome. Rivard, Carol. *Journal of School Health*. v49, n2, p96–98, Feb 1979 (EJ 202 425; Reprint: UMI).

Although fetal alcohol syndrome is a preventable disease, it is hard to control because identification of the alcoholic mother is difficult.

180. Hazards and Benefits of Drug Interaction. Labianca, Dominick A. *Intellect*. v106, n2395, p401–03, Apr 1978 (EJ 182 848; Reprint: UMI).

Most cases of drug toxicity are direct consequences of drug misuse—either intentional or inadvertent. Discusses two types of drug interaction—synergistic and antagonistic. The former produces a combined effect greater than the sum of the effects of the individual drugs concerned; the latter is produced when the desired action of one drug is diminished or completely eliminated by the action of another drug.

181. Health Implications of Marihuana Use: A Review. Petersen, Robert C. *American Biology Teacher*. v41, n9, p526–29, Dec 1979 (EJ 214 989; Reprint: UMI).

Summarizes what is known about the effects of marihuana use on health. The topics included are its chemistry and the metabolism; the effects of acute intoxication on learning, memory, intellectual performance, driving, and other skilled performances; and effects on lungs, brain, heart, and other systems.

182. Jimson "Loco" Weed Abuse in Adolescents. Shervette, Robert E., III et al. *Pediatrics*. v63, n4, p520–23, Apr 1979. (Available from: Arthur Retlaw and Associates, Inc., Suite 2080, 1603 Orrington Avenue, Evanston, IL 60201.)

Over a three-year period, 29 adolescent patients were hospitalized because of intentional Jimson weed ingestion. Their records were reviewed for the presence of signs and symptoms of atropine/scopolamine toxicity, clinical course, treatment, and outcome.

183. Marijuana Revisited. Archer, James, Jr.; Lopata, Ann. *Personnel and Guidance Journal*. v57, n5, p244–50, Jan 1979 (EJ 195 896; Reprint: UMI).

This review examines recent research on the psychological effects of marihuana. The article contains material on potency, research problems, use patterns in the United States, and expectancy, as well as a review of research on acute effects, including psychosis, toxic delerium, acute anxiety, and brain damage. Nonacute effects are also examined, with material on studies of amotivational syndrome, intellectual functioning, memory, sexual activity, and driving. Research on marihuana's relationship to other drugs and to criminal behavior is also evaluated. Implications for counselors are discussed.

184. Parental Smoking Affects Children. *Science News*. v113, n22, p361, Jun 1978. (EJ 185 746; Reprint: UMI).

Research done by workers at Harvard Medical School suggests that passive exposure to cigarette smoke can impair breathing in children ages five through nine. Lung flow rates (breathing ability) decreased for children with smoking parents, and significantly if the children also smoked.

185. Some Unsettling Thoughts about Settling in with Pot. Hawley, Richard A. *Independent School*. v38, n2, p29–30, 33–35, Dec 1978 (EJ 204 092; Reprint: UMI).

Popular culture now considers marihuana harmless, but research shows it has definite physiological and neurological effects, effacing memory and attention, and producing cell damage and learning deficits. Young people turn to pot to escape the emotional pressures of adolescence. Parents and schools can help adolescents by setting firm prohibitions.

186. Study Finds Sleeping Pills Overprescribed. *Science*. v204, n4390, p287–88, Apr 20, 1979.

Sleeping pills, the most prescribed medication in the world, are more dangerous and less useful than either physicians or patients realize, according to a recent report by the Institute of Medicine of the National Academy of Sciences. Both barbiturates and their chief alternatives, benzodiazepines, have hazards.

MICROFICHE

187. Cutting Tobacco's Toll. World Watch Paper 18. Eckholm, Erik. Mar 1978, 42p. Sponsoring agency: Worldwatch Institute, Washington, DC (ED 156 970; Reprint: EDRS—HC not available; also available from Worldwatch Institute, 1776 Massachusetts Avenue NW, Washington, DC 20036)

This pamphlet discusses the "unnatural" history of tobacco, the broadening medical indictment, world smoking trends, who profits, and public policy and public health. Equalling a fourth of the global military budget, consumer expenditure on cigarettes ensures that powerful, strongly motivated interests will struggle to keep global cigarette sales on the rise. This is true despite the fact that the World Health Organization has said that the control of cigarette smoking could do more to improve health and prolong life than any other single action in the whole field of preventive medicine.

188. Drug Users and Driving Behaviors. Research Issues 20. Austin, Gregory A., Ed. et al., Documentation Associates, Los Angeles, CA Jun 1977, 182p. Sponsoring agency: National Institute on Drug Abuse (DHEW/PHS), Rockville, MD (ED 159 548; Reprint: EDRS; also available from Superintendent of Documents, US Government Printing Office, Washington, DC 20402, stock no. 017-024-00640-8).

A major factor in the American public's concern over unconventional drug use is its effect on traffic safety. This volume contains summaries of the latest experimental and epidemiological research on the interactions between drugs and driving behaviors. The experimental studies deal with the effects of drugs and cognition, coordination, reaction time, and other psychomotor functions, all of which are related to driving performances.

189. The Fetal Alcohol Syndrome Public Awareness Campaign, 1979: Progress Report concerning the Advance Notice of Proposed Rulemaking on Warning Labels on Containers of Alcoholic Beverages and Addendum. Department of the Treasury, Washington, DC; National Institute on Alcohol Abuse and Alcoholism (DHEW/PHS), Rockville, MD, Feb 1979, 251p (ED 179 287; Reprint: EDRS; also available from Superintendent of Documents, US Government Printing Office, Washington, DC 20402, stock no. 048-012-00048-5).

This report provides expert opinion on the problems of fetal alcohol syndrome (FAS) and ways to inform the public of teratogenic risk of alcohol consumption during pregnancy. In the absence of firm evidence that moderate drinking of alcoholic beverages leads to FAS and uncertainty concerning the effectiveness of labeling of alcoholic beverages, a decision on these problems was made by the Department of the Treasury, Bureau of Alcohol, Tobacco, and Firearms. It was decided that the bureau would work with appropriate federal agencies, with members of all segments of the alcoholic beverage industry, and with other interested groups to develop and implement a program of public education rather than require product labeling at this time. The report includes summaries of experts' comments and an outline of the plan of action to educate the public. Addenda to the report include a review of scientific findings related to alcohol ingestion and fetal outcomes, plus the full texts of the experts' reports. Extensive references to the related literature are included.

190. Marihuana and Health. Fourth Annual Report to the U.S. Congress from the Secretary of Health, Education, and Welfare, 1974. Petersen, Robert C. et al., National Institute on Drug Abuse (DHEW/PHS), Rockville, MD, 1975, 74p (ED 120 624; Reprint: EDRS).

This report examines the extent and nature of marihuana use in the US. It presents information on the social and psychological influences as well as the toxicological and pharmacological effects. It also analyzes effects on behavior and discusses therapeutic aspects of the drug.

191. Marihuana and Health: In Perspective. Summary and Comments on the Fifth Annual Report to the U.S. Congress from the Secretary of Health, Education, and Welfare, 1975. National Institute on Drug Abuse (DHEW/PHS), Rockville, MD, 1975, 19p (ED 123 224; Reprint: EDRS).

This booklet on marihuana and health begins with general observations made at a press briefing by the director of the National Institute on Drug Abuse, followed by questions and answers. The last section contains a summary and overview of the Fifth Annual Report to the US Congress from the Secretary of Health, Education, and Welfare. The information in this section includes a discussion of the extent and nature of marihuana use. Next are discussions of the chemistry and characteristics of cannabis, animal research, human effects and health implications, other chronic human effects, and therapeutic aspects of marijuana.

192. Marihuana and Health. Sixth Annual Report to the U.S. Congress from the Secretary of Health, Education, and Welfare, 1976. National Institute on Drug Abuse (DHEW/PHS), Rockville, MD, 1976, 51p (ED 138 553; Reprint: EDRS; also available from Superintendent of Documents, US Government Printing Office, Washington, DC 20402).

This edition, the sixth in the series of annual reports, is a nontechnical summary updating developments in marihuana research with selected references from the fifth edition. Areas of discussion include: (1) nature and extent of marihuana use in the United States; (2) marihuana use among high school seniors; (3) an overview of use trends; (4) predicting marihuana use; (5) chemistry and metabolism of cannabis; (6) animal research; (7) human effects; (8) special health problem areas; (9) overseas chronic user studies; (10) psychopathology; (11) complex psychomotor performance in driving and flying; (12) tolerance and dependence; (13) therapeutic aspects; and (14) future research directions. Progress in the marihuana research programs has underscored the need for more subtle understanding of marihuana use and its possible implications. List of references is included.

BOOKS

193. Alcoholism: Development, Consequences, and Interventions. Estes, Nada J.; Heinemann, M. Edith. St. Louis, MO: C.V. Mosby Company, 1977, 332p.

This book is intended to contribute to the theoretical knowledge of alcoholism workers so that the needs of people with alcohol related problems may be met with greater understanding. Contributors to the book represent a variety of disciplines and address a broad spectrum of topics. Part One deals with developmental perspectives of alcoholism, including criteria for its diagnosis. Part Two focuses on the consequences of excessive alcohol on various body systems. Part Three deals with alcohol problems in special groups such as teenagers, women, and American Indians. Part Four provides an array of interventions used in various stages of the illness and for family members.

Drug Rehabilitation Methods

JOURNAL ARTICLES

194. Adolescent Drug Abuse: Etiological and Treatment Considerations. Amini, Fariboz et al. *Adolescence.* v11, n42, p281–99, Sum 1976.

Issues involved in treating adolescent drug abusers and literature describing abuser personality traits are examined. The Youth Service at Langley Porter Institute and the problems encountered and solutions attempted there are discussed. The importance of residential as opposed to outpatient treatment and honesty in staff/patient relationships is emphasized.

195. The Effects of an Education Intervention Program for Juvenile Drug Abusers and Their Parents. Iverson, Donald C. et al. *Journal of Drug Education.* v8, n2, p101–11, 1978.

The Juvenile Intervention Program utilizes the principles of family involvement and peer pressure throughout the program, while the basis of the program involves the education of the participants in such areas as family architecture, family communication patterns, and drug knowledge. Parents have benefited from the program but no immediate change was evidenced by the juveniles.

196. Family Therapy with Adolescent Drug Abusers: A Review. Baither, Richard C. *Journal of Drug Education.* v8, n4, p337–43, 1978.

This paper presents a brief review of literature concerning the current status of family therapy in the treatment of drug-abusing adolescents. The method of approach was to survey and summarize findings and statements found in the literature. The need for a systematic approach to therapy is emphasized.

197. Group Vocational Rehabilitation Counselling for Drug Abusers as an Outreach Technique in the Schools. Roskin, Gerald et al. *Drug Forum: The Journal of Human Issues.* v7, n1, p35–40, 1978–79.

In working with drug-abusing youths over the past several years, the authors have utilized a program of vocational rehabilitation counselling in groups. This article is a description and discussion of the development and operation of this program.

198. Theoretical and Clinical Approaches to the Treatment of Adolescent Drug Addiction. Deangelis, G.G. *American Journal of Occupational Therapy.* v30, n2, p87–93, Feb 1976.

Careful consideration of the psychoanalytical, social and psychological dynamics of youth can help in the formulation of tenable hypotheses that may be used in part to structure treatment programs. This paper explores these considerations and presents a treatment approach based on a fusion between client and therapist lasting long enough for the client to work through related emotional and interpersonal problems.

199. A Treatment Approach for Children of Alcoholics. Kern, Joseph C. et al. *Journal of Drug Education.* v7, n3, p207–18, 1977.

Treatment agencies that ignore needs of children of alcoholics are inadvertently breeding a second generation of alcoholics. This paper reports on an effort to mount an education/prevention effort with children of alcoholics and their mothers. Each session is described in detail and recommendations for programing offered.

200. Treatment of Adolescent Alcoholism. Unger, Robert A. *Social Casework.* v59, n1, p27–35, Jan 1978.

The author explores the growth of adolescent alcohol abuse; causal factors; definitions and dynamics of teenage alcoholism; treatment goals and methods for the alcoholic adolescent; and the necessary family and social support systems for the young drinker in treatment.

MICROFICHE

201. An Approach for Casual Drug Users. Technical Paper. Bloom, Erwin S., Ed., National Institute on Drug Abuse (DHEW/PHS), Rockville, MD, 1977, 37p (ED 154 317; Reprint: EDRS; also available from Superintendent of Documents, US Government Printing Office, Washington, DC 20402, stock no. 017-024-00626-1).

This publication was written to respond to the fact that many drug treatment centers receive inappropriate referrals of casual or recreational marijuana users from the courts for treatment as an alternative to jail. A drug-abuse task force recommended that agencies give priority to abusers of the high-risk categories and to compulsive users of drugs of any kind. It also suggested the concept of an alternative educational model for casual users of low-risk drugs and recommended the adoption and implementation of such a structure throughout the country. In this way, more appropriate services will be provided to casual drug abusers. Educational services can be provided either as an additional program track at a treatment facility or as a specialized educational service operated by community agencies not directly involved in treatment. This monograph examines four examples of alternative educational programs currently in operation. The programs described in this monograph provide one example of alternative programing which can be established to meet a community need and to provide humane, inexpensive, and individualized services to the casual drug abuser.

202. Empirical Approaches to the Treatment of Alcohol Abuse: Alternatives to Abstinence. Nelson, Ronald G.; Janzen, William P., Alabama University, Department of Psychology, 1977, 52p. Sponsoring agency: National Institute of Mental Health (DHEW), Rockville, MD (ED 158 200; Reprint: EDRS).

This report presents research studies from the past 15 years which indicate that some alcoholics have been able to return to controlled moderate drinking after behavioral treatment. Presented in this report are: (1) the techniques used to train alcohol abusers to drink moderately; (2) the research methodologies used to measure the treatment effects of controlled drinking programs; (3) a discussion of the characteristics of controlled drinking candidates; (4) two sample optional controlled drinking programs. It is hoped that if treatment with options other than abstinence is made available, many alcoholics who are currently untreated will seek and receive help.

203. An Evaluation of a Treatment Program for Drug Dependent Youth.* Lyles, Jerry Lee, Indiana University, 1976, 75p (773302; Reprint: DC).

The current increase in drug abuse among adolescents has resulted in an increase in treatment programs focusing on this group. This investigation was an analysis of one such program, the Vernon Project for Drug Dependent Youth (VPDDY), located at Vernon, Texas. The research questions were: is the program effective in changing the personalities, as measured by the Minnesota Multiphasic Personality Inventory (MMPI), of the addicts treated there, and, are there two different subgroups present in the adolescent addict population?

Data used in this research were obtained from the records of the psychology department at VPDDY, the addicts' medical record chart and a behavior monitoring system maintained as an integral part of the total program. The follow-up data were collected by the field counselors in vocational rehabilitation. All patients are tested by the VPDDY psychology department on admission to the facility, then retested with the MMPI prior to their discharge.

The results of this study indicate that the program at VPDDY is effective in changing the personalities, as measured by the MMPI, of the addicts treated there. Different treatment outcomes were indicated for the two subgroups within the total population. The existence of two subgroups was strongly supported by the data, with one of the subgroups demonstrating significantly greater change on their MMPI scores. At the time of discharge the two subgroups were more alike than on admission. Conclusions drawn on these results are: that a treatment program for adolescents needs to provide different treatment modalities for the subgroups found; programs need to offer longer-term inpatient treatment with active follow-up programs in the addict's home community, i.e. halfway house, for those addicts with greater personality deficits and a short-term treatment program for those addicts with few personality deficits.

204. Evaluation of Drug Abuse Services Program (DASP).† California State Department of the Youth Authority, Sacramento, Oct 1978, 53p (PB-297 973/ OST; Reprint: NTIS).

The California Youth Authority's Drug Abuse Services Program (DASP) came into being June 15, 1977, through funding from the State Office of Narcotic and Drug Abuse. The program aims at identifying hard-core abusers of opiate, depressant, stimulant, and hallucinogenic drugs within the Youth Authority population and at providing treatment and rehabilitative services for them following their release on parole. It was designed as an interim replacement for the previous Community-Centered Drug Program (CCDP) and is a direct descendant of the latter program.

205. Group Interaction as a Treatment Modality for Adolescents Involved in the Use of Drugs.* Moore, Johnna Lee, Claremont Graduate School, 1978, 123p (7814845; Reprint: DC).

Group interactions with peers and the sense of identity many people derive, as a result of close attachments with friends, were viewed as a possibility modality for the treatment of drug dependent adolescents, if properly structured and implemented within the noncurricular programs of secondary schools.

Specifically, it was the purpose of this study to compare, analyze, and evaluate methods of treatment for adolescents involved in the use of dangerous drugs and narcotics. A secondary aim of the research was to identify the means by which school personnel and the existing educational framework of the public school were adaptable to an innovative approach toward drug habilitation and substance abuse control.

Groups of identified, drug involved adolescents were established at four different high schools within one school district. These "rap" sessions (as termed by the students) were voluntary and under the guidance of a certified member of the staff. Comparisons were made by establishing a control group, randomly selected, with drug abusive tendencies and by the use of numerous evaluative tools to measure the degrees of differences in terms of: attitudes, values, arrests, absences, achievement, and drug related behaviors. Standardized tests were also administered to comparison groups, during the research year, and most instruments were pre/ post assessments.

The conclusions were factually based; however, it was important to recognize that within the scope of this study, many variables were operative. Most often, attempts were made to support stated outcomes by using more than one evaluative instrument to measure the findings. An action research design and descriptive analytical method of reporting were employed to detail the outcomes of this study.

The conclusions were more positive for the treatment groups, when compared to the control group subjects; for example, a rap participant became more involved in school activities and attendance records, by pre/post comparisons, were measurably better than those of the control group.

Familial relationships, for the treatment subjects, registered positive gains in attitudes toward mothers; however both comparison groups deteriorated in their feelings toward fathers. The data were also supportive of the hypothesis that friends (peers) exercised considerable influence on one another, even more so than did parents or other adults. While attitudes and values were difficult to assess at any level of confidence, the rap members experienced more positive gains than the control in these areas.

Finally, three critical research outcomes emerged and were positively supported by the findings. These included the following: (1) peer groups were successfully employed as a part of the drug abuse treatment modality reported; (2) the rap approach was a significant factor toward the reduction of drug related behaviors previously reported for these students; (3) schools were conducive settings for the treatment modality described in this study.

206. Juvenile Court Alcohol School Evaluation Interim Report.† Glines, Stephen W.; Byrd, Roy N., Utah Highway Safety Office, Salt Lake City; National Highway Traffic Safety Administration, Washington, DC, Sep 1977, 169p (PB-294 790/1st; Reprint: NTIS).

The Utah Juvenile Court Alcohol School is an educational program attended by random juveniles convicted of alcohol offenses and their parents. The evaluation of the program compares the impact of the school with the impact of a subsidiary treatment and the standard court procedures. This is in the first interim report of the evaluation, covering 30 percent of the projected data. The final evaluation report will be used to specialize the "referral to treatment process" and update the school's curriculum so that it encompasses those elements which most effectively impact recidivism.

207. A Model for a Family Systems Theory Approach to Prevention and Treatment of Alcohol Abusing Youth. Spiegel, Renee; Mock, William L. 1977, 27p (ED 166 624; Reprint: EDRS).

A description of the Youth Services Demonstration Project currently being conducted at Alcoholism Services of Cleveland is presented. The family systems approach model used by the project incorporates the following procedures into a multiphase program: (1) assessment and contracting sessions; (2) selection of one of three possible treatment courses; and (3) follow-up and evaluation of the program. Special issues related to the implementation of this family systems approach include acceptance of the family focus, counselor awareness, choice of cotherapist, and flexibility in treatment planning. Each phase of the treatment is described in detail for the reader.

208. A New Rehabilitation Program for Young Drug Abusers in a Psychiatric Hospital.† Karras, Athan; Cohen, Melvin, Long Island Jewish-Hillside Medical Center, Glen Oaks, NY; Office of Human Development, Washington, DC, Rehabilitation Services Administration, Mar 1977, 112p (PB-264 287/4ST; Reprint: NTIS).

The Strauss Cottage program was developed to meet the need for a vocationally oriented program for treating the emotionally disturbed individual who also abused drugs. Total treatment time was 9 to 12 months, the first 3 months spent in the inpatient phase and the remaining months spent in intensive aftercare. Vocational objectives were achieved by integrating them within the structure of a psychiatric unit operating as a behaviorally oriented therapeutic

community. Effectiveness of the program has been compared to conventional psychiatric services available to drug abusers randomly assigned to other units of the hospital. The results of 6 and 12 months follow-up interviews indicate no differences at 6 months, but significant differences at 12 months, Strauss patients showing improved functioning and less substance abuse than controls.

209. Outcomes in Alcoholism Treatment. Stambul, Harriet B.; Armor, David J., Rand Corporation, Santa Monica, CA, Aug 1977, 43p; pages 39–43; may not reproduce clearly due to type (ED 163 377; Reprint: EDRS; also available from The Rand Corporation, Santa Monica, CA 90406).

Alcoholism researchers in the past 35 years have emphasized abstinence as the major criterion of treatment success. In recent years, however, this emphasis has been questioned and from the current debate over treatment goals and outcome measures at least two areas of controversy have emerged. The first, called the "abstention/moderation" controversy, questions whether some alcoholics can return to and maintain normal or controlled drinking, and discusses the implications of this outcome for treatment goals. The second involves the broadening of outcome measures to include a wide spectrum of social and psychological behavior, including attitudes and self-concept, job and marital stability, and earnings or income from employment. Research on various aspects of these two areas has been conducted, but a resolution of the conflicts has not yet emerged.

210. A Rural Communities Response to Drug Abuse. Jacobs, Peter J. Sep 1977, 14p; Paper revised for the Rural Sociological Society Annual Meeting (Madison, WI, September 1977) (ED 143 470; Reprint: EDRS).

The upward economic flux of Pike County is having a dramatic impact on the traditional morals and values held by the established community. Drug availability has increased proportionately with improved highway systems, accessibility of money, and increasing numbers of youth with their own cars. Although 75 percent of the population live in isolated areas, there are only nine deputies covering the area to prevent or divert sales and exchanges of drugs. This also increases the illicit drug traffic. Thus in 1974, an educational/preventive drug treatment program for Pike County was implemented. The program offers individual, group, and family counseling; drug education to schools and community; criminal justice referral/intake; drug diversion/prevention; crisis intervention; speakers bureau; recreation; and a hot line, to be established this fiscal year. Sometimes the drug council works with other community agencies to help a client. The program serves the prescription drug abuser as well as the illicit drug abuser. At the local level, the program is governed by a council, comprised of interested citizens, which is regionally responsible to the Paint Valley Mental Health and Mental Retardation Board located in Chillicothe, Ohio. The program has established a healthy relationship with the judicial system, hospitals, and schools. The most difficult problem encountered has been the lack of resources. The community has been very responsive and supportive of the program, which has begun its third year of services to Pike County.

211. A Study of Factors Relating to Drug Abuse and Treatment Results in a Selected High School Population.* Bethea, Charles William, Michigan State University, 1975, 231p (7612399; Reprint: DC).

This study had two central thrusts. Its primary purpose was to identify what individual changes result from group counseling for drug abusers. Secondly, an attempt was made to describe psychosocial differences between drug-abusing youth and their peers who were not involved in drug use or abuse.

In order to extract appropriate data, this study has tested individuals who met predetermined criteria of drug abuse before and after peer group counseling experience. Among the variables examined were self-concept; ability to cope with anxiety; social skills; social attitudes towards the family, school, and authority; and several forms of substance use.

The treatment subjects were 38 high school students from a conservative, all-White, marginally employed community of blue collar workers. Subjects completed standardized tests and also a student survey which assessed attitudes regarding the family, social agencies, and drug-use behavior. The tests utilized were the Tennessee Self-Concept Scale, State-Trait Anxiety Inventory, and Fundamental Interpersonal Relationships Orientation-Behavior. A cross-section of 136 youths from the high school attended by the treatment subjects was selected for purposes of comparison.

The treatment consisted of six weeks group counseling augmented by any necessary individual, legal, medical, educational, or vocational assistance. Counseling strategies consisted of enabling clients to see self-defeating behavior and attitudes. New alternatives were posed by the individuals themselves with the group's support. Tasks which were to test out these alternatives were attempted between sessions.

Following the six week treatment, another six to eight weeks were allowed to elapse. Clients were then retested with the standardized tests. A brief questionnaire was administered to assess drug-taking behavior. In addition, a one- to two-hour interview was conducted with each subject by a staff member with whom a prior relationship and trust existed. Information obtained from this interview aided understanding of statistical findings.

Nine null hypotheses were developed in order to consider possible differences regarding social deviancy, self-concept, anxiety coping, interpersonal skills, and drug-use behavior. Five dealt with variances in scores between the treatment and comparison groups, and four related to the treatment group's pre- and posttest scores.

Significant findings were obtained in several categories, both due to treatment and between experimental and comparison groups: (1) Treatment and comparison groups differed only in regard to the former's greater nonmedical drug use and in wanting other people to assume much of the decision making in their lives. (There was also a consistent although nonsignificant pattern of greater social deviancy by the former.) (2) Individuals in treatment reported more ease in handling short-term anxiety, increased interpersonal skills, and reduced nonmedical use of drugs.

BOOKS

212. **Drug Dependence and Its Treatment.** Roessler, Richard et al. Washington, DC: American Psychological Association, 1976, 71p.

The purpose of the review was to draw together in one source recent information on treatment and rehabilitation of drug abusers. In order to provide readers with a more in-depth feeling for the literature, the format of a 123-item annotated bibliography was chosen. Special emphasis was placed on annotating articles from 1970 to mid-1974. Research studies are presented in terms of purpose, sample, method, results, and conclusions; descriptive articles are abstracted in a paragraph format. Material in the bibliography introduces the reader to a representative sample of the work done in drug rehabilitation during the early to mid-1970s. The table of contents includes topics such as drug treatment, drug-abuse prevention, drug addicts, treatment of drug abuse, and follow-up studies.

213. **Reaching Out: Helping Young People in Trouble.** Sexton, Brendan John; Sexton, Patricia Cayo. New York: Schocken Books, 1975, 248p.

Reaching Out is a personal statement that provides a framework for dealing, in a community setting, with the needs and problems of young people—in and out of trouble. It is a distillation of the principal author's experiences in helping to found and ultimately directing a successful nonresidential therapeutic community for young drug abusers and troubled youths in his community.

Among the subjects discussed in this book are the needs and feelings of young people; various approaches to therapy; adolescent relationships and their interaction with parents, teachers, police, and other adults; the mythology and reality of addiction and its effect on societal concerns such as crime and race relationships; and the specifics of starting and running a community drug program, including advice on organization, funding, and administration.

214. **So, You're Going to Counsel the Drug Abuser?** Trione, Verdun. New York: Vantage Press, 1975, 203p.

The author reviews selected research on the facts and history of drug abuse, as well as legal issues and educational practices. Viewing addiction as a form of adaptation to one's environment, he advocates a counseling approach which helps the drug abuser to adopt a new lifestyle outside the drug culture.

Drug Legislation

JOURNAL ARTICLES

215. **Case against Decriminalization of Pot.** Steffenhagen, R. A. et al. *Journal of Drug Education.* v8, n2, p93–99, 1978.

Decriminalization of marihuana is not enough. Full legalization is needed to remove marihuana users from the drug culture where they now associate with users of other illegal, but more dangerous, drugs.

216. Color It Black: The Failure of Drug Abuse Policy.
Lewis, David L. *Social Policy.* v6, n5, p26–32,
Mar–Apr 1976.

Notes that those who know drugs and users firsthand see the
law enforcement-medical/maintenance system which has evolved in
America as ineffective, hypocritical, and cruel. The drug user
remains the archetypal pariah.

**217. Decriminalizing Possession of All Controlled
Substances.** Kurzman, Marc G. *Journal of the
American College Health Association.* v26, n6, p312–
16, Jun 1978 (EJ 191 477; Reprint: UMI).

Presents excerpts from the Minnesota Bar Association's Blue
Ribbon Committee report of findings and recommendations for
decriminalizing possession of small amounts of heroin and other
controlled substances.

**218. Drug Education: A Case Study of Legislative Intent
and Perceived Effect.** Reasons, Charles E.; Seem,
John. *Drug Forum: The Journal of Human Issues.* v7,
n2, p181–95, 1978–79.

Interview data indicate that Nebraska's statutory provision of
drug education for those convicted of possession or sale of illegal
drugs does not deter illicit drug use. A comparison of instructors'
and participants' responses to the same questions reveal major
ideological differences regarding drug policy in general, and
marihuana policy specifically. Both instructors and offenders felt
that the drug education was not a deterrent, yet it helped some and
should be kept, in a modified form.

219. Marijuana and the Law: What Young People Say.
Hays, J. Ray et al. *Journal of Drug Education.* v5, n1,
p37–43, 1975.

This research presents data on the extent of drug use by high
school students in Texas and these students' attitudes concerning
change in the marihuana law. Results show more students consider
drug use to be a social problem than a legal problem; 35 percent
preferred less severe penalties for marihuana use or legalization.

220. A New Prohibition for Teen-Agers. Beck, Melinda;
Malamud, Phyllis. *Newsweek.* v93, p38, Apr 2, 1979.

Massachusetts is the sixth state to raise its minimum drinking
age in the last 2½ years, and battles are brewing in more than a dozen
other states over bills to boost the age higher than 18. But there are
many opponents to this trend, and no definite proof that higher
drinking ages ease teenage alcohol abuse.

221. Raise the Legal Age for Drinking? Holland, Bertram
H.; Cheney, Bradford T. *US News and World Report.*
v86, p61–62, Apr 16, 1979.

Bertram H. Holland of the Massachusetts Secondary School
Administrators Association argues that the legal drinking age should
be raised beyond 18 in order to get liquor out of the high schools.
Bradford Cheney, a college student-leader insists that raising the
drinking age is simplistic, for it would do nothing to stop youngsters
from drinking.

222. Subjective Perception of Deterrence. Teevan, James
J., Jr. *Journal of Research in Crime and Delinquency.*
v13, n2, p155–64, Jul 1976.

High school students were questioned about their perceptions
of the certainty and severity of punishment for marihuana use and
shoplifting. Respondents who perceived a higher certainty of
punishment engaged in less marihuana use and shoplifting; those
who perceived a higher severity of punishment were not deterred.

223. States Cork Jug on Teen-Age Drinkers. *US News
and World Report.* v87, p5, Sep 3, 1979.

Like other states recently, Illinois has just raised its legal
drinking age (for wine and beer) back to 21.

**224. When It Became Legal to Drink at 18 in
Massachusetts and Maine: What Happened?**
Zylman, Richard. *Journal of Alcohol and Drug
Education.* v23, n3, p34–46, Spr 1978 (EJ 189 493;
Reprint: UMI).

Lowering the age at which youth may use beverage alcohol
legally in Massachusetts and Maine has had no important effect.

MICROFICHE

**225. Alcohol and Drug Abuse Education Amendments
of 1978; Hearing before the Subcommittee on
Alcoholism and Drug Abuse of the Committee on
Human Resources, United States Senate, Ninety-
Fifth Congress, Second Sesson on S. 2915.** Congress
of the US, Washington, DC, Senate Committee on
Human Resources, 1978, 70p; contains some small
type (ED 172 130; Reprint: EDRS).

The Subcommittee on Alcoholism and Drug Abuse of the
Senate Committee of Human Resources exists to review the
federally funded alcohol- and drug-abuse education and prevention
programs for youth. The purpose of this hearing was to consider S.
2915, a bill to renew and revise the Alcohol and Drug Abuse
Education Act. Specifically, it suggests extending the authorization
of appropriations for carrying out the provisions of this act. To this
end, testimony of witnesses regarding various aspects of alcohol and
drug education programs for youth is presented. Also included are
an amended version of the proposed bill, complete texts of the
witnesses' statements, and additional information such as
supporting tables and charts.

**226. Drug Abuse Office, Prevention, and Treatment
Amendments of 1978. Hearing before the
Subcommittee on Alcoholism and Drug Abuse of
the Committee on Human Resources, United States
Senate, Ninety-Fifth Congress, Second Session on
S. 2916.** Congress of the US, Washington, DC, Senate
Committee on Human Resources, Apr 1978, 289p;
some pages are of marginal reproducibility due to
small print size (ED 178 831); Reprint: EDRS).

The purpose of the testimony presented before the Subcommittee on Alcoholism and Drug Abuse in April 1978 was to amend the drug-abuse office and treatment act of 1972, thereby extending assistance programs for drug-abuse prevention, education, treatment, rehabilitation, and other purposes. Speakers represented such organizations as National Institute on Drug Abuse; Alcohol, Drug Abuse, and Mental Health Administration; and Rural Alcohol and Drug Agencies.

227. Effects of Labeling the 'Drug-Abuser': An Inquiry.† Williams, Jay R., National Institute on Drug Abuse, Rockville, MD, Division of Research, Mar 1976, 50p (PB-249 092/8ST; Reprint: NTIS).

This monograph is a literature review and analysis of the effects on adolescent self-concept and subsequent behavior stemming from arrest or apprehension on a drug-use charge. It is addressed to the social issue of whether apprehension, in the respect that it labels the adolescent as deviant, may actually produce more deviant behavior as a result of the labeling.

228. Federal Strategy for Drug Abuse and Drug Traffic Prevention 1979. Strategy Council on Drug Abuse, Washington, DC, 1979, 76p (ED 178 844; Reprint: EDRS; also available from Superintendent of Documents, US Government Printing Office, Washington, DC 20402, stock no. 052-003-00640-5).

This represents an approach to the nation's drug-abuse problem and reflects the views of departments and agencies involved in the federal drug control and prevention effort, public interest groups and members of Congress. It describes a comprehensive strategy for federal activities relating to drug-abuse prevention and control. Major topics include: (1) the nature and extent of the drug problem; (2) drug-abuse treatment, rehabilitation, and prevention; (3) domestic drug law enforcement; (4) international efforts at control; and (5) special analyses of marijuana, PCP, and cocaine.

229. Legal Aspects of Drug Abuse. Sloat, Robert S. May 1978, 30p; Paper presented at the Annual International Convention, The Council for Exceptional Children (56th, Kansas City, May 2–5, 1978, Session Th83) (ED 153 433; Reprint: EDRS).

Discussed from a teacher's perspective are the legal and cultural ramifications of drug abuse. The importance of teachers' examining their own values concerning drug use is emphasized. Also reviewed is the history of drug use and of narcotics legislation. Recommendations concerning legislative reform are discussed.

230. Marijuana: A Study of State Policies & Penalties. Peat, Marwick, Mitchell and Co., Columbia, MD, Nov 1977, 389p. Sponsoring agency: National Institute of Law Enforcement and Criminal Justice (Department of Justice/LEAA), Washington, DC (ED 155 530; Reprint: EDRS; also available from Superintendent of Documents, US Government Printing Office, Washington, DC 20402, stock no. 027-000-00601-9).

This study is a comprehensive analysis of issues concerning marihuana that are of importance to state policymakers. It reviews the medical, legal, and historical dimensions of marihuana

possession and use which state officials have considered. Attention is directed to the experience of eight states that have eliminated incarceration as a penalty for private possession of small amounts of marihuana as well as to the experience of states that have not passed such decriminalization laws. The study provides a comprehensive, independent, and objective analysis of the issues under examination. It does not, however, make policy recommendations but instead leaves the evaluation of data and development of specific policy options to state officials. The assessment of the experience with the recently passed decriminalization laws is based on the best data now available rather than on trend data or longitudinal analysis. Further assessments, based on more substantial and longer-term data, will determine whether or not the impact of the new laws over time on the criminal justice and health care systems and on wages is consistent with the patterns observed to date.

231. The Nation's Toughest Drug Law: Evaluating the New York Experience. Final Report of the Joint Committee on New York Drug Law Evaluation. Mar 1978, 168p; for related document see entry 232. Sponsoring agency: National Institute of Law Enforcement and Criminal Justice (Department of Justice/LEAA), Washington, DC (ED 159 530; Reprint: EDRS—HC not available; also available from Superintendent of Documents, US Government Printing Office, Washington, DC 20402, stock no. 027-000-00648-5).

This volume presents the results of a three-year study of the impact of New York State's strict drug law, which was enacted in 1973. The study was undertaken by the Joint Committee on New York Drug Law Evaluation, established by the Association of the Bar of the City of New York and the Drug Abuse Council, Inc. The volume has three main sections. The first section explores the effects of the 1973 drug law on drug use, crime, cost to the state, incarceration of young people, recruitment of informants, and rate of commitments to state prisons. The second section attempts to account for the disappointing results of the 1973 drug law. The criminal justice process as a whole did not seem to increase the threat to the offender. Court delays also reduced the threat. The third section contains observations and lessons for the future. It examines the difficulties of implementation, what could have been done to improve implementation, and possibility for future improvement.

232. Staff Working Papers of the Drug Law Evaluation Project. A Companion Volume to the Final Report of the Joint Committee of New York Drug Law Evaluation. Mar 1978, 328p; for related document see entry 231. Sponsoring agency: National Institute of Law Enforcement and Criminal Justice (Department of Justice/LEAA), Washington, DC (ED 159 529; Reprint: EDRS—HC not available; also available from Superintendent of Documents, US Government Printing Office, Washington, DC 20402, stock no. 027-000-00647-7).

The papers in this volume were prepared as part of an evaluation of the effects of the strict 1973 New York state drug laws. The first paper explores the effects of the laws on heroin use. It analyzes the trends of various indicators of heroin use in New York state over a period of several years. In order to isolate movements unique to New York, these trends are compared with those of comparable indicators for other East Coast states and cities that were not directly affected by the new drug laws. The second paper is on crime committed by narcotics users in Manhattan. It presents the findings of a study of changes in the magnitude of felony crimes committed by narcotics users in Manhattan between 1971 and 1975. The crimes included are all felonies which directly affect victims. The third paper explores the effects of the 1973 drug laws on the New York state courts. It is concerned primarily with implementation of the statutes dealing with possession or sale of dangerous drugs. The last paper is on sentencing patterns under the 1973 New York state drug laws.

BOOKS

233. Drug Use by High School Students in an Environment of Shifting Legal Penalties: Some Concommitants of Changes in the Legal Status of Marijuana. Supplement Abstract Service. Stuart, Richard B. et al. Washington, DC: American Psychological Association, 1976, 122p.

In Ann Arbor, Michigan, penalties for the possession of small amounts of marihuana were changed three times in four years. This provided an opportunity to assess the relationship between changes in the legal status of marihuana and the use of marihuana and five other classes of drugs. Data were collected by anonymous self-report questionnaires completed by 3,940 high school students in Ann Arbor and in three neighboring communities over the four-year period. Changes in the legal status of marihuana appeared to have little impact upon its use by high school students. Also, during the time that the possession of marihuana was decriminalized, use of hard drugs remained stable. Analysis of the combinations of drugs used casts doubt upon the "escalation" theory of cumulative drug use. Students' decisions to use drugs were shown to be influenced by many factors, including their information about drugs, their attitudes toward drugs in society, their past experiences with drugs, and their perception of their friends' use of drugs. Finally it was found that students' attitudes toward decriminalization of the possession of drugs were highly selective.

DRUGS AND THE SCHOOLS

Administrative Concerns

JOURNAL ARTICLES

234. Adolescent Alcohol Involvement Scale—Measuring Adolescents Use and Misuse of Alcohol. Mayer, John; Filstead, William. *Journal of Studies on Alcohol.* v40, n3, p291–300, Mar 1979.

The 14-item Adolescent Alcohol Involvement scale is presented, with reliability/validity data.

235. The Alcoholics on Your Staff: How to Find Them, How to Help Them, and Why You'll Profit from Doing Both. Cramer, Jerome. *American School Board Journal.* v164, n8, p49–52, Aug 1977 (EJ 164 142; Reprint: UMI).

Strong programs to help alcoholics can result in savings of both money and lives.

236. Applicability of Alcohol and Drug Abuse Confidentiality Laws to the School System. Coggins, Patrick C. *Journal of the International Association of Pupil Personnel Workers.* v23, n1, p80–82, Jan 1979.

Recommends five guidelines for schools to follow in applying federal and state alcohol- and drug-abuse confidentiality laws. Views these laws in the context of increasing litigation over students' rights.

237. The Child, School, Alcohol, and Abuse. Worrell, D. Frank. *School Guidance Worker.* v32, n2, p43–47, Nov 1976.

Explains some of the problems encountered by children who live with addicted parents. Also emphasizes some ideas that are required to teach or treat these children successfully.

238. A Cooperative Approach toward Children from Alcoholic Families. Hecht, Murray. *Elementary School Guidance and Counseling.* v11, n3, p197–202, Feb 1977.

Studies have shown that children of alcoholics are more apt to exhibit problems of delinquency, anxiety, depression, neurosis, sexual confusion, and hostility than are children of other families. An integrated team approach to early identification and intervention with children of alcoholics, in a familiar setting such as school, will be helpful in arresting further pathological development. It remains to devise methods for involving parents who, typical of alcoholics, deny their problem and its effect on their children.

239. Dealing with Youngsters Who Drink. Milbauer, Barbara. *Teacher.* v93, n6, p49–51, Feb 1976.

Elementary school alcoholics are not anonymous. Article suggests methods for identifying the signs and taking action to solve the problems suffered by young alcoholics.

240. Detecting Drugs in School: The Legality of Scent Dogs and Strip Searches. Flygare, Thomas J. *Phi Delta Kappan.* v61, n4, p280–81, Dec 1979 (EJ 211 060; Reprint: UMI).

The legality of warrantless searches of students depends on the kind of search that takes place and what happens to any evidence obtained during the search. The case of *Doe* v. *Renfrow* is discussed.

241. The Development of Attitudinal Measures toward Alcohol Education in the School and in the Home. Finn, Peter. *Journal of Drug Education.* v8, n3, p203–19, 1978.

A series of alcohol education seminars for parents was conducted to develop, pretest, and test an alcohol education attitudes questionnaire, which can be used to evaluate the attitudes of parents, teachers, students, and others toward alcohol education in the school and in the home. The questionnaire is included.

242. Drug Education for Administrators. Hackett, Peter; McKeon, Thomas, L. *NASSP Bulletin.* v60, n402, p78–85, Oct 1976.

The formulation of a drug policy and the implementation of that policy in a firm but fair manner are the responsibility of the school administrator. Authors give serious consideration to this responsibility.

243. **The Drug Problem and Youth: The Need for School-Based, Humanistic Approaches to Prevention and Early Intervention.** *Drug Forum: The Journal of Human Issues*. v4, n3, p233–40, 1975.

In order to ameliorate the drug problem as it is affecting schoolage youth, school-based approaches to prevention and intervention need to be adopted. Such approaches also need to be responsive to the needs of those who have engaged in various forms of drug-taking behavior. They need to include appropriate counseling, care, or referral to care, as well as efforts aimed at redirecting youthful energies along more personally fulfilling and socially beneficial lines.

244. **Drugs in Suburban Schools.** Mullis, B. J. *NASSP Bulletin*. v64, n432, p112–14, Jan 1980 (EJ 214 235; Reprint: UMI).

The most effective way to eliminate drug abuse on school property is to rigidly enforce the rules and bring in the policy when necessary.

245. **Guidelines for School-Police Cooperation in Drug Abuse Policy Department.** Langer, John H. *Journal of School Health*. v46, n4, p197–99, Apr 1976.

Guidelines are presented for developing a school drug-abuse policy in cooperation with community health agencies and police.

246. **Handling Drug Use in Schools.** Hoch, Loren L.; Olszowy, Janice. *NASSP Bulletin*. v63, n426, p71–75, Apr 1979 (EJ 197 931; Reprint: UMI).

The prompt, fair handling of students involved in the use and abuse of drugs in the school setting is effective in altering the behavior of students. Guidelines are presented for a written policy.

247. **Heisner Report: There's 100-Proof Help for Alcoholic Teachers.** *Instructor*. v87, n9, p26–27, Apr 1978 (EJ 176 177; Reprint: UMI).

Briefly discusses the problem of alcoholic teachers and how they can be helped.

248. **How Do the Schools View Substance Education and Prevention?** Vissing, Yvonne M. *Journal of Drug Education*. v8, n4, p267–77, 1978.

The use of substance (drug and alcohol) abuse prevention and education is commonly found in the school. In order to determine what substance services are currently being provided, and to see what services appear desirable for implementation in the schools, this assessment was conducted on schools in a two-county metropolitan area.

249. **In the Wayzata Schools They Do More than Just Talk about Alcohol and Drug Problems.** Brodie, Thomas A.; Manning, William O. *American School Board Journal*. v163, n11, p46–48, Nov 1976.

Wayzata's chemical dependency program regards alcohol and drug abuse as a treatable illness. Chemically dependent students and employees are recognized and helped by specially trained counselors.

250. **Kojack in Your Classrooms May Be Enough to Make You Lose Your Hair.** Doran, Bernadette. *American School Board Journal*. v165, n8, p20–24, Aug 1978 (EJ 184 769; Reprint: UMI).

Discusses the practice of using undercover narcotics agents in the schools, a practice that has not yet been tested in the courts.

251. **Legal Authority for Schools and Colleges to Control Student Use of Drugs.** Phay, Robert E.; Winn, Edward L. *School Law Bulletin*. v7, n2, p1, 3–6, Apr 1976.

Courts seldom overturn school board punishment of students for drug abuse; in fact, relatively few cases even reach the courts. Problems usually arise from poorly written statutes and board regulations that are either vague or inconsistent with statutory requirements.

252. **Teenage Alcoholism—Detecting Those Early Warning Signals.** Dykeman, Bruce F. *Adolescence*. v14, n54, p251–54, Sum 1979 (EJ 211 983; Reprint: UMI).

This article describes attitudes and behaviors common to all alcoholics and some of the symptoms most frequently associated with the teenage alcoholic.

253. **Thinking about Drinking: Helping the Troubled Employee.** Oliver, David G. *Independent School*. v38, n1, p17–19, Oct 1978.

Because of the concern over student alcohol abuse, the school employee with a drinking problem sometimes is neglected. This article discusses this aspect of alcohol use in the schools, and offers some suggestions on how best to address the problem. A model organizational policy statement on employee alcoholism is appended.

254. **To Permit or Prohibit Smoking in High Schools: It's a Burning Issue.** Brody, Judith A. *American School Board Journal*. v164, n5, p19–21, May 1977.

This author considers the dilemma of school boards either to provide an ethical example by banning student smoking or to "accept reality" and permit it. A school which has adopted each position is described. Related questions of smoking education and the effects of teachers who smoke are discussed.

255. **What Can Be Done about Smoking in the Schools?** Fox, Alice. *Health Education*. v9, n3, p4–5, May–Jun 1978 (EJ 187 876; Reprint: UMI).

Whether for or against permitting smoking in the schools, school districts should forcefully present the dangers of smoking in their health education programs.

256. **Why Kids Use Drugs and What That Means for Schools.** Morse, Jeffrey. *Education Digest*. v42, n4, p48–50, Dec 1976.

The author outlines a variety of reasons which can lead youngsters to take drugs: isolation, lack of purpose, fun, thrill seeking, and rebellion. He suggests that schools avoid hard-line, inflexible policies for dealing with drug users. Instead, these students should be treated as kids who have made a mistake and provided with attention and support in finding new ways to meet their emotional needs. This article is reprinted from *Illinois School Board Journal*, v64, p20–23, May–Aug 1976.

MICROFICHE

257. Administrator's Handbook for Crime Prevention and Drug Education. Texas Education Agency, Austin, Division of Crime Prevention and Drug Education, Jul 1975, 42p; for related document see entry 343 (ED 146 521; Reprint: EDRS).

Acts of three Texas Legislatures have mandated that the schools of Texas provide a program for all public school students, grades K–12, in crime prevention and drug education. To assist schools in formulating a philosophy about and in developing appropriate programs and techniques for drug education and crime prevention programs, the Texas Education Agency has developed a series of supportive publications. The ''Administrator's Handbook for Crime Prevention and Drug Education'' is one of this series and is designed to assist educators in developing a comprehensive program for their school district. In an attempt to accommodate the varied program needs of school districts, this guide contains information and activities useful to the board of school trustees, superintendent, and other educators in planning a delivery system for crime prevention and drug education. Because any type of education program requires extensive planning and delineation of goals, objectives, priorities, and alternative ways of achieving objectives, these guidelines provide suggestions and ideas suitable for developing or modifying a crime prevention and drug education program.

258. Alcohol Abuse Prevention: A Comprehensive Guide for Youth Organizations. Boys' Clubs of America, New York, 1978, 166p. Sponsoring agency: National Institute on Alcohol Abuse and Alcoholism (DHEW/PHS), Rockville, MD (ED 173 450; Reprint: EDRS—HC not available; also available from Boys' Clubs of America, 771 First Avenue, New York, NY 10017).

This guide, the culmination of a three-year Project TEAM effort by the Boys' Clubs of America, describes numerous strategies for developing an alcohol-abuse prevention program. The core of this guide consists of program models developed by the Boys' Club project at seven pilot sites. The models presented cover the following areas: peer leadership, peer consulting, arts and crafts, cultural exploration, media strategy, values clarification, and community service. Specific objectives and activities for developing and implementing each of the models are outlined. Suggestions for starting a prevention program, developing project staff, getting teenagers involved, and working with the program models are presented. Suggestions are also made concerning program objectives and planning, evaluation concepts and techniques, program funding, and publicity. In addition, facts and myths about alcohol and alcohol abuse are discussed and a resource list is provided.

259. Conducting Followup Research on Drug Treatment Programs. Johnston, Lloyd D., Ed. et al. 1977, 203p. Sponsoring agency: National Institute on Drug Abuse (DHEW/PHS), Rockville, MD (ED 153 099; Reprint: EDRS; also available from Superintendent of Documents, US Government Printing Office, Washington, DC 20402, stock no. 017-024-00631-9).

This manual is a technical resource for helping drug treatment program directors decide whether to do a follow-up of a client population and, if so, how to do one. Each chapter was written by a particular set of authors. However, the points contained in the chapters had to receive the general agreement of a committee whose membership included representatives not only from the research community, but also from the National Institute on Drug Abuse (NIDA) and the treatment community. After completing the first three chapters, the reader should have the information needed to determine whether to do a follow-up, and how to plan it in detail and make staffing assignments, if the decision is to proceed. The remaining chapters provide detailed guidance for implementing each of the research stages. A few of the areas covered are: techniques for successfully locating respondents, interviewing techniques, confidentiality, guidelines for preparing the data for analysis and conducting the analysis, and suggestions on how a report might be organized. The appendix includes many specific examples of interview questions and interviewing training materials.

260. Criteria for Assessing Alcohol Education Programs. California State Department of Education, Sacramento, 1976, 29p. Sponsoring agency: California State Office of Alcoholism, Sacramento (ED 154 293; Reprint: EDRS—HC not available; also available from Publication Sales, California State Department of Education, P.O. Box 271, Sacramento, CA 95802).

Alcohol abuse has become the number one drug problem in the United States. In 1973 the California State Board of Education adopted guidelines for drug education programs in schools, and those guidelines can also be used with alcohol education programs. This document provides criteria by which individual schools, school districts, and communities can assess their alcohol education programs, and measure them against the California guidelines.

261. Developing School Drug Policy: A Guide for Administrators. Maine State Department of Educational and Cultural Services, Augusta, 1975, 47p (ED 112 520; Reprint: EDRS—HC not available).

This administrator's guide is intended to aid local school administrators who formulate policies and procedures for dealing with drug-involved students. The guide suggests alternatives for those engaged in such policymaking rather than mandating a single course of action for all school districts. The guide is not intended to limit a community's prerogative to determine its own rules and regulations under existing state and federal law. Drug policies should be flexible and possess a high degree of individual application, as simplified, rigid, and general policies are frequently unworkable. Any action designed to help students meet and cope with their problems must steer a course between two concerns: what is best for the individual and what is most desirable for the total school population. In the sections on individual topics—the role of school personnel with respect to confidentiality, pupil records, the school's relationship with the policy, student rights, procedures regarding suspension and expulsion, and procedures regarding readmission—an attempt is made to state the issue clearly, to refer to pertinent law, to suggest possible approaches to policy, and to explain, where necessary, the reasons for the approaches taken. A sample school policy is appended.

262. Drug Abuse Instrument Handbook: Selected Items for Psychosocial Drug Research. Research Issues 12. Nehemkis, Alexis, Ed. et al. Documentation Associates, Los Angeles, 1977, 340p. Sponsoring agency: National Institute on Drug Abuse (DHEW/PHS), Rockville, MD (ED 154 304; Reprint: EDRS; also available from Superintendent of Documents, US Government Printing Office, Washington, DC 20402, stock no. 017-024-00533-9).

Identifying, acquiring, and developing valid and reliable instruments are major problems facing researchers who study psychosocial drug use and abuse. This handbook is designed to help eliminate these problems. It is intended to serve as a basic reference tool by identifying existing instruments and suggested items for the creation of new instruments. Over 2,000 items from 40 instruments are included, categorized according to the areas they assess. The instruments from which they were selected have been found to discriminate between drug users and nonusers, or have identified different drug-user types. Many of the instruments were developed specifically for drug research; others were developed first for use in other fields. It is hoped that this unique handbook will facilitate contact between instrument developers and users, and enable other investigators to compare and build upon previous research.

263. Drug Abuse Prevention in Atlantic County, New Jersey: A Status Report of School Based Prevention Practices as Viewed by Secondary School Principals.* Miller, Joel Robert, Rutgers University, The State of New Jersey G.S.A.P.P., 1979, 185p (8002177; Reprint: DC).

The major purpose of this investigation is to provide a status report on drug-abuse prevention practices conducted within the secondary schools of Atlantic County, New Jersey, as of August 1978. Based on a review of the pertinent literature, expert opinion, local socioeconomic characteristics, and community dynamics, it is argued that the prevailing cultural pattern in Atlantic County is conducive to the development and persistence of maladjustment and drug abuse among adolescents in particular.

A review of the drug-abuse prevention literature suggests that principals' involvements in school-based prevention is a major determinant in the viability of prevention programs. Moreover, the attitudes of principals toward prevention practices may be shaped by many factors, including the perceived seriousness of the problem and an appreciation of the prevention field in general. Accordingly, the purpose of this study is to examine the perceptions of secondary school principals with respect to the problem of drug abuse and the programs and practices designed to prevent student drug abuse.

It is hypothesized that there would be incongruities between principals' beliefs, on the one hand, and available data reflecting drug-abuse trends, on the other. If principals' perceptions were to become more accurate regarding the status of drug abuse, those efforts toward prevention might increase. In the present study, 28 questions were designed to elicit the principals' perceptions in three broad areas: (1) the seriousness of the drug-abuse problem in the schools and surrounding communities; (2) prevention services as extant within the school; and (3) adequacy of prevention agents within the school and community as perceived by the principals.

Thirteen middle school principals and seven high school principals participated in a 29-item questionnaire survey, which was conducted by telephone interviews during the summer of 1978. The findings suggest that principals have inaccurate perceptions of the drug-abuse problem in their schools and in the community at large. It would appear that both the involvement of school principals and the information they possess are limited, despite the fact that they are mandated by the state of New Jersey to provide suitable drug-abuse prevention programs. Within the limitations of the present study, it is recommended that county planners and public school officials endeavor to increase the accuracy of principals' perceptions. Appropriate mechanisms for the implementation of such programs are suggested.

264. An Employee Alcoholism Program for Public Education.* Harris, Jimmy Dale, University of Idaho, 1976, 200p (7619895; Reprint: DC).

The purpose of the study was to develop and test an alcoholism training model which would aid public school administrators and supervisors to identify and ameliorate problems related to alcohol abuse among public school employees.

A model program was constructed using a systems approach. In order to empirically evaluate the model, a training program based on the model program was developed and tested. The training model consisted of placards, film, slides, case studies, and an overhead transparency lecture on the policy, principles, and procedures relating to an employee alcoholism program. The model program, training program, and testing instruments were submitted to a panel of experts for evaluation on whether the training program met stated objectives and on the adequacy of specific components. Suggestions for the implementation of such a program were included. Public school administrators and supervisor volunteers were randomly assigned to groups based upon a modified pretest/training/posttest design. The testing instrument required respondents to indicate their perceptions about variables which operate within an employee alcoholism program. Each response was weighed on a scale of 1 to 5 with an assumption of equal intervals. A t test was used to analyze the data for statistical significance.

The statistical analysis of the data indicated that public school administrators and supervisors significantly ($p < 0.05$) changed perceptions in nine areas of knowledge, awareness, and understanding related to an employee alcoholism program.

265. A Manual for Managing Community Alcohol Safety Education Campaigns. National Highway Traffic Safety Administration (DOT), Washington, DC, Office of Driver and Pedestrian Research, Jan 1978, 54p (ED 159 575; Reprint: EDRS; also available from Superintendent of Documents, US Government Printing Office, Washington, DC 20402, stock no. 1978-0-256-039).

This guide offers help to community members for establishing an alcohol safety education program. Emphasis is placed upon the development of a communications plan, including defining objectives, identifying target audiences, and enlisting community support. The manual can be used to manage community alcohol safety education campaigns.

266. Programming Community Resources; A Training Program for Alcohol Program Administrators. National Center for Alcohol Education, Arlington, VA, 1978, 135p; some small print may be marginally legible. Sponsoring agency: National Institute on Alcohol Abuse and Alcoholism (DHEW/PHS), Rockville, MD; University Research Corporation, Washington, DC (ED 172 050; Reprint: EDRS).

This guide is designed to upgrade and/or develop the assessment and negotiation skills of management personnel who are involved in developing and coordinating resources among community agencies to provide comprehensive services for individuals with alcohol problems. This training program addresses the following topics: (1) community assessment, (2) target problem identification and analysis, (3) planning and conducting interagency negotiation, and (4) group problem-solving techniques. Resource materials, assessment forms, and evaluation instruments are provided in the appendices.

267. The Public Schools and Problem Drinking of Professionals: Development of Policy Guidelines.* Scott, Joel Edward, Arizona State University, 1978, 137p (7911134; Reprint: DC).

A review of the literature revealed that alcoholism/problem drinking was a recognized problem in business and industry. The study problem was to determine whether a problem with alcoholism/problem drinking existed among educators and, if so, to determine what was being done about the problem. The study posed these questions: (1) What are key leaders' perceptions of alcoholism/problem drinking among professional educators in the district? (2) Do a school board policy and a formal administrative procedure exist for alcoholism/problem drinking among professional educators? (3) If a school board policy and an administrative procedure exist, were the bargaining units for teachers and administrators involved in policy and procedures development? (4) If there is no school board policy or formal procedure, is there an informal procedure for dealing with alcoholics/problem drinkers? (5) Is there a relationship between the perception of alcoholism/problem drinking and the respondent's position in the school district or the location of the school district? (6) Did the interviews reveal a need for guidelines for policy development in the area of alcoholism/problem drinking?

A structured interview instrument was developed, reviewed by a panel, and field tested to elicit responses to the questions. A county was selected that would yield the most representative data. The personnel determined to have the information necessary were the superintendent, business manager, and business director of each of the school districts in the county. Nineteen superintendents, seven personnel directors and thirteen business managers were interviewed. The interview data were treated by frequency counts, percentages, and nonparametric tests, chi square, Binomial and Fisher's exact probability.

The conclusions were: (1) Alcoholism/problem drinking was not perceived by key leaders to be a problem of significance. (2) No school district had a school board policy or formal procedure for dealing with alcoholic/problem drinking professional educators. (3) While many of the school districts had an informal policy, the majority did not have an informal policy for dealing with alcoholic/problem drinking professional educators. (4) The perception of alcoholism/problem drinking by position and location revealed agreement except that suburban/rural districts used the criteria of

personality problems and conflicts in their informal procedure. (5) A need for guidelines for policy development in the area of alcoholism/problem drinking was identified.

The implications of the study were that alcoholism/problem drinking was not addressed or ignored. There was a discrepancy between perception of those interviewed and general research. An informal policy tends to be subjective. Alcoholism/problem drinking affects job performance, so to improve the quality of instruction and administration, policy and procedures need to be developed. A trend of alcoholism assistance programs is emerging in education. Finally, proposed guidelines for policy development were recommended.

268. Quality Assurance for Alcohol, Drug Abuse, and Mental Health Services: An Annotated Bibliography. Towery, O. B. et al., National Institute of Mental Health (DHEW), Rockville, MD, 1979, 31p. Sponsoring agency: Department of Health, Education, and Welfare, Washington, DC (ED 179 905; Reprint: EDRS).

This is a comprehensive bibliography for all those in the alcohol, drug-abuse, and mental health fields who are developing and implementing programs for assuring quality in the services they provide. A major problem is the newness of the language and the unfamiliarity with procedures required by the government and others seeking accountability from services providers. Many entries concern the Professional Standards Review Organization (PSRO) Program and its background. Other entries cite experiences of model quality assurance programs, program evaluations, medical records, and confidentiality.

269. Why Evaluate Drug Education? Task Force Report. Southern Regional Council, Atlanta, GA, 1975, 40p. Sponsoring agency: National Institute on Drug Abuse (DHEW/PHS), Rockville, MD (ED 119 052; Reprint: EDRS; also available from Superintendent of Documents, US Government Printing Office, Washington, DC 20402, stock no. 017-024-00461-8).

This publication provides some guidance to alcohol and drug education program administrators by clarifying the different levels of evaluation and the kinds of learning that can occur at each level. While it outlines the components and considerations for evaluation, it does not define a step-by-step procedure. In short, it serves as a diet rather than a recipe. A second objective for the publication is to take away the threatening overtones to the word evaluation by showing the benefits to be gained and by pointing out the value that negative findings have for the ultimate success of a program. This book contains four sections: Why Evaluate?; Guidelines for Impact Evaluation; Suggestions for Process Evaluation; and Evaluation of Drug Programs (synopses of some examples of evaluations of alcohol and drug education programs). The section of the book dealing with impact evaluation was developed by a task force sponsored by the Southern Regional Education Board project, Enhancing Drug Education in the South. The task force included state-level program directors, representatives from federal agencies concerned with alcohol and drug education, and people with expertise in program evaluation.

BOOKS

270. Drug Abuse Prevention in Your Community.
Rockville, MD: National Institute on Drug Abuse,
1978, 25p. (Also available from Superintendent of
Documents, US Government Printing Office,
Washington, DC 20402, stock no. 017-024-00790-1).

This pamphlet provides recent information on commonly used
drugs as well as guidelines and resources for a community drug-
abuse prevention effort.

Drug Education: Perspectives and Approaches

JOURNAL ARTICLES

271. Adolescent Smoking: Onset and Prevention.
McAlister, Alfred L. et al. *Pediatrics*. v63, n4, p650–
58, Apr 1979 (Available from Arthur Retlaw and
Associates, Inc., Suite 2080, 1603 Orrington Ave.,
Evanston, IL 60201).

The report presents a behavioral scientist's perspective on the
problem of preventing smoking and other self-destructive behaviors
in adolescents.

272. Alcohol: You Can Help Your Kids Cope. Finn,
Peter. *Instructor*. v85, n3, p76–78,83–84, Nov 1975.

The author asserts that most children will come in contact
with alcohol during their elementary school years and that it is the
task of the schools to facilitate their development as responsible
drinkers or abstainers, who can cope with alcohol abusers around
them. He outlines the goals of alcohol education and two teaching
strategies: spontaneous discussion and subject area integration. He
also gives attention to the problems of objectivity and of dealing with
two special groups of children—those from abstinent families and
those from families with problem drinkers.

**273. Alcohol Education in the School Curriculum: The
Single Discipline vs. the Interdisciplinary
Approach.** Finn, Peter. *Journal of Alcohol and Drug
Education*. v24, n2, p41–57, Win 1979 (EJ 202 388;
Reprint: UMI).

Several examples of how alcohol education can be integrated
into social studies, English, foreign language, and art classes are
offered along with a discussion of the advantages and disadvantages
of the single discipline and the interdisciplinary approach to alcohol
education.

274. Approaching Drug Education with Skepticism.
Brown, W. Cecil. *School Guidance Worker*. v32, n2,
p16–22, Nov 1976.

Out of the overwhelming number of drug education
programs, this paper attempts to ferret out the basic issues.
Prevention approaches based on decision making, self-concept, and
behavior therapy are critiqued from an ethical standpoint.

275. Are Drug Education Programs Effective? Barresi,
Charles M.; Gigliotti, Richard J. *Journal of Drug
Education*. v5, n4, p301–16, 1975.

The effects of expert speakers in producing change in drug
attitudes, opinions, and knowledge of high school students were
evaluated with a quasi field experiment. Three different treatment
groups (expertise areas) and a control group were employed. The
results indicate that such traditional drug education programs have
no change effect.

**276. Awareness and Creative Choice: Alternatives to
Drugs.** Irwin, Samuel et al. *Contemporary Drug
Problems*. v4, n1, p35–56, Spr 1975.

The authors suggest that the source of dependencies and
abusive behaviors lie in the negative conditioning of the individual.
They advocate a drug education program which focuses on
improving the individual's self-awareness and self-trust through
such techniques as relaxation, concentration, meditation, centering,
and self-observation.

277. Beyond Drug Education. Robinson, Paul E. *Journal
of Drug Education*. v5, n3, p183–91, 1975.

Rather than teach people about drugs, this author maintains
that we should stress education of the self. Our goal should be to help
people to think intelligently and rationally, to control their
destructive impulses, to make wise decisions, to resist peer pressure,
and to understand their values, needs, and desires.

278. Booby Traps in Drugs Educations. Swanson, Jon
Colby. *Journal of Drug Education*. v6, n4, p297–300,
1976.

Conditional thinking helps us avoid some pitfalls in drug-abuse education programs. Some of the more common reactions and overreactions within drug education programs are discussed.

279. The Case for Having the Public Schools Teach Our Youngsters How to Drink. Hames, Lee N. *American School Board Journal.* v163, n3, p38–41,43, Mar 1976.

The author asserts that since youngsters are going to drink no matter what adults say, the schools should teach students how to make wise decisions about alcohol and how to use it safely. He makes suggestions for implementing an alcohol education program that has strong parent and student involvement.

280. A Comparison of Three Drug Information Presentations. Hewitt, Davis; Nutter, Richard W. *Journal of Drug Education.* v9, n1, p79–90, 1979.

Knowledge and attitudes of technical college students were compared after exposing them to drug education programs in three formats: lecture, mixed media, and an agency film program. Results of a questionnaire show format has little effect on knowledge or attitude. Recommendations are made for future drug information programs.

281. Complexities of Smoking Education. Neeman, R. L.; Neeman, M. *Journal of School Health.* v45, n1, p17–23, Jan 1975.

This article discusses problems involved in the design of effective health education programs addressed to smoking prevention. Individual, peer, and family influences on smoking are considered.

282. Considerations and Issues in a Drug Abuse Program for the Mentally Retarded. Sengstock, Wayne L. et al. *Education and Training of the Mentally Retarded.* v10, n3, p138–43, Oct 1975.

The problem of drug abuse is presented along with the motivational forces generally found to be behind drug use. Current and past programs in this area have generally not been successful. The reasons for these failures are discussed and suggestions to help the educator deal with this problem are described.

283. The Counselor's Role in Alcohol Education Programs. Lee, Essie E. *School Counselor.* v23, n4, p289–91, Mar 1976.

This article reviews a study by Lee, Fishman, and Shimmel which examined drinking patterns of juniors and seniors in high school. The article then goes on to make suggestions about alcohol education programs and the counselor's role in those programs.

284. A Critique of Traditional Drug Education Programs. Mathews, Walter M. *Journal of Drug Education.* v5, n1, p57–64, 1975.

This article classifies traditional drug education approaches into seven styles and two modes. The author is critical of each style, but presents his model for the use of administrators and drug educators. A review is presented of some studies which are critical of the factual approach to drug education.

285. Current Status and Problems of Alcohol Education in the Schools. Milgram, Gail Gleason. *Journal of School Health.* v46, n6, p317–20, Jun 1976.

Problems of definition, goals, societal ambivalence, content, teacher training, needs of students, and grade level force one to admit that alcohol education is not yet a reality and an evaluation of any success in terms of prevention is impossible.

286. Does Alcohol Education Prevent Alcohol Problems? Need for Evaluation. Cooper, A. Mitch; Sobell, Mark B. *Journal of Alcohol and Drug Education.* v25, n1, p54–63, Fall 1979.

This paper critically examines the evidence for the alleged failure of alcohol education to prevent alcohol problems and concludes that an indictment of primary prevention methods is not warranted at this time. A number of recommendations regarding methodological characteristics of an adequate test of the effectiveness of alcohol education are then presented and discussed.

287. Drug Abuse: A Problem of Socialization. Simmonds, Robert M. *Journal of Drug Education.* v8, n4, p299–303, 1978.

If society is to deal effectively with drug abuse among juveniles and young adults, we must understand underlying causal factors and construct viable alternatives which are antithetical to drug attitudes. This article contains a general guideline for developing a school drug education program.

288. Drug Abuse Is Alive and Well. Frank, Peter R. *Educational Forum.* v42, n4, p459–67, May 1978 (EJ 184 464; Reprint: UMI).

After years of work in drug-abuse prevention and education, the author concludes that drug-abuse education has failed. He says that children need early decision-making opportunities to form values, and describes how drug use and abuse are promoted by intense industry advertising.

289. Drug Abuse Prevention: A Human Development Model for Defining the Problem and Devising Solutions. Sugarman, Barry. *Drug Forum: The Journal of Human Issues.* v6, n4, p387–97, 1977–78.

Drug abuse is frequently the result of deficits in human development process and is one of several behavior patterns with which the individual attempts to fill an "emotional vacuum." Effective drug-abuse prevention must involve the improvement of environment. A distinction is made between primary prevention, secondary prevention, and rehabilitation.

290. Drug Cognitive Structures and Strategies: With Special Reference to Drug Education Programs. Fiddle, Seymour. *Journal of Drug Education.* v8, n2, p151–60, 1978.

We need much more research about cognitive structures guiding drug takers, that is, maps which help them decide what drugs are to be used for their effects, which drugs to use together or separately, and factors influencing those effects. Some further assumptions of drug education programs are listed, and some hypothetical cognitive strategies are suggested.

291. Drug Education: A Cultural Perspective, an Educational Model and an Implementation Scheme. Floyd, Jerald D.; Lotsof, Antoinette B. *Journal of Drug Education.* v8, n4, p357–68, 1978.

Examines attitudes towards drug use and challenges many of the traditional assumptions relating to this critical area. Based on this examination, a new set of goals for drug education is suggested. An approach to drug education that is more in touch with the realities encountered by school-aged children is discussed.

292. Drug Education: For Whom? Hochhauser, Mark. *Journal of Alcohol and Drug Education.* v23, n3, p24–33, Spr 1978.

Traditional preventive drug education programs have been directed towards elementary and secondary school students; such programs will not be maximally effective unless they become available to more individuals who may develop drug-abuse problems, not merely those who are most easily surveyed. Such an approach requires specific training on the undergraduate and graduate level for those involved in drug education, with particular emphasis on the development of lifetime drug education programs.

293. Drug Education: Reducing or Increasing Drug Consumption? Serdahely, William J.; Behunin, Oral. *Journal of Alcohol and Drug Education.* v23, n1, p8–19, Fall 1977 (EJ 175 597; Reprint: UMI).

A college drug-education course is examined to determine whether (1) it affected students' consumption of drugs, and (2) whether drug consumption is stimulated by such a course. It was concluded that consumption was not significantly reduced, while the use of amphetamines slightly increased.

294. The Effects of Fear Appeal and Communication upon Attitudes toward Alcohol Consumption. Fritzen, Robert D. *Journal of Drug Education.* v5, n2, p171–81, 1975.

This study examines the relationship between two independent variables, the fear appeal of the message and the character of the communicator; and the attitudes, behavior, and information retention of seventh- and eighth-grade pupils with respect to the consumption of alcoholic beverages. Findings indicate that high fear messages from a nonalcoholic communicator resulted in more conservative attitudes toward alcohol but not in actual behavior change.

295. The Effects of Students' Perception of a Speaker's Role on Their Recall of Drug Facts and Their Opinions and Attitudes about Drugs. McCleaf, James E.; Colby, Margaret A. *Journal of Educational Research.* v68, n10, p382–86, Jul–Aug 1975.

The ascribed social role of a speaker and his ascribed experience with drugs contributed to significant differences in student recall of drug information. Sex of the respondent was found to have a significant effect on students' scores on the Drug Opinion and Attitudes Test. One implication drawn from the study was that, of the types of speakers studied, a law enforcement officer is probably the least effective in conveying drug information.

296. The Failure of Our School Drug Abuse Programs. Bard, Bernard. *Phi Delta Kappan.* v57, n4, p251–55, Dec 1975.

Although some nontraditional drug education programs work, most programs are either ineffective or actually increase the use of drugs, because their content and presentation styles are neither realistic nor honest.

297. The Growing Problem of Teenage Drinking. Petrillo, Thomas J. *Today's Education.* v67, n3, p85–86, Sep–Oct 1978 (EJ 198 780; Reprint: UMI).

Ways in which teachers can improve attitudes of students toward drinking and prevent teenage alcoholism are discussed.

298. "If We Could Make It So": Drug Education for Exceptional Children. Floyd, Jerald D.; Lotsof, Antoinette B. *Journal of Drug Education.* v7, n1, p63–70, 1977.

This detailed position paper reflects upon traditional and contemporary drug education with particular attention to programs in schools. An effective educational approach is presented by integrating critical issues with a practical rationale for developing drug education programs to meet the unique needs of exceptional children.

299. Impact and Roles of Drug Information in Drug Education. Goodstadt, Michael S. *Journal of Drug Education.* v5, n3, p223–33, 1975.

Evidence is presented elucidating the role of knowledge about drugs in facilitating or impeding drug use. The issues considered include (1) the role of drug information in previous education programs, (2) the source and uses of drug information, (3) the impact of this information, and (4) the alternative roles for drug information.

300. Implications of Drug Education Teaching Methods for Drug Usage. Serdahely, William J. *Journal of Alcohol and Drug Education.* v25, n1, p1–6, Fall 1979.

The hidden curricula of dichotomous drug education teaching methods are discussed. It is suggested that the hidden curriculum of the traditional drug education teaching style, the lecture/examination approach, reinforces some of the qualities which are characteristic of substance abusers. On the other hand, it is proposed that the hidden curriculum of nontraditional teaching methods is more likely to teach attributes consistent with the appropriate use of substances.

301. Instructional Practices of Drug Education Teachers. Valente, Carmine Michael. *Health Education.* v7, n2, p32, Mar–Apr 1976.

Demographic characteristics and instructional practices are reported for 73 public school drug education teachers. Little demographic difference was found among teachers. Drug education usually occurred in health and social studies classes. Participation in a drug workshop was a primary factor in motivating teachers to teach about drugs.

302. Life Style and Cigarette Smoking: A Challenge for the School Counsellor. Langford, E. Robert. *School Guidance Worker*. v32, n2, p5–9, Nov 1976.

The author suggests that a critical factor in influencing healthful lifestyles among young people is a counselor's example. The counselor who continues to smoke loses an effective form of counseling.

303. The "No Win": Drug Education Evaluation Problems. Swanson, Jon Colby. *Journal of Drug Education*. v8, n2, p125–29, 1978.

Confusion on the goals of prevention and treatment has led some schools to define the nature of their drug-abuse education program in such fashion that they cannot reasonably expect success. Drug-abuse prevention goals are the domain of education. New models for evaluating such goals need to be developed.

304. Our Children Are Going to Pot: Comments from a Health Educator. Apgar, Fred M. *Journal of School Health*. v50, n1, p40–41, Jan 1980.

Health education seems to have focused on the cognitive aspect of drug abuse in the past. But now, educators and society as a whole should direct their efforts at identifying the underlying causes of drug abuse and addressing these needs. Particular attention should be given to the family and to the emotional and social development of young people.

305. Prevalent and Preferred Styles in Drug Education. Antonow, Walter et al. *Journal of Drug Education*. v6, n2, p117–25, 1976.

A survey of prevalent and preferred drug education styles revealed that a significant difference exists between the present approach to drug education and the preferred. The attitudes of the drug education specialists were found to be in congruence with the national attitudes toward the above-mentioned areas: the preaching and scaring models were rejected in favor of a supportive, affective, involved mode.

306. Prevention of Alcoholism—A Teaching Strategy. Cappiello, Lawrence A. *Journal of Drug Education*. v7, n4, p311–16, 1977.

Programs of alcohol education, or education on alcoholism, should have three main objectives: (1) information about alcohol and alcoholism, (2) case findings, and (3) prevention. The subject is an extremely complex one, calling on the skills of many different disciplines for the gathering of research data and the treatment of the patient.

307. Primary Prevention Education. Mannello, Timothy. *Journal of Alcohol and Drug Education*. v24, n1, p39–57, Fall 1978 (EJ 198 801; Reprint: UMI).

Alcohol-abuse prevention education encourages participants to make choices, to set safe drinking standards, and to detect questionable practices before they lead to problems.

308. Recent Trends in Alcohol Education. Blane, Howard T. *Health Education*. v7, n3, p36–38, May–Jun 1976.

There are two basic trends in alcohol education—one aiming at containment and control, the other envisioning a society in which alcohol is morally neutral, its use integrated into activities that reflect social solidarity, and in which drinking is not associated with social hazard.

309. The Role of Persuasive Communications in Drug Dissuasion. Schlegel, Ronald P. *Journal of Drug Education*. v7, n3, p279–90, 1977.

This report presents an experimental study in which changes in marihuana attitudes and smoking intentions were attempted using the formal communication approach. Several currently useful generalizations derived from past research and the present study are suggested.

310. Should Alcohol Education Be Taught with Drug Education? Finn, Peter. *Journal of School Health*. v47, n8, p466–69, Oct 1977 (EJ 172 782; Reprint: UMI).

At the present time, the soundest instructional approach in helping students to clarify their attitudes and behaviors toward alcohol use/abuse is to separate it from other components of drug education.

311. Smoking Intervention; Comparing Three Methods in a High School Setting. Greenberg, Jerrold S.; Deputat, Zenon. *Journal of School Health*. v48, n8, p498–502, Oct 1978 (EJ197 191; Reprint: UMI).

This study compared smoking intervention programs that use (1) a scare approach, (2) a facts approach, and (3) a values approach. It was concluded that a more lasting change in smoking behavior and attitude results from a smoking intervention program that uses affective educational activities such as values clarification and discussions pertaining to feelings and emotions as they relate to cigarette smoking.

312. Teaching Drug Education in a Meaningful Manner. Harris, W. H. *Physical Educator*. v35, n4, p183–86, Dec 1978.

Just as the pendulum of drug education swung to the far extreme of facts-only programs in the 1960s and early 1970s, there may be a trend today to swing to the far extremes of affective education programs. Maybe a blending of the two polarities would be the most effective approach.

313. Which Way Drug Education? Wepner, Stephen F. *Journal of Drug Education*. v9, n2, p93–103, 1979.

Reviews history of drug programs and offers a plan to decrease adolescent drug abuse by utilizing an array of noneducational resources including youth-oriented media. Achieving this goal will permit educational programs to shift their energies and resources back to primary prevention and away from intervention and treatment.

314. The Youthful Drug Abuser and Drug Abuse Education—Closing the Credibility Gap. Nail, Richard L.; Gunderson, E. K. Eric. *Journal of Drug Education*. v5, n1, p65–74, 1975.

The goal of this report is to briefly summarize the state of drug-abuse education, with frequent reference to authoritative figures in the field. Personal decision making is discussed, along with advantages and hazards concerning reliance on youthful attempts to reach independent conclusions regarding drug use. The significance of the mass media in disseminating drug-abuse information is pointed out. Authoritative evidence appears to make a case for an unemotional, honest, and informative presentation of drug-abuse topics.

MICROFICHE

315. Cigarette Warning Labels as Educational Devices. Newman, Ian M. et al. Oct 1978, 23p; Paper presented at the Annual Meeting, American School Health Association (Dearborn, MI, October 12, 1978) (ED 166 131; Reprint: EDRS).

This paper reports an investigation on the educational impact of warning labels on cigarette packages on adolescents. Subjects were asked to identify the locations of warning labels on cigarette packages and advertising and to restate the warning label. Results indicated that official warnings may be well known in general terms but poorly known in specific terms. It is suggested that if mass public warning statements about health are educational devices, they should be developed and pretested with care and evaluated before they are widely disseminated.

316. Comparison of Recovered Alcoholic and Non-Alcoholic Communicator in Alcohol Education.† Clark, Susan G.; Porter, JoAnn, Fairfax Alcohol Safety Action Project, VA; National Highway Traffic Safety Administration, Washington, DC; Virginia Highway Safety Division, Richmond, Apr 1977, 16p (PB-293 727/4ST; Reprint: NTIS).

The study was designed to test one aspect of presenting alcohol information to high school students; namely, does a recovered alcoholic have more influence on attitudes and knowledge about alcohol than a nonalcoholic. Three groups of high school students were given knowledge and attitude pretests. Material was presented to Group A by a person introduced as a recovered alcoholic. Group B's material was presented by the same person, but who was not introduced as a recovered alcoholic. Group C had no information presented, and it acted as a control. Analysis of variance indicated a significant increase in knowledge in the experimental groups, but the characteristic recovered alcoholic was not influential. Attitudes changed only slightly, but in the direction opposite of that predicted. Policy implications for alcohol education programs were discussed.

317. A Conceptual Model of Drug Use and Its Implications for Special Educators. Lotsof, Antoinette; Floyd, Jerald D. Apr 1976, 15p; Paper presented at the Annual International Convention, The Council for Exceptional Children (54th, Chicago, IL, April 4–9, 1976) (ED 122 512; Reprint: EDRS).

Such drug education approaches as scare tactics have proved unsuccessful in the past, and a new educational model based on the health concept has been developed. The health concept model includes social, physical, mental, and emotional growth and development, decision making, and interpersonal and intrapersonal interactions. Before applying the model, a basic understanding of human needs and types of drug use is needed. Meaningful learning experiences for working out drug-use patterns should include goals with the following characteristics: they should be stated in terms of the learner; they should include cognitive, affective, and action domains; and they should identify the desired end results in terms that have clear meaning to the student.

318. Drug Abuse Prevention: The Awareness, Experience, and Opinions of Junior and Senior High School Students in New York State. Report No. 2 of Winter 1974/75 Survey. Dembo, Richard et al. New York State Office of Drug Abuse Services, Albany, May 1976, 43p; for related document see entry 55 (ED 140 174; Reprint: EDRS).

This report represents an attempt to measure young people's awareness of and attitude toward the prevention efforts their schools have undertaken in terms of the prevalence and incidence of drug use. It also seeks to learn which prevention program topics the students desire. Further, the report addresses the issue of the credibility of various sources of information on drugs and the people who are, in the eyes of youngsters surveyed, the helpers. This information has direct pragmatic value, since it speaks to drug and alcohol use from a perspective that should yield pathways to timely and meaningful intervention.

319. The Drug Education Controversy: Attitudes of Educators and Experts. Research Bulletin Vol. 12, No. 2. Webb, Rodman B.; Legg, Sue M., Florida Educational Research and Development Council, Gainesville, 1978, 52p; may be marginally legible due to small print (ED 158 201; Reprint: EDRS—HC not available; also available from FERDC, c/o Lee County School Board, 2055 Central Avenue, Ft. Myers, FL 33901).

In this study 651 teachers, administrators, and guidance counselors working in 16 randomly selected Florida junior high schools, middle schools, and senior high schools gave their opinions on drug education, school policies for drug offenders, and the causes of drug abuse. Drug education experts throughout the country also responded to the same questions. The survey showed that the opinions of educators differ markedly from the opinions of drug education experts and that there is more agreement in opinion among experts than among educators. The survey also showed that educator attitudes can be a source of resistance to effective drug education as it is defined by experts because: (1) educators are more likely than experts to see drug use as immoral and as a result of parental permissiveness; (2) educators are more likely to believe that schools cannot help drug users; and (3) educators take a more punitive approach to drug users than do experts. Incorporating this information on educator and expert attitudes toward drug education, the survey authors present an evaluation checklist for a drug education program.

320. A Framework for Developing Drug Abuse Prevention Strategies for Young People in Ghetto Areas. Dembo, Richard; Burgos, William. Jan 1976, 24p; Paper presented at the Annual Meeting of the American Educational Research Association (San Francisco, CA, April 19–23, 1976) (ED 124 821; Reprint: EDRS).

The present paper considers critical factors in the experience of young people that need to be taken into account in order to understand them and to develop prevention programs. Drawing on research and the literature on socialization, social psychology, and drug abuse, an ethnographically informed social context model of the actor is developed and its implications for prevention activities among ghetto youths examined.

321. Health Education: Drugs and Alcohol; An Annotated Bibliography. ERIC Clearinghouse on Teacher Education, Washington, DC, 1975, 33p. Sponsoring agency: National Education Association, Washington, DC (ED 104 841; Reprint: EDRS—HC not available; also available from NEA Publications, Order Department, The Academic Building, Saw Mill Road, West Haven, CT 06516, stock no. 1351-4-00).

This document begins with an article on what drug abuse is and how educators can deal with it. The annotated listing which follows is divided into sections on drug abuse, drug education, alcohol abuse, alcohol education, and venereal disease. Journal articles constitute the majority of the generally post-1971 entries; research studies, books, curriculum manuals, and bibliographies are also included. The reference section of this document was developed by the ERIC Clearinghouse on Teacher Education from a computer search of the ERIC database. The references are composed of abstracts of ERIC documents as they appear in *Research in Education* (RIE). Annotations of journal articles have been taken from *Current Index to Journals in Education* (CIJE).

322. Health Education: Smoke Stop Programming. Johnson, Ray. 1977, 8p; Paper presented at the Annual Convention, American School Health Association (Atlanta, GA, October 12–16, 1977) (ED 150 116; Reprint: EDRS).

The author examines the traditional emphasis of health educators in preventive approaches to smoking behavior and suggests (through a brief literature review) specific techniques that may be useful in aiding those who would stop smoking.

323. It Starts with People: Experiences in Drug Abuse Prevention. Resnik, Henry S., Porter, Novelli and Associates, Inc., Washington, DC, 1978, 84p; some parts may reproduce poorly due to print quality. Sponsoring agency: National Institute on Drug Abuse (DHEW/PHS), Rockville, MD, Division of Resource Development (ED 167 851; Reprint: EDRS).

The question of drug-abuse prevention is examined in this booklet. Addressing itself to a variety of disciplines and professions, the book reveals the effectiveness of prevention programs implemented in classroom, school, and community settings. It draws on the experiences of several dozen drug-abuse prevention programs that were either visited or assessed as part of an intensive research and review process. Strategies and educational techniques for prevention programs are emphasized, and organizational models for schools, communities, and minority groups are presented. The emphasis is on how individual people can reach across age and social barriers to work with youth and help them live without drugs.

324. Prevention of Alcoholism with Implications for Elementary and Secondary School Education.* Owen, Roger D., University of Oregon, 1976, 229p (774749; Reprint: DC).

Four-year longitudinal interviews with Oregon alcohol educators and an examination of literature from within and external to the field of alcoholism are employed to review the possible causes why alcoholism education in the schools has failed to reduce the incidence of the problem. Emphasis is given to the constraints which have operated currently and historically and which have been major factors responsible for this failure.

Among them are: the governmental-industrial complex, the assumption of a rational model of man, poor accountability in the schools and among the alcoholologists. The schools are seen as instrumental in creating deviant behavior in a large number of students, of maintaining a nonredemptive posture, and further stigmatizing children with spoiled-image programs, and furthering their negative self-concepts.

The second objective is the elaboration of conditions that must be present for alcohol-education-as-prevention to occur. Implications are presented for a nonspecific primary prevention program based on behavioral competency training. This is intended to emphasize its disparity from the other nonspecific primary prevention program with currency: values clarification.

Values clarification has many common attributes with guided group interaction, which may best be considered verbal competency training, though usually programed to junior high and high school students where such training may not have its greatest impact. It is a strategy based on many of the dynamics of insight therapy which has questionable value for the population at risk. Sensitivity training and similar strategies are not seen as effective with children whose negative self-concept has been reinforced throughout their prior lives.

The strategies of behavioral competency training are based on the assumption that a person's life experiences provide the major definition of his/her self-concept. This conceptualization borrows from the thesis that youth need to develop a sense of competence, belongingness, usefulness, and personal potency to achieve legitimate adult identities. It also is derived from the Life Skills program used currently in schools in Calgary, Alberta, Canada, which places emphasis on the development of "personal power." Phases of a behavioral-competency-structured training program include self-exploration, planning or goal setting, and action. Instructional strategies and methods then may be implemented and adjusted for each grade level.

Changes within the teacher-training curriculum are seen as requisite to: (1) provide teachers with sufficient skills to raise self-esteem in children who have already developed academic low-certain self-concepts and (2) maintain the integrity of each student in the status system of the school. The teacher with these skills coupled with the nonspecific primary prevention strategies based on behavioral competence building is seen as having greater opportunity to decrease the incidence of alcoholism and related forms of deviance.

325. Primary Prevention in Drug Abuse: An Annotated Guide to the Literature. Messolonghites, Louisa, Comp., National Institute on Drug Abuse (DHEW/PHS), Rockville, MD, Division of Resource Development, 1977, 212p (ED 153 513; Reprint: EDRS; also available from Superintendent of Documents, US Government Printing Office, Washington, DC 20402, stock no. 017-025-00561-4).

This annotated guide is a first attempt to canvass and organize the growing body of literature and resources available to workers in the field of primary drug-abuse prevention. Major topics covered include: history, strategies, and policies of drug-abuse prevention; education and training; community action; multimedia information sources; evaluation; additional readings; and state and federal contacts and coordinators.

326. A Skeptical Look at Drug Education. Brown, W. Cecil. Jul 1977, 19p; Paper presented at the Annual Conference on Alcohol and Drug Dependencies (12th, Winnipeg, Manitoba, Canada, July 10–15, 1977) (ED 151 623; Reprint: EDRS).

This paper argues that attempts to prevent nonsanctioned drug use through education have spawned a variety of programs and prescriptions. Sophisticated and ideosyncratic vocabularies have been used to describe the various recommendations. The literature refers to developing self-concept, mental health, and decision-making skills. References are made to the communication-persuasion model, induced-cognitive dissonance, confluent education, values education, and assertiveness training—all in the name of preventing some vaguely conceived drug problem. The author asserts that virtually every activity with a psychological or educational sound has been offered in such convincing terms that little scrutiny has been made of their premises, potential, or educational integrity. The paper focuses on two issues. First, since self-concept development is a prominent feature in current drug education programs, it is argued that these approaches are based on questionable assumptions and erroneous extrapolations. Their validity is therefore in doubt. Second, the issues of educational integrity and ethical responsibility is considered in relation to many

prominent approaches to drug education. Hidden beneath the euphemisms, the author claims, are attempts to create compliant behavior through deception and bias. The common attempt to create compliant behavior in these programs is presented as antithetical to education itself.

BOOKS

327. Drug Abuse Prevention: Perspectives and Approaches for Educators. Corder, Brice W. et al. Dubuque, IA: Wm. C. Brown Co., 1975, 123p.

This is a practical guide for planning school drug education programs. It provides background on the drug question and suggestions for developing and evaluating programs that go beyond the facts-only approach to drug education.

328. Drugs in the Classroom: A Conceptual Model for School Programs. Cornacchia, Harold J. et al. St. Louis, MO: Mosby, 1978, 2d ed., 335p.

The main emphasis in this volume is on the *conceptual model* of a school drug program and its implementation. Part one covers the dilemma faced by the schools. Part two discusses the drug scene: a current synthesis of pharmacological, psychological, and sociological aspects of drugs; rehabilitation and treatment resources; and the law and law enforcement procedures. In part three is found a *conceptual model* of the school drug program, which includes (1) formal and informal drug education with specific suggestions for curriculum development and practical ideas (values clarification, decision making, mental health) for use by classroom teachers; (2) drug services to identify drug abusers and procedures for helping these students; (3) school atmosphere needed to understand student unrest, what to do about the physical and emotional needs of students, and provision for humanism in the school; and (4) coordination of the school drug program necessary for an administrative structure to develop policies and procedures, to conduct inservice programs, and for other purposes. Part four provides evaluation guidelines and suggestions for use by teachers, administrators, and others, with illustrative procedures.

Drug Education: Inservice Training

JOURNAL ARTICLES

329. Behavioral Objectives for the Drug Education Preparation of K–3 Elementary School Teachers. Cohen, Stuart J. *Journal of Drug Education.* v7, n1, p1–14, 1977.

This report identifies training behavioral objectives in drug education for K–3 teachers.

330. Drug Education for Teachers: Its Effects on Attitudes and Instruction. Weiner, Marc A. et al. *Drug Forum: The Journal of Human Issues.* v6, n3, p279–88, 1977–78.

A major response to the increased use of drugs among the nation's youth has been a demand for the inclusion of formal drug education in the public school curriculum. This paper partially examines whether or not there are differences in fact between trained and untrained teachers in two basic areas: (1) their knowledge about drugs, and (2) their attitudes about school drug policy and drug education. Trained teachers were more knowledgeable, but, in the area of attitudes about school drug education and drug policy, less difference could be related to the amount of teacher training.

331. An Evaluation of Workshops Designed to Prepare Teachers in Alcohol Education. Rankin, William L. et al. *Journal of Alcohol and Drug Education.* v23, n3, p1–13, Spr 1978.

An experiment was conducted to determine the effectiveness of training workshops for teachers who were subsequently to implement an alcohol education curriculum for grades K–12. The objectives of the four-day workshops were: (1) to provide information regarding alcohol and alcoholism, community alcoholism treatment resources, and materials of the new curriculum; (2) to effect attitudes favorable to responsible uses of alcohol; (3) to train teachers in coping skills; and (4) to train teachers in techniques for conducting open-ended discussions. As measured by the instruments developed for this project, the workshops did increase knowledge and change attitudes about responsible uses of alcohol. The workshops were, however, mostly unsuccessful in changing other related attitudes, and in improving coping skills and discussion-leading abilities.

332. Training Teachers for Drug Abuse Prevention: A Humanistic Approach. Safford, Philip L. et al. *Journal of Drug Education.* v5, n4, p335–49, 1975.

Based on recognition of the apparent inadequacy of didactic methods in drug-abuse education, a staff development model was planned and implemented which sought to bring about the personal involvement of teachers and students. The program involves inservice training, curriculum development, and affective education. Evaluation suggests program goals are being realized.

MICROFICHE

333. Alcohol Abuse Training Related to Minority Populations. Handbook: Blacks. Porter, Thomas L. et al., Southern Area Alcohol and Education Training Program, Inc., Atlanta, Ga, 1977, 34p. Sponsoring agency: National Institute on Alcohol Abuse and Alcoholism (DHEW/PHS), Rockville, MD (ED 177 229; Reprint: EDRS—HC not available; also available from Southern Area Alcohol Education and Training Program, Inc., 4875 Powers Ferry Road, NW, Atlanta, GA 30327).

The intent of this manual is to provide counselors with essential background information about alcohol abuse among Blacks and with a practical, workable model for organizing and structuring a training program. A general discussion of Black self-awareness in relation to alcohol abuse is presented. An approach to counseling and serving the Black alcoholic is suggested. A model program for training persons who will be working with Black alcoholics and alcohol abusers is outlined. A general alcohol

education program for use in training alcohol-abuse counselors is also outlined. Included is a Black vocabulary test and an alcohol awareness test that can be used for pretraining assessment of the counselor's needs and posttraining evaluation of the effectiveness of the program. A bibliography of pertinent printed materials and a list of available films and audiovisual aids are provided.

334. Alcohol Abuse Training Relevant to Minority Populations. Handbook: Native Americans. Southern Area Alcohol and Education Training Program, Inc., Atlanta, GA, 1977, 27p. Sponsoring agency: National Institute on Alcohol Abuse and Alcoholism (DHEW/PHS), Rockville, MD (ED 173 494; Reprint: EDRS—HC not available; also available from Southern Area Alcohol Education and Training Program, Inc., 4875 Powers Ferry Road, NW, Atlanta, GA 30327).

The intent of this manual is to provide counselors with essential background information about alcohol abuse among American Indians and with a practical, workable model for organizing and structuring a training program. The nature and extent of alcohol abuse among American Indians and the particular pattern of drinking behavior observable among them are discussed. A model program for training persons who will be working with American Indian alcoholics and alcohol abusers is outlined. In addition, a modular outline of a general alcohol education program for use in training alcohol-abuse counselors is presented. Included is an alcohol awareness test which can be used for pretraining assessment of the trainers' needs and posttraining evaluation of the effectiveness of the program. A bibliography of pertinent printed materials and a list of available films and audiovisual aids are provided.

335. Alcohol Abuse Training Relevant to Minority Populations. Handbook: Spanish Speaking. Southern Area Alcohol and Education Training Program, Inc., Atlanta, GA, 1977, 29p. Sponsoring agency: National Institute on Alcohol Abuse and Alcoholism (DHEW/PHS), Rockville, MD (ED 173 493; Reprint: EDRS—HC not available; also available from Southern Area Alcohol Education and Training Program, Inc., 4875 Powers Ferry Road, NW, Atlanta, GA 30327).

The intent of this manual is to provide trainers with essential background information about alcohol abuse among Spanish-speaking Americans and with a practical, workable model for organizing and structuring a training program. The nature and extent of alcohol abuse among Spanish-speaking Americans and the particular patterns of drinking behavior observable among this group are discussed. A model program for training persons who will be working with Spanish-speaking alcoholics and alcohol abusers is outlined. A modular outline of a general alcohol education program for use in training alcohol-abuse trainers is also presented. Included is an alcohol awareness test which can be used for pretraining assessment of the trainers' needs and posttraining evaluation of the effectiveness of the program. An annotated bibliography of pertinent printed materials and a list of available films and audiovisual aids are provided.

336. Alcohol Abuse Training Relevant to Minority Populations. Trainer Manual, Trainee Handbook. Southern Area Alcohol and Education Training Program, Inc., Atlanta, GA, 1977, 102p. Sponsoring agency: National Institute on Alcohol Abuse and Alcoholism (DHEW/PHS), Rockville, MD (ED 173 495; Reprint: EDRS—HC not available; also available from Southern Area Alcohol Education and Training Program, Inc., 4875 Powers Ferry Road, NW, Atlanta, GA 30327).

This training manual presents current information about alcohol abuse and alcoholism among minority populations. It is designed to aid counselors employed in alcohol-abuse programs. Areas discussed in this report include: interpersonal communication, knowledge of alcohol abuse and alcoholism, evaluation and assessment, planning, referral, counseling, and treatment. Specific topics addressed include physiological, psychological, and sociological/anthropological approaches to alcoholism, resources, public relations, vocational rehabilitation, legal aspects, instructional planning research, and funding resources. Strategies for training counselors and implementing treatment and/or prevention programs which are relevant to the needs of minority group alcoholics and alcohol abusers are also outlined.

337. Basic Substance Abuse Counselor's Training Course; Individual Counseling Skills and Client Management. Trainer's Manual [and] Resource Manual. Salisbury, DeRoss; Kamar, Normandie, Indiana State Department of Mental Health, Indianapolis, Dec 1978, 595p. Sponsoring agency: National Institute on Drug Abuse (DHEW/PHS), Rockville, MD, Division of Resource Development (ED 173 717; Reprint: EDRS; also available from Superintendent of Documents, US Government Printing Office, Washington, DC 20402; The National Drug Abuse Center for Training and Resource Development, 656 Quince Orchard Road, Room 607, Gaithersburg, MD 20760, publication no. 79-153T).

The Individual Counseling Skills Training Course is a three-unit, 11-day course for alcoholism and drug counselors. One unit, dealing with individual counseling skills and client management, is presented here. The course was originally conceived for paraprofessionals in frontline counseling positions who have little or no formal academic training. It can also be adapted for homogeneous groups of professionals. The authors strongly recommend that the training be carried out in a residential setting. The format involves the use of both a trainer (who makes authoritative presentations of subject matter) and a facilitator (who uses both directive and nondirective techniques to guide the group process). Topics covered include the whole self, somatic awareness, principles of behavior change in counseling situations, and cognitive and affective closure. An accompanying resource manual for use by participants offers pretraining questionnaires, objectives, suggested activities, and additional reading.

338. The Development and Field Testing of a Competency-Based Teacher Education Module in Drug Abuse Education for Prospective Elementary School Teachers* Kesselschmidt, Norma Laks, Columbia University Teachers College, 1977, 226p (7714733; Reprint: DC).

The purpose of this study was to develop and field test a competency-based teacher education module in drug abuse education for prospective elementary school teachers.

The competencies developed by the investigator for this study were: Competency I—the teacher identifies the sociological problems affecting children (including miscellaneous drugs, alcohol, tobacco), and Competency II—the teacher utilizes the school situation to apply subject matter information (including curriculum development, clinical experience, assessment).

A concise statement, including a rationale and list of prerequisites, was developed for each of the competencies in the module. During two workshops the competencies were validated by health educators, classroom teachers, and administrators. These competencies were translated into behavioral objectives. Preassessment instruments, utilizing teacher-made criteria for scoring, were developed by the investigator. A list of learning activities intended to facilitate mastery of the objectives was compiled. Those activities believed to most effectively develop the objectives were included in the module. Postassessment instruments either identical or parallel to the preassessments were developed. Remediation consisted of a selection from the "additional" activities or the repetition of a previous activity. The format of the module and the components were assessed by a panel of experts and appropriate revisions were incorporated.

The setting for the field testing was a preservice undergraduate health course. This study's population consisted of 14 students identified as prospective elementary school teachers. Student achievement was measured through a comparison of pre- and postassessment scores. Student reaction to the module experience was measured through an anonymous questionnaire.

Examination of the data related to student achievement showed that no student demonstrated competency on any of the pretests. This reaffirms the lack of accurate information possessed by the prospective teachers. The data related to the number of students passing the posttests showed that 21 of the 26 posttests attempted were passed by 13 or more students on the first trial. Further examination showed that all of the students attempting a posttest after remediation activities demonstrated competency. The data imply that mastery of the objectives was facilitated, in this population, by learning activities.

Student reaction measured through an anonymous questionnaire produced general agreement that more time was needed than was available in a summer session course, and there was too much work for the number of credits allocated to this experience. There was agreement that the rationale for Competency I needed to be revised to promote clearer understanding and a higher level of motivation. Most of the students found Competency II to be more interesting, relevant, and enjoyable than Competency I.

339. Doing Drug Education: The Role of the School Teacher. Southern Regional Education Board, Atlanta, GA, 1975, 32p. Sponsoring agency: National Institute on Drug Abuse (DHEW/PHS), Rockville, MD (ED 119 051; Reprint: EDRS; also available from Superintendent of Documents, US Government Printing Office, Washington, DC 20402, stock no. 017-024-00460-0).

Enhancing Drug Education in the South was a project conducted by the Southern Regional Education Board in 1971–74. The project held regional conferences that brought together people in the SREB region with state-level responsibility for planning alcohol and drug education programs in an effort to find solutions to common problems such as coordination and program evaluation.

SREB convened a task force of eight people with expertise in teaching and in preparing teachers for drug education. The task force first met early in April 1972 to determine what kinds of skills students need to live successfully in a drug-oriented society, and what classroom activities would be most effective in meeting these needs. With this as a basis, the second session, held at the end of April, concentrated on determining the competencies—knowledge, skills, values, and attitudes—needed by a teacher who would carry out the activities. This report reflects the deliberations of two workshops that focused on teacher training for the role of drug educator in schools. The objective of these two sessions was not to design a curriculum or training program, but rather to determine what competencies a teacher needs to serve as an effective drug educator. Furthermore, the task force defined ''drug educator'' as a role that any teacher might assume, whether his primary assignment be English, social studies, science, or health.

340. Drugs in Perspective: Trainer's Manual and Resource Manual. Link, William E. et al., National Drug Abuse Center for Training and Resource Development, Gaithersburg, MD, 1979, 874p. Sponsoring agency: National Institute on Drug Abuse (DHEW/PHS), Rockville, MD, Division of Resource Development (ED 177 448; Reprint: EDRS; also available from Superintendent of Documents, US Government Printing Office, Washington, DC 20402, stock no. 1724-00344).

This manual is designed to train those helping professionals working with youth overseas, military personnel, and community service organizations in the area of drug-abuse prevention and treatment. The resource modules focus on the following areas of concern: (1) introduction to prevention and treatment, (2) perspectives on substance use and abuse, (3) social and historical contexts for understanding American substance abuse, (4) substance actions, (5) understanding the phenomenon of substance abuse, (6) treatment approaches, (7) prevention approaches and strategies, and (8) closure and evaluation. The trainer's manual provides guidelines and suggestions for lectures, demonstrations, guided group discussions, task group exercises, and optional reading assignments.

341. Drugs, Society and Personal Choice: A Summer School for Teachers. Ramsey, G. Ross; Barnes, Lesley. May 1976, 68p; Paper presented at the Annual Convention of the Canadian Guidance and Counseling Association (Halifax, Nova Scotia, May, 1976) (ED 136 128; reprint: EDRS).

The paper is designed to familiarize the reader with the historical development, planning, implementation, and evaluation components of a drug information course offered to teachers in Nova Scotia. The paper presents the course plan, highlights of previous summer school experiences, and anticipated further directions.

342. Facts about Drug Abuse: Trainer's Manual. Link, William E. et al., National Drug Abuse Center for Training and Resource Development, Gaithersburg, MD, Nov 1977, 413p; pages III 37–51 not filmed due to copyright. Sponsoring agency: National Institute on Drug Abuse (DHEW/PHS), Rockville, MD (ED 170 637; Reprint: EDRS; also available from Superintendent of Documents, US Government Printing Office, Washington, DC 20402).

Following an introductory survey of the course, this modular drug-abuse trainer's manual contains all course-specified materials. These materials are: the course goals and objectives; time/activity sheets; trainer guidelines, process notes, and exercise instructions; detailed lectures and supplementary information. The time/activity sheets contain the training schedule with time allocations, training tasks with the materials and equipment needed, training activities that specify expected trainer and trainee behaviors, and logistical details. Actual course topic areas are: historical evolution of drug use; types of drugs; drug effects; alcohol and marihuana; social and legal responses to drug use; treatment efforts; drug myths; drug dependence; the evolution of polydrug abuse; and the roles of families, schools, communities and peer groups related to drug-abuse prevention. Additional items discuss feedback and evaluation by trainers.

343. A Framework for Crime Prevention and Drug Education in Texas: Desirable Teacher Competencies. Texas Education Agency, Austin, Division of Crime Prevention and Drug Education, Jun 1975, 39p; for related document see entry 257 (ED 136 098; Reprint: EDRS; also available from Texas Education Agency, Division of Crime Prevention and Drug Education, 201 East Eleventh Street, Austin, TX 78701).

This manual provides guidelines for both teachers and students, developed by the Texas Education Agency for their program of crime prevention and drug education. It enumerates the necessary teacher competencies in skills and attitudes in the secondary school, directed toward bringing about desired student activities. A glossary of pertinent terms is also included.

344. Group Process in Alcohol Education. American Driver and Traffic Safety Education Association, Washington, DC, 1978, 49p (ED 166 575; Reprint: EDRS—HC not available; also available from American Driver and Traffic Safety Education Association, 1201 Sixteenth Street, NW, Washington, DC 20036).

This manual describes group process and relates it specifically to alcohol education and to a pilot study conducted in cooperation with the Milwaukee Public Schools. It reports on an effort to prepare teachers to use group process techniques in alcohol education, and on their subsequent use of the process with their high school students. The manual could be a valuable resource for those who prepare teachers to meet classroom responsibilities. The first part presents strategies for the classroom. It gives an overview of group process, discussing why it is worth trying, and how to prepare, use, and evaluate it. A subsection on techniques for alcohol education explores decision making, and offers discussion hints and suggested activities. The second part describes the pilot study. It discusses an inservice workshop, describing teacher preparation and data collection, and comparing teachers' preconceptions with their experiences after using the material. This second part concludes with a discussion and recommendations; it recaps the project design, and presents pros and cons of the group process approach.

345. Humanizing Preservice Teacher Education: Strategies for Alcohol and Drug Abuse Prevention. ERIC Clearinghouse on Teacher Education, Washington, DC, Dec 1977, 94p. Sponsoring agency: National Institute of Education (DHEW), Washington, DC; Office of Education (DHEW), Washington, DC, Alcohol and Drug Abuse Education Program (ED 147 281; Reprint: EDRS).

This document presents summary reports of six demonstration projects and one research project engaged in primary prevention of alcohol and drug abuse. The goals of these seven projects were the same, though each evolved and worked differently: (1) reinforcement of nonuse of alcohol and drugs; (2) discouragement of experimentation; and (3) prevention or early intervention in the destructive use of all substances. The programs focused very little on drug use and abuse, per se, but attempted to deal with causes rather than symptoms. The final aim of these projects was to find ways to humanize teacher education, to change prospective teachers who would create a humanistic environment in the schools so that students would no longer feel the need to seek external gratification through drug abuse. The six demonstration projects are summarized in reports entitled: (1) Preservice Model Project (sponsored by Life Resources and Boston College); (2) Humanizing Environment and Educational Development (Mankato, Minnesota, State University); (3) HIP—An Alternative Program for the Preparation of Elementary Teachers (University of Missouri—Columbia); (4) A Competency-Based Affective Program for Preservice Teachers (University of Houston); (5) USDE Drug Abuse Prevention Demonstration Project (University of Northern Iowa); (6) The Drug Education Program (University of California at Santa Cruz). The research project report is entitled "Self-Knowledge Education as an Approach to Drug Abuse Education," and was conducted by the University of Massachusetts. A summary of significant features of all seven reports is presented in an afterword, as well as possible future action in the area.

346. National Institute on Drug Abuse Training Grants Directory. Mitchell, Lonnie E., National Institute on Drug Abuse (DHEW/PHS), Rockville, MD, Apr 1979, 27p. Sponsoring agency: Department of Health, Education, and Welfare, Washington, DC (ED 177 430; Reprint: EDRS; also available from Superintendent of Documents, US Government Printing Office, Washington, DC 20402).

This catalog lists for individuals, universities, colleges, and single state agency directors, training grants supported by the National Institute on Drug Abuse. The four different types of grants described are developmental, career teacher, individual fellowship, and institutional research training grants. Each section is divided alphabetically by state. Because the training grants are a component of the National Manpower and Training System (NMTS), the first half of the directory is a description of NMTS in order to place the grants in their proper context. The NMTS description provides a historical perspective, including the system's development and structure, and its activities in the Manpower Training Branch, National Drug Abuse Center, Regional Support Centers, State Training Support Program, Career Development Centers, Health Professions Education Program, Developmental Training Grants Program, Research Fellow Training Grants Program, Federal Agency Manpower Training Group, and contracted services.

347. Suggestions to Maximize Implementation of Inservice Programming for Health Related Instruction. Shute, Robert E. Apr 1977, 19p; Paper presented at the Annual Meeting of the American Educational Research Association (New York, April 4–8, 1977) (ED 137 274; Reprint: EDRS).

A rationale, a model, and several suggestions are presented for increasing and maintaining the rate of classroom implementation of new teacher skills developed through inservice training programs. Because the health-related instructional areas have received insufficient attention in posttraining studies, the suggestions are presented in the context of drug education. Suggestions include: (1) inform all of the involved groups—students, teachers, parents, school officials, community members—of the drug education curriculum and make them aware of each stage of program implementation; (2) gain cooperation and assistance for program implementation; (3) ensure commitment of the various groups involved; (4) train all groups to deal with drug-related questions; (5) maintain contact with all involved groups; (6) anticipate trouble areas; (7) be experimental, but not sloppy; (8) be realistic—expect things to go wrong; and (9) listen to others. These suggestions are considered to transcend the drug education context in which they were researched; further research is needed to substantiate claims of their effectiveness for other health-related areas of inservice instruction implementation.

348. You, Youth, and Prevention; Trainer Manual and Session Outline Cards. National Center for Alcohol Education, Arlington, VA, 1979, 163p; audiovisuals not included. Sponsoring agency: National Institute on Alcohol Abuse and Alcoholism (DHEW/PHS), Rockville, MD (ED 174 908; Reprint: EDRS; also available from Superintendent of Documents, US Government Printing Office, Washington, DC 20402, stock no. 017-024-00898-2).

This program is designed for personnel working in alcohol service agencies who are responsible for planning and implementing prevention programs for youth. The training is most appropriate for the person who is just starting to plan a prevention program and who has only minimal experience in prevention work with youth. Training skills and experience in planning and managing prevention programs, equally important to the successful delivery of this training program, are discussed. Skill building is a focus in the directing of role play and simulation activities, group discussion, individual problem solving, lectures, and brainstorming. Specific suggestions on how to deploy the training staff are included in the refresher material on training techniques. Also included is a set of outline cards to be used by the trainer during sessions.

BOOKS

349. Drugs and the Coach. Clarke, Kenneth S. Washington, DC: American Alliance for Health, Physical Education, and Recreation, rev. ed., 1977, 70p.

The purpose of this publication is to provide the school coach with a perspective for becoming involved in drug education. It discusses the use of drugs in athletics, the use of street drugs by athletes, and how the coach can utilize "teachable moments" to help players with drug problems.

Drug Education: Program Descriptions and Evaluations

JOURNAL ARTICLES

350. The Alcohol and Drug Abuse Education Program.
Spillane, James. *American Education.* v14, n8, p50–51, Oct 1978.

Describes USOE's Alcohol and Drug Education Program (ADAEP), which offers regional training and technical support to local team efforts. Schools using the program are listed, and a few are described. ADAEP's 1977–78 program grants are listed.

351. Anti-Drug Abuse Commercials. Feingold, Paul C.; Knapp, Mark L. *Journal of Communication.* v27, n1, p20–28, Win 1977.

This experiment presented a series of antiamphetamine/antibarbiturate persuasive commercials to high school students. Messages were varied according to: (1) the threat of serious vs. minimal harm; (2) explicit vs. implicit conclusions; and (3) presentation as a monologue or dialogue. The messages had a boomerang effect, decreasing rather than increasing subject's negative attidues toward drugs.

352. Community Involvement in Alcohol Education.
Savage, Tom V., Jr. *Clearing House.* v51, n7, p349–50, Mar 1978 (EJ 182 683; Reprint: UMI).

In Spokane, Washington, an alcohol education program has developed prevention methods for alcohol abuse by getting the community, the schools, and higher education to cooperate. Discusses the program's main components—teacher and community education.

353. Comprehensive Alcohol Education: A New Approach to an Old Problem. Gonzalez, Gerardo M.; Kouba, James M. *NASPA Journal.* v16, n4, p7–13, Spr 1979 (EJ 200 906; Reprint: UMI).

This is a program model for responsible decision making on alcohol use. The intent is to encourage a philosophy about alcoholic beverages using a consistent example of moderate use. Moral implications are left to the individual. Drinking is not viewed as proof of adulthood, virility, or social acceptability.

354. Comprehensive School-Based Smoking Prevention Program. Botvin, Gilbert J.; Eng, Anna. *Journal of School Health.* v50, n4, p209–13, Apr 1980.

The purpose of this study was to test the effectiveness, with students in grades 8–10, of a comprehensive smoking prevention program which focused primary attention on the principal social and psychological variables believed to be involved in the onset of cigarette smoking. The results indicate that there were significantly fewer new experimental smokers among the students who participated in the smoking prevention program than among a comparable group of students in a control group, both at the time of posttest 1 and three months later at the time of the follow-up, posttest 2. Thus far, over a period of six months, the psychosocial smoking prevention program tested in this study has succeeded in reducing the incidence of new experimental smoking by nearly 70 percent.

355. Developing a Teen-Peer Facilitator Program. Pyle, K. Richard. *School Counselor.* v24, n4, p278–81, Mar 1977.

Peer-facilitator and/or peer counseling programs are having a real impact in schools. Guidelines provided in the article were found to have value in development and implementation of the program at Buchholy High School, Gainesville, Florida. More than 2,200 students, 120 teachers, 80 parents, and 9 administrators have been involved.

356. Drug Abuse and Your Child: What Can the Schools Do? Kearney, Artie L. *School Counselor.* v26, n3, p187–90, Jan 1979 (EJ 195 800; Reprint: UMI).

The staff of Wisconsin's Cooperative Educational Service Agency Number Eight has developed a drug prevention education program that operates under the premise that drug abuse is a "people problem" and people who have problems with drugs are people with personal problems—the symptom is drug abuse.

357. Drug/Alcohol Education—A New Approach for Schools. Rose, Shirley E.; Duer, William F. *Education.* v99, n2, p198–202, Win 1978 (EJ 196 706; Reprint: UMI).

Drug programs are changing from legalistic, pharmaco-logical, factual presentations to humanistic, experimentally based inquiry formats. The study reported here describes a humanistic/inquiry approach field tested in a middle school and demonstrating the success of curricula providing for decision making, self-concept enhancement, and interpersonal relationship activities facilitated by trained and committed teachers.

358.   Drug Education to Date: A Review. Randall, Diana; Wong, Martin R. *Journal of Drug Education.* v6, n1, p1–21, 1976.

A comprehensive review is presented of drug education programs for school students from 1967 to date. In general it was found that the great bulk of drug education programs reported were lacking in any meaningful evaluation that would provide data for guidance in the design of future programs.

359.   The Effect of Transcendental Meditation upon Modifying the Cigarette Smoking Habit. Ottens, Allen J. *Journal of School Health.* v45, n10, p577–83, Dec 1975.

A smoking treatment based on Transcendental Meditation (TM) was compared to a more traditional program using group discussion of self-control techniques. Both treatments were equally effective in reducing cigarette consumption.

360.   Enlisting Youth against Drugs and Drinking. Wittish, Linda. *American Education.* v15, n5, p15–18, Jun 1979.

In the Savannah, Georgia TRENDS program, high school students volunteer to teach sixth graders about drugs, utilizing a values education approach.

361.   Evaluating the Effect of a One-Day Drug Education Program on High School Journalists. Haskins, Jack B. *Journal of Drug Education.* v9, n3, p263–71, 1979.

Evaluates a one-day drug education program, embedded in a week-long workshop for high school journalists. Results indicate a one-day program is probably insufficient to change entrenched attitudes and behavior, and such programs may have unintended side effects. Good program evaluation research cannot be planned as an afterthought to the program.

362.   Evaluation of a Self-Development Approach to Drug Education: Some Mixed Results. Jackson, Javon; Calsyn, Robert J. *Journal of Drug Education.* v7, n1, p15–28, 1977.

A 50-hour self-development approach to drug education (STRIDE) which included values clarification, empathy training, drug information, with considerable peer interaction was evaluated by means of a true experiment. No differences were found between treatment and no-treatment groups in terms of drug usage, drug knowledge, and self-esteem.

363.   Freedom Road School: The Truth behind the Name. Fox, Terry C. *Journal of the International Association of Pupil Personnel Workers.* v20, n3, p151–53, Jun 1976.

This article describes Freedom Road School where high school age students with drug associated problems continue their education while receiving professional therapeutic treatment.

364.   Health and Drug Education—A Regional Approach. Clements, Mary. *Educational Leadership.* v35, n4, p314–17, Jan 1978 (EJ 171 597; Reprint: UMI).

Describes the Values Clarification Project and the Berkeley Health Curriculum Project, two educational programs being used by southwest Iowa schools in order to reduce drug abuse.

365.   Health Education through Entertainment: A Multimedia Campaign. Kelly, Nancy M. *Journal of the American College Health Association.* v26, n5, p248–52, Apr 1978 (EJ 187 748; Reprint: UMI).

This paper reports on a multimedia approach to alcohol education in the context of developing positive patterns of social interaction leading to personal and social health.

366.   Here's Looking at You: A School-Based Alcohol Education Project. Mooney, Carol et al. *Health Education.* v10, n6, p38–41, Nov–Dec 1979.

Describes the validated K–12 alcohol education curriculum developed by the Educational Service District (ESD) 121 in Seattle, Washington. The program, which comes in a series of curriculum kits for specific grade levels, emphasizes flexible instructional methods and content focusing on alcohol information, decision making, coping skills, and self-concept. Teacher preparation (20–32 hours) is required for implementation. Some evaluation findings are presented.

367.   Increasing Alcohol Awareness: A Drinking Demonstration. Mascalo, Alison. *Journal of College Student Personnel.* v20, n5, p454–55 Sep 1979.

In an effort to increase alcohol awareness among students at Salisbury State College, the counseling services staff staged a drinking demonstration. The purpose of the three-hour program was to enable students to learn how they performed different tasks at various degrees of intoxication. Five students and one member of the housing staff participated as drinkers; each was assigned a nondrinking partner responsible for ''baby-sitting'' during and after the event. It was judged that the informal and nonthreatening tone of the program facilitated learning.

368.   Middle School Curriculum Change: An Action-Oriented Cooperative Drug Education Pilot Project. Moyer, David H.; Simon, Robert K. *Adolescence.* v10, n39, p313–26, Fall 1975.

Describes the assumptions and processes of the development and implementation at Bayard Middle School's Cooperative Drug Education Pilot Project. Instructional approaches and some course content are outlined.

369.   Modeling: Prevention Showcase. *Health Education.* v10, n4, p30–31, Jul–Aug 1979 (EJ 213 525; Reprint: UMI).

Descriptions are given of model programs for the prevention of drug abuse.

370. Outdoor Education: A Neglected Resource for Combating Internal Pollution. Gemake, Josephine Stahl; Patti, Anthony V. *Communicator*. v9, n2, p19–21, Spr–Sum 1978 (EJ 189 338; Reprint: UMI).

Defining internal pollution as "the contamination and abuse of the human body through the habitual use of substances taken to relieve anxieties and tensions," this article asserts that outdoor education experiences can combat internal pollution through active physical, social, and intellectual involvement, promoting the security of belonging, achieving, and coping.

371. PAL, a Plan for Prevention of Alcohol Abuse: Some Evaluative Afterthoughts. Calmes, Robert E.; Alexander, Sharon D. *Journal of Alcohol and Drug Education*. v23, n1, p2–7, Fall 1977.

The PAL (Prevent Alcoholism) procedure consisted of a director working with several high school drama groups to produce original slide/tape productions communicating the students' own ideas about responsible decision making concerning alcohol use. The program was found to have real psychological benefits to the student participants, developing their altruism, moral reasoning, and role-taking abilities.

372. Peer Models Prevent Smoking among Pre-Adolescents. Williamson, John A.; Campbell, Lloyd P. *Clearing House*. v53, n8, p360–62, Apr 1980.

A model antismoking program was developed which was predicated upon maximum appeal to fifth- and sixth-grade youngsters. Teams of high school seniors presented the program, which included audiovisual aids and science experiments. Posttest scores indicated that the elementary students who experienced the program had significant attitude change over the control group. They were more knowledgeable about the hazards of smoking and had less tendency to perceive smoking as a grown-up activity.

373. Playing against Drugs. Hoyt, Jane Hauser. *American Education*. v12, n10, p21–25, Dec 1976.

In the belief that if children feel good about themselves they'll have no need for drugs, schools in Appleton, Wisconsin, have built a model prevention program.

374. A Prevention Program with Punch—The National PTA's Alcohol Education Project. Kimmel, Carol K. *Journal of School Health*. v46, n4, p208–10, Apr 1976.

Describes the volunteer effort of the PTA to provide alcohol education to students, schools, and parents. Their program is entitled "Alcohol: A Family Affair."

375. The Primary Prevention Project. Bauer, David G. *Health Education*. v7, n2, p9, Mar–Apr 1976.

The author evaluates the effectiveness of a school-based program of values clarification aimed at producing responsible alcohol use. Although the quantity of alcohol consumed did not decline, more responsible use was indicated through fewer traffic deaths and accidents and fewer incidences of irresponsible social actions.

376. A Program in Alcohol Education Designed for Rural Youth. Fullerton, Madonna. *Journal of Alcohol and Drug Education*. v24, n2, p58–62, Win 1979

The program described is based upon the premise that a person's thoughts, feelings, and emotions are self-controlled.

377. Project Youth: An Approach to Drug Abuse. Ryan, William P.; Hettena, Charlotte. *Elementary School Guidance and Counseling*. v10, n4, p270–78, May 1976.

The authors describe a drug prevention program for preadolescent children. The program tends to achieve its aims through the use of small-group work and positive peer influence, development of positive self-concept, and problem solving. Evaluation shows that it is influential in changing student characteristics.

378. School-Based Health Education Project: Implementation Stage II. Seffrin, John R. et al. *Health Education*. v10, n3, p12, May–Jun 1979 (EJ 207 189; Reprint: UMI).

Two units of the School-Based Health Education Project in Howard County, Indiana, require revision, according to test results. The Little Smoky unit on smoking for second graders stresses the effects of smoking on the body systems while the Counter Conscious unit examines the uses of over-the-counter substances.

379. A School-Community Approach to Alcohol Education. DiCicco, Lena et al. *Health Education*. v8, n4, p11–13, Jul–Aug 1977 (EJ 170 695; Reprint: UMI).

Program goals, content, and methods are described for the Cambridge and Somerville Alcohol Program for Alcoholism Rehabilitation (CASPAR), a community-school collaborative effort stressing alcohol education as opposed to alcoholism education with its scare tactics.

380. A Small Group Approach to Youth Education about Alcohol. Kunkle-Miller, Carole; Blane, Howard T. *Journal of Drug Education*. v7, n4, p381–86, 1977.

A small-group affective education approach to teaching high school youth about alcohol stresses group exploration of student-generated questions and concerns by creating an atmosphere of free emotional interchange in which students can sort feelings, facts, and myths.

381. Smoking Cessation in High School. Mills, Davis et al. *Health Education*. v9, n3, p5–7, May–Jun 1978 (EJ 187 877; Reprint: UMI).

Youth Quit Smoking Programs are discussed, and it is noted that senior high school students can get involved in planning, implementing, and evaluating smoking cessation programs.

382. Student-Designed Smoking Education. Wexler, Henrietta. *American Education*. v14, n8, p49, Oct 1978.

Briefly describes six smoking education projects funded by the National Interagency Council on Smoking and Health. All six were designed and developed by young people. Contact addresses are provided for each project.

383. Students Can Be Effective Change Agents. Wright, Johnny. *NASSP Bulletin.* v63, n424, p44–49, Feb 1979 (EJ 196 055 Reprint: UMI).

A student participatory model, developed to combat a drug problem, could be helpful in solving other school problems.

384. A Systematic Approach to Alcohol Education. Craig, Jerrine; De Lint, Jan. *Journal of Alcohol and Drug Education.* v23, n2, p38–46, Win 1978.

The authors examine the way in which 14 different agencies, some of them research institutes and government information departments, responded to three questions about alcohol and alcoholism that are very frequently asked of such agencies. Only two of the sources responded to all three questions, and only one, the American Medical Association, did so in a fairly complete and direct way. It was concluded that more care is needed in ensuring that popular education materials respond to expressed information needs.

385. A Systems Model for Cigarette Smoking Educations. Swanson, Jon Colby; Gajda, Robert S. M. *Journal of Alcohol and Drug Education.* v22, n2, p23–27, Win 1977.

The design, application, and evaluation of an eco-model for cigarette smoking education is proposed. It emphasizes to the smoker the consequences of smoking to the health and functioning of him/herself and those around him/her.

386. Thinking about Drinking: Teaching Tomorrow's Drinkers. Stephen, Arville I.; DiMella, Nancy C. *Independent School.* v38, n1, p11–13, Oct 1978.

A program geared toward students in grades 4–8 is described. It integrates information about alcohol use and abuse into the existing curriculum.

387. Thinking about Drinking: The Hidden Questions. Kubler-Merrill, Alexandra. *Independent School.* v38, n1, p14–16, Oct 1978.

A program geared toward high school students is described. It is independent of the curriculum, and goes beyond discussions of alcohol use to tackle the larger issues of life, death, and well-being.

388. To Help Schools Combat Smoking. Baker, Leonard S. *American Education.* v14, n8, p18–23, Oct 1978 (EJ 200 750; Reprint: UMI).

Describes the national antismoking campaign in terms of various school projects funded by the US Department of Health, Education, and Welfare, coordinated by its Office on Smoking and Health. Projects include utilizing peer counselors, demonstrating what smoking does to the body, and showing how to deal with social pressures.

389. Treatment vs. Prevention of Smoking. Heit, Phil; Gibson, Jim. *Health Education.* v9, n3, p8–9, May–Jun 1978 (EJ 187 878; Reprint: UMI).

A model smoking cessation clinic for students is described.

390. Utilizing a Health Behavior Model to Design Drug Education/Prevention Programs. Iverson, Donald C. *Journal of Drug Education.* v8, n4, p279–87, 1978.

The underlying philosophical and practical problems encountered when designing drug education/prevention programs are reviewed. The Health Belief model which emphasizes personal susceptibility to health problems, is described and its most relevant components are outlined. The drug education material and teaching methodology which complement the model are reviewed as well.

MICROFICHE

391. Alcohol Education Programming at the University of Massachusetts, Amherst, and Evaluation of Results to Date. Kraft, David P. et al. Aug 1977, 30p; Paper presented at the Annual Convention of the American Psychological Association (San Francisco, CA, August 26–30, 1977). Sponsoring agency: National Institute on Alcohol Abuse and Alcoholism (DHEW/PHS), Rockville, MD (ED 150 506; Reprint: EDRS).

This report describes the Demonstration Alcohol Education Project at the University of Massachusetts. A basic assumption of the program is that most people can learn to drink sensibly. Rather than being abstinence-oriented, it seeks to foster responsible decisions about alcohol use, including comfortable drinking and nondrinking behaviors. It uses a variety of approaches to promote this idea. The three major categories of approach are: (1) community development (responding to the needs and wants of target populations); (2) extensive approaches (posters, pamphlets, and special displays); and (3) intensive approaches (small discussion groups to help individuals examine and modify their attitudes and behavior). The program's objectives and methodology are presented in detail, as well as a description of results which demonstrate its effectiveness.

392. Alternatives for Young Americans: A Catalog of Drug Abuse Prevention Programs. Applied Management Sciences, Inc., Silver Spring, MD; Chinese Culture Foundation, San Francisco, CA, 1979, 357p. Sponsoring agency: National Institute on Drug Abuse (DHEW/PHS), Rockville, MD, Division of Resource Development (ED 177 443; Reprint: EDRS; also available from Superintendent of Documents, US Government Printing Office, Washington, DC 20402, stock no. 017-024-00855-9).

This reference book contains resumes of program descriptions geared toward youth and adults who need or want information on drug-abuse prevention programs, locally or nationally. Several major entries include: (1) national program models, (2) evaluated alternative programs from all states, and (3) descriptions of prevention programs. All section entries are identified by state and listed alphabetically according to program title. Each entry conveys the following information to the user: program name entry, address, phone number and hours available of the contact person, and the general program description. Unique features and/or operational instruments are offered as supplementary material whenever necessary.

393. An Alternatives Prevention Approach to Drug Abuse.* Busse, Wilma Joan, Western Michigan University, 1979, 132p (80 02732; Reprint: DC).

The purpose of this study was to investigate the effectiveness of a primary prevention alternatives strategy with undergraduate college students. The prevention approach was examined to determine its effect upon the students' drug knowledge, drug attitudes, drug-use behavior, and participation in alternative behaviors.

The design used was the pretest/posttest control group design There were five groups and two group leaders. The five groups consisted of two reinforcement of alternatives groups, two placebo/ discussion groups and one control group. A total of 67 volunteer subjects were randomly assigned across the five groups. The reinforcement and placebo/discussion groups were exposed to six two-hour group sessions over a six week period. The control group underwent only pre- and posttesting. Subjects in the reinforcement groups received positive verbal reinforcement from the leader for participation in drug alternative behavior and antidrug attitudes. The placebo group subjects did not receive positive verbal reinforcement from the neutral leader but were permitted to discuss any drug-related topic.

The scales employed for pre- and posttesting were the Pennsylvania State University Drug Education Evaluation Scales developed by Swisher and Horan in 1973. The specific scales include a drug knowledge scale, drug attitude scale, and a personal drug-use inventory. In addition, a Modified Pennsylvania State University Personal Drug Use Scale, developed by Evans and D'Augelli in 1975, was used to measure drug use and frequency of drug use. An alternatives behavior scale, developed by the author, was used to measure participation in drug alternative behavior. Two psychological inventories, the California Personality Inventory and the Mooney Problem Checklist, were administered to determine the overall psychological adjustment of the subjects prior to treatment.

No significant treatment effects were found. The implications of these results for counselor educators and college student personnel professionals are discussed and additional research is recommended.

394. Change in Factual Knowledge and Reported Use of Illicit Drugs Resulting from the Viewing of a Motion Picture.* Sohn, Mark Fohs, University of Maryland, 1975, 127p (7618840; Reprint: DC).

In this study a drug education film was shown to a group of college students for the purpose of determining the effect of the film on factual knowledge and reported use of illicit drugs. It was assumed that the usefulness of a film could be measured by testing subjects with regard to knowledge of facts about and reported use of drugs. The film used in this study was ''Students Look at Drugs,'' produced by the Eli Lilly Company. The specific questions addressed in this study were: (1) Does one presentation of a drug education film produce a 15 percent minimum immediate increase in factual knowledge about illicit drugs? (2) Does the single

presentation of a drug education film produce a 15 percent minimum increase in factual knowledge about illicit drugs 14 days after the film showing? (3) Is reported drug use significantly higher or lower 14 days following the single presentation of a drug education film?

Initially, a pilot study was conducted to assess the entertainment value of the films, the appropriateness of the test instruments, and logistical problems that might be encountered.

The main study was conducted with 166 subjects from Northern Virginia Community College. The subjects were randomly assigned to an experimental and control group. This was the first step in making use of the posttest only, control group design, a true experimental design. While the control group saw a placebo film, the experimental group saw a drug film. Similarity of entertainment value of the two films had been established during the pilot study. Immediately following the film presentation all subjects took the immediate posttest, selected to assess knowledge of facts. Two weeks later the delayed posttest was administered to assess level of knowledge and reported use.

For each research hypothesis the difference in group mean scores was compared with the t test. A significant difference was found for hypothesis one only. A 15 percent difference in group scores was not achieved for any hypothesis.

The data do not support the isolated use of ''Students Look at Drugs'' for educational purposes. No conclusions were drawn regarding the film's usefulness as a teaching aid. However, the learning that did result from this film exposure suggests that the film had some educational value.

It was concluded that film viewing did not result in a 15 percent increase in factual knowledge or a decrease in reported use. The findings of the study concur with many nonempirical evaluations which suggest that a large number of these films should not be the sole input in educational programs. It was also concluded that the method used is a valid one for assessing the effectiveness of other drug education films.

395. Comparative Effectiveness of Smoking Prevention Programs. Jason, Leonard A.; Mollica, Mark. Sep 1979, 23p; Paper presented at the Annual Convention of the American Psychological Association (87th, New York, September 1–5, 1979) (ED 179 862; Reprint: EDRS).

Given the documented link between smoking and later debilitating health conditions, a need exists to investigate educational programs aimed at reducing rates of smoking among school age children. An entire class of ninth graders was involved in a treatment condition featuring either role playing and discussion or discussion only. While both treatments effectively reduced levels of smoking among inchoate smokers, few changes were noted for youngsters manifesting more long-term, entrenched habits. Levels of smoking for children monitored in a control school remained about the same. These data suggest that early preventive programs might be most efficacious in curtailing smoking among school age children.

396. The Effect of a Relational Drug Education Program on the Degree of Alienation and Attitudes toward Drugs among Junior High School Students.* Brand, Ira, Rutgers University, State University of New Jersey, 1976, 158p (7627305; Reprint: DC).

A variety of drug education programs have developed, each with a new thrust or set of procedures to reduce drug abuse. The focus of the present study is to evaluate the success of a relational approach to drug education.

The major characteristics of the relational drug education program are as follows: (1) It was student oriented. Students had input into program planning and selected their teachers. (2) Students and teachers coplanned activities. (3) The program emphasized a humanistic philosophy with an emphasis on values rather than drug knowledge. (4) Students were encouraged to air their feelings about the school through rap sessions. (5) The program provided supporting services to students beyond the 9 A.M. to 3 P.M. school day. These included tutorial assistance and outside agency referrals by the school guidance counselor. (6) Parents were encouraged to participate in activities with students.

Five major hypotheses guided the study. They were: (1) Students completing a relationally oriented drug education program will show less sense of normlessness than students not completing such a program. (2) Students completing a relationally oriented drug education program will show less sense of powerlessness than students not completing such a program. (3) Students completing a relationally oriented drug education program will show a greater antidrug attitude than students not completing such a program. (4) Students who have a lower sense of normlessness will show a lower prodrug attitude. (5) Students who have a lower sense of powerlessness will show a lower prodrug attitude.

The school selected for the study was one with a history of drug use and one in which a relational drug education program was about to be introduced. The study utilized a pretest/posttest control group design. The sample consisted of 120 ninth-grade junior high school students, divided into three groups. Eighty of the 120 students were randomly selected from among volunteers for the drug education program. These 80 students were randomly divided into experimental and control groups, with each group consisting of 20 males and 20 females. A second control group comprised of 20 male and 20 female students was randomly selected from among nonvolunteers to the program. The treatment was a relational drug education program intended to improve interaction between students and teachers for the purpose of reducing student prodrug attitudes and feelings of alienation.

The Attitude toward Drugs Scale (ATD) and the Pupil Attitude Questionnaire (PAQ) were administered to the experimental and control groups at the beginning and conclusion of the drug education program, which lasted for a period of about five months.

None of the first three hypotheses was confirmed. A relationally oriented drug program had no significant effect on student attitudes toward drugs or student sense of alienation. Hypotheses predicting a correlation between student attitudes toward drugs and alienation were completely supported only for the females. The results do not support the effectiveness of the relational drug education program. A more refined program utilizing such approaches as student/teacher planning as well as content-oriented drug education should be developed and tested. It seems apparent that more research is needed before any definitive models for drug education can be confidently recommended.

397. The Effect of a Three-Day Minicourse on Knowledge and Attitudes about Drinking and Driving of High School Driver Education Students.* Masten, Frank Lamont, University of Missouri—Kansas City, 1979, 84p (7918414; Reprint: DC).

With the expectation of reducing the number of alcohol-related traffic fatalities among teenagers, federal funds were allocated to the state of Missouri. These funds were used to support the effort of the Missouri Department of Elementary and Secondary Education in cooperation with the Missouri Safety Center to develop a curriculum about drinking and driving and to promote its teaching in the high schools of Missouri.

After a study of existing curricula and their results, a curriculum was developed. This curriculum emphasized activities which were purported to change attitudes because research suggested that attitude was the critical factor in changing drinking/driving behavior.

The curriculum was introduced to high schools throughout the state of Missouri at a series of two-day workshops. At these workshops representatives of the area schools simulated the classroom activities and curriculum materials were distributed when available. Ninety-seven percent of the high schools in the state were represented at these workshops. The workshop participants were asked to administer a pretest and posttest to their classes before and after they taught the curriculum.

It can be concluded that the curriculum does effect learning achievement. However, the curriculum did not result in a more positive attitude. This casts some doubts on the effectiveness of activities that are purported to change attitudes when used in the context of drinking and driving. Since the change in learning achievement or attitude was not as great as in other studies, it may be that the skill and enthusiasm for the techniques taught in the workshop dissipate quickly. This suggests that longitudinal studies should be done on the effectiveness of the teachers' workshops.

398. The Effects of a Simulation Game on Knowledge Retention and Attitude Change among Convicted First Offense Drinking Drivers.* Stember, Thomas Patrick, United States International University, 1977, 192p (7909844; Reprint: DC).

The aim of the study was to investigate the effectiveness of using a simulation game strategy to increase knowledge retention concerned with the effects of alcohol on driving and its relationship to accidents, to induce positive attitude change concerned with drinking and driving, and to elicit an increase in statements related to self-perception of not being rearrested in the future for driving while intoxicated. The subjects were convicted first offender drinking drivers. It was hypothesized that the simulation game strategy, as compared to a lecture film strategy, would produce a more positive shift in the dependent variables of knowledge retention, attitude toward drinking and driving, and self-perception of the likelihood of being rearrested in the future for driving while intoxicated.

A randomized control group posttest-only design was utilized with the experimental treatment being a simulation game entitled "The DWI Game." The simulation game was designed, developed, and validated specifically for use with the DWI population. The simulation game was introduced during the fourth session of an ongoing drinking and driving education class in Montclair, California. The playing time took 1½ hours with 30 subjects grouped into six groups of five persons each playing the simulation game. The control group received a lecture/film presentation during the fourth session, a presentation typically employed in the Montclair drinking and driving education course.

Significant differences were found to support two of the three hypotheses and a significant difference was also found for one of the three items in the third hypothesis. It was found that Drinking and Driving Knowledge Inventory scores increased significantly for the experimental group as a result of playing the simulation game. A similar result was found for the Drinking and Driving Opinion Survey. The experimental group showed significant attitude change in a positive direction as compared to the control group. On item 3 on the Behavioral Description Scale (What do you believe are your chances of being rearrested on a DWI charge within the next year?), a significant difference was found to exist in favor of the experimental group. On item 4 (How difficult will it be to change the behavior that led to your arrest?) and item 5 (How valuable do you feel this course has been for you?), no significant difference was found to exist between the two groups.

399. The Effects of Learning When to Be Uncertain on Children's Knowledge and Use of Drugs. R and D Memorandum No. 144. Sieber, Joan E. et al., Stanford University, Stanford Center for Research and Development in Teaching, May 1976, 52p. Sponsoring agency: National Institute on Drug Abuse (DHEW/PHS), Rockville, MD (ED 126 187; Reprint: EDRS).

The first attempt believed to be ever made by drug prevention researchers to investigate the long-term effects of a school-based curriculum that may have affected student's decisions on the use of drugs is reported here. This final report contains a short section in nontechnical language describing the study and its results, and a longer section providing the detail and language characteristic of a research report. The evidence from this study indicates that a curriculum that taught students to recognize when it is warranted to be uncertain has a desirable effect three years later on those students' beliefs and behavior concerning drugs. The curriculum was not developed for the purpose of drug-abuse prevention and contained no examples or exercises dealing with drug-abuse prevention. The most interesting finding, from the standpoint of drug-abuse prevention, is the pattern of correlations indicating that students who can recognize when it is warranted to be uncertain about drugs report less hard drug use and more soft drug use. Another important outcome of the study is the finding that warranted uncertainty is a reliable construct which, irrespective of training, affects self-reported drug use. The discovery that drug use may be significantly affected by a relatively brief classroom-based training exercise that does not contain information about drugs has interesting implications for the development of prevention strategies.

400. Effects of the School Health Curriculum Project Heart Unit and Demographic Variables on Cigarette Smoking Attitudes of Lower Socioeconomic Sixth Grade Students. Redican, Kerry J. et al. 27p (ED 146 129; Reprint: EDRS).

The effects of an administration of the School Health Curriculum Project Heart Unit to a group of 145 sixth-grade students of lower socioeconomic status were examined. The Heart Unit was administered over a period of nine weeks, five times per week, one hour per day. Participants were divided into separate treatment and control groups and the scores achieved by each on pre- and posttest administrations of the Teenage Self-Test on Smoking were analyzed. These analyses indicated that the only variables affecting performance on the cigarette smoking attitude inventory after exposure to the experimental curriculum were sex, residency status, best friend's smoking status, and older siblings' smoking status. Welfare status and parental smoking behavior did not appear to influence achievement on posttest mean scores. A significant difference was noted at the .05 level between pre- and posttests of the students participating in the Heart Unit. Therefore, the curriculum appeared to have an effect on the experimental groups reflected in the significant difference between pre- and posttest mean scores. Based on these findings, it was concluded that: (1) the School Health Curriculum Project Heart Unit can be effectively

implemented in lower socioeconomic schools; (2) females achieved significantly higher posttest mean scores than males; (3) welfare status does not influence posttest mean scores of those students exposed to the curriculum unit; (4) best friend's smoking behavior can influence a student's performance on the self-test on smoking; (5) older siblings at home who smoke can exert a negative influence on a student's performance on the self-test; and (6) parental smoking behavior does not exert an influence on student's performance with respect to the self-test.

401. An Evaluation of a School-Community Team for the Primary Prevention of Drug Abuse.* Stokely, Barbara Lafot, University of Southern California, 1978. (Available from Micrographics Department, Doheny Library, USC, Los Angeles, CA 90007.)

Primary drug prevention refers to meeting basic needs before abuse occurs, in contrast to treatment and rehabilitation. The purpose of this study was to evaluate the development of a school/community team formed to design and implement an innovative program for the primary prevention of drug abuse. The team, organized in a small, middle-class suburban community, was formed on the rationale of social systems theory. It was trained through a program conducted by the California State Department of Education Health Services.

A dual approach to evaluation was used to assess the team's progress. The first method was a conventional descriptive evaluation, including an assessment of the needs and demographics of the community pertinent to primary prevention. The goals and objectives of the team were described as were the activities designed to implement objectives. An evaluation instrument was administered to rate objectives in order of need for operationalized improvement.

The second method involved an analysis of the dynamics of team development based on qualitative field research. The techniques of participant observation and intensive interviewing were employed to develop an analysis of the determinants and indicators which influenced the team's functioning as an innovative subsystem.

The two most successfully operationalized objectives were a feedback system for increased student participation in responsible decision making at the target high school and a rap room using paraprofessionals as counselors at the target intermediate school. Objectives rated as needing most improvement were: (1) more organized public relations; (2) greater involvement of students in overall planning; and (3) further development of three promising new programs: evening school activities, peer counseling, and a family communication training series. Continued program funding was deemed a major future objective for the team.

Results of the field work methodology suggested that the team did not sufficiently prepare the community to receive an innovative program of primary prevention. Criteria for team member selection failed to include representation from established community power blocks. After the initial and predictable stage of conflict which inevitably accompanies change, this community's diffusion rate for innovation was quite rapid. Hypotheses to account for this rate include similar norms and values of the community and the team, moderation of innovations, openness of the community, and team effectiveness. Indirect indicators of the team's success include increased articulation between target schools, increased articulation among community agencies, dissemination of portions of the design to other systems, publication of articles, and use of team skills to design a comprehensive community mental health program. These outcomes and the relatively low need for operationalized improvement suggest the team should be rated as highly effective in its implementation of a primary prevention program.

Special attention should be paid to the following factors which influence team success: (1) the necessity of preparing the community and establishing the need for innovation through a comprehensive and organized public relations campaign; (2) the advisability of including key members of the established community power structure on the team; (3) the need for thorough preparation of team members to cope with the political ramifications of innovation; (4) the importance of establishing congruence between the norms and values of the community and the team for optimal diffusion; (5) the importance of maintaining balance between the stability and conservatism of the community and the innovativeness of the team for optimal diffusion; (6) the advisability of providing adequate support for the team to ensure its survival, particularly in early stages, and (7) the importance of guarding against working in isolation and the need for continuous, effective linkage between the team and other subsystems of the community.

402. A Film and Teacher's Resource Booklet in Drug Abuse Education for Secondary School Students.*
Martin, John Joseph, Columbia University Teachers College, 1975, 183p (763266; Reprint: DC).

The purpose of this study was to produce a 16mm sound, motion picture film and *Teacher's Resource Booklet* for the initial student motivation toward group discussion in a high school unit of instruction on drug abuse.

Research of the literature indicated that the majority of existing drug-abuse films were either inaccurate, distorted, outdated, or conceptually unsound; that drug education programs of the informative type may not be as effective as educators hoped they would be; that the film medium can be an excellent tool for stimulating discussion and focusing interest if it is made personally relevant to students, accurate, and up-to-date in the information presented; and that on the high school level more emphasis should be placed upon individual attitudes about drugs and the behavior that is motivated by those attitudes. Additional research involved discussions with various secondary school drug education teachers and high school students to determine what they felt would be an interesting and useful film in a drug education unit.

With the above research as a basis, a rough script for the film "Minus Two" was prepared. The medical and drug-related facts were checked out with doctors, law enforcement officers, and former drug addicts. The script was read to a number of high school classes. As the script was being finalized, decisions were being made as to what limitations there would be regarding the actual production costs and availability of motion picture equipment. Eventually, various organizations and individuals donated their time, equipment, and talents toward the production.

The completed film "Minus Two" was shown to several groups of drug education teachers and high school students. A 10-point questionnaire on various aspects of the film was submitted to these students. The results were very favorable. The teachers gave a number of suggestions that helped develop the contents for the *Teacher's Resource Booklet*. The total package of film and teacher's booklet was reviewed by two drug-abuse specialists.

The film "Minus Two" was produced as a stimulus to motivate students to group discussion. It is not a film of drug facts. It does not preach or even state clearly a fact or a principle. Rather, it employs subtle visual techniques and emotion-laden scenes to show two adolescents caught up in drug abuse and to confront its viewers with the task of learning from this visual experience. The film must be previewed and the *Teacher's Resource Booklet* read carefully, for

the sound track of this film and its visuals do not prescribe a principle. Such principles must come from the follow-up discussion. With this film different approaches can be used for students of different ages, cultural backgrounds, and levels of drug sophistication.

Emphasis has been placed on the motivational aspects of drug use—why people use drugs, what they hope to accomplish, and what they hope to escape. With the film as a starting point, free-flowing dialogue between students and teacher will, hopefully, follow in an atmosphere of tolerance for all points of view, free of moralizing and shock reactions.

403. Guide to Alcohol Programs for Youth. Maloney, Susan K., National Clearinghouse for Alcohol Information (DHEW/PHS), Rockville, MD, 1976, 30p (ED 142 900; Reprint: EDRS).

This program guide was prepared by the National Clearinghouse for Alcohol Information of the National Institute on Alcohol Abuse and Alcoholism. Its purpose is to assist program planners in the development of strategies to minimize the abuse of alcoholic beverages by youths. It provides information and direction to: (1) youth-serving organizations wanting to add an alcohol education component to ongoing programs; (2) educational institutions wanting to examine alcohol use among their students and develop strategies to minimize its abuse; and (3) any community group interested in directing their resources to reducing alcohol abuse by young people. It might also be of value to alcohol program planners and community or private foundations. The booklet is designed to be adapted to the needs of the individual community. Topics covered include trends in drinking behavior, strategies for change, implementation considerations, and program development. The guide also includes a list of programs and contact addresses.

404. A Primary Prevention Drug Education Program for School Children: An Attempt at Evaluation.
Lopez, Thomas S.; Starkey, Kathryn T. Apr 1976, 14p; Paper presented at the Annual Meeting of the American Educational Research Association (San Francisco, CA, April 19–23, 1976) (ED 124 860; Reprint: EDRS).

Recently programs for primary prevention of drug and alcohol abuse have centered in the affective domain. Value sharing training for teachers is intended to change classrooms and students. Fifth and sixth graders were given pre/post measures of self-esteem and risk-taking attitudes. Value clarification behaviors of teachers were analyzed. Children grew in self-esteem and had a more positive attitude toward risk taking. Value sharing activities did not increase after teacher training.

405. Recommendations for the Revision of "Teaching about Drugs: A Curriculum Guide K–12."*
Harvilla-Ellis, Nancy Theresa, Indiana University, 1979, 193p (8003461; Reprint: EDRS).

In order to ascertain the strengths and weaknesses of the curriculum guide, *Teaching about Drugs,* research focused on the construction of a survey instrument to generate data relevant to the stated problem.

A closed format questionnaire was constructed utilizing consistent structured responses plus one concluding free response item. Items for the instrument were derived from open-ended responses from an exploratory study conducted by the American School Health Association and from desirable criteria of curriculum guides gleaned from texts. The instrument was refined utilizing feedback from a competent jury and a pilot study.

Of 283 potential respondents, 118 instruments were returned of which 65 were usable. There were 38 usable elementary level instruments and 27 usable adolescent level instruments.

Frequency and percent of responses were calculated for each part of the instrument: background information of respondents, suggested curriculum, teaching aids and review papers, and overall evaluation of the guide. All but the background data were analyzed according to the elementary and adolescent levels of the guide. Pearson product moment correlation coefficients indicated the relationship between individual items in an area of the instrument and an overall assessment of that area. This internal check for consistency of responses provided data relevant to reliability.

Generally, it was found that suggested objectives, content, learning activities, and resources and materials were well-perceived but could be improved or updated. Teaching aids and review papers were considered to be relatively helpful but also in need of minor revisions. The most frequent overall assessment of the guide was ''good'' by both levels of respondents. Internal consistency of responses was apparent.

406. The Secondary School Drug and Narcotic Education (DANE) Program: The Team Approach. Blankenship, Betty; Gould, Nancy Gibson, San Diego City School District, CA, 1975, 262p; for related document see entry 441 (CM 000 980; Reprint: SMERC—HC not available).

The DANE (Drug and Narcotic Education) Program uses itinerant teachers, working with the regular staff, to provide an opportunity for secondary school students to discuss and understand the drug scene as they see it. This manual covers: (1) the DANE concept; (2) administration and staffing; (3) secondary school information; (4) DANE counseling; (5) drug and narcotic information; (6) most often asked questions; (7) drug and narcotic laws; and (8) drug terminology.

407. Social Work in Family Life Enrichment: The Children of Alcoholics—A Montessori Approach. McDonald-Jay, Celynn. Oct 1977, 15p (ED 159 532; Reprint: EDRS—HC not available; also available from American Montessori Society, 150 Fifth Avenue, New York NY 10011).

This model proposes a Montessori schooling approach for the children of alcoholics because this approach helps the child develop his self-esteem and concentration; acquire a sense of order, mastery, and control over his environment; and separate fact from fantasy. The model assumes that alcoholic parents, responding to the debilitative effects of alcohol abuse, have difficulty interpreting reality to their children and are ineffective as appropriate role models for their children. The model further proposes that, when an alcoholism program expands its role as therapeutic agent to include the children of clients, treatment of the alcoholic parent and family life are enhanced. Also included in this paper are descriptions of: (1) how the model was generated; (2) historical data regarding the Montessori approach; (3) aspects of the Montessori approach particularly relevant to the needs of children of alcoholics; and (4) a Montessori curriculum and classroom environment.

408. Statement before the Subcommittee on Alcoholism and Drug Abuse, Committee on Human Resources, United States Senate. Nowlis, Helen H. Mar 1977, 18p (ED 142 878; Reprint: EDRS).

The Drug Education Program is funded by Education Personnel Development funds from the Office of Education. Its goals are: (1) reinforcing nonuse of drugs, (2) discouraging experimentation, and (3) preventing or intervening in destructive uses of all substances. Its philosophy emphasizes both use and nonuse of substances as behavior and looks to behavioral and social sciences for ways of understanding and influencing those behaviors. This paper reports on the activities of the program since its inception in 1970. After setting up some pilot programs, the group decided that its most effective role would be one of leadership, training, and resources. It therefore set up a network of five regional resource centers, which offer training to small teams from many local communities. During training, teams are exposed to a broad range of activities, including needs assessment, program planning, team building, group, individual, and peer counseling alternatives to substance abuse, communication skills, problem solving, decision making, and conflict resolution skills, and skills in marshalling local support for their programs. After returning to the community, teams implement counseling, teacher training, workshops, and other activities suited to their area's needs. Many teams have been successful, but the need in this area is still very great.

409. Substance Abuse Prevention Education Program. 1974–75 Evaluation Report. Michigan State Department of Education, Lansing; Michigan State Department of Public Health, Detroit, Nov. 1975, 98p (ED 119 055; Reprint: EDRS).

The Substance Abuse Prevention Education (SAPE) program aims at: (1) having a direct impact on young people to prevent substance abuse; (2) working with school teachers, parents, and other citizens to develop specific skills that will facilitate substance-abuse prevention; and (3) providing program participants with better understanding of the nature of substance abuse, its causes, and its prevention. The SAPE program engaged in the following activities during 1974–75: (1) the introduction of basic substance-abuse educational ideas to participant groups; (2) provision of information and consultation to interested schools and citizens; (3) specific training programs geared to school staffs to improve in-school curricula and teaching formats, relative to substance-abuse prevention; (4) the setting up of student service centers; (5) the training of a cadre of paraprofessional citizen-trainers; (6) involvement of the entire family in substance-abuse prevention; and (7) working with schools and school districts on policies and procedures which facilitate a school climate conducive to substance-abuse prevention. The seven program activities received emphasis in the order mentioned as far as percent of staff-time was concerned. Most participants expressed satisfaction and said they felt the program helped them considerably.

410. Teen Involvement for Drug Abuse Prevention. Administrator's Guide. Conroy, Gladys E.; Brayer, Herbert O. 1978, 39p. Sponsoring agency: National Institute on Drug Abuse (DHEW/PHS), Rockville, MD (ED 154 318; Reprint: EDRS).

The Teen Involvement program is implemented primarily by youth, with guidance and direction from qualified, concerned adults. It aims at preventing substance abuse by utilizing positive youth-to-youth communications. Junior and senior high school students are trained to discuss causes of drug abuse and ways of preventing it with students in grades 4–12. The program's creators have sought to involve youth in an effort to improve decision-making capabilities, develop better organized values, and reduce and prevent substance abuse among young people. Selected students, called teen advisors, serve as role models for younger students. After carefully supervised training, they visit elementary school classrooms on a regularly scheduled basis. Similar programs can be started by interested administrators in their own settings.

411. U.S. Office of Education Alcohol and Drug Training and Resource Center Program. Pizza, Joan G. 1978, 158p; master's thesis, University of Maryland (ED 159 538; Reprint: EDRS—HC not available).

This descriptive paper of the US Office of Education, Alcohol, and Drug Training and Resource Center Program represents the first, general documentation of the program. The writer's experiences in the national office of the program have formed the framework and perspective through which information collected from other sources was filtered, chosen, and organized. These sources include works of personnel in the National Office and Training Centers, literature from other US Governmental agencies, and studies in education, human development, and school systems change. The paper includes: (1) an overview of the USOE Training and Resource Center Program, which is designed to assist schools to develop appropriate local programs aimed at preventing drug and alcohol abuse and other destructive behavior; (2) the premises and working assumptions of the USOE Training and Resource Center Program; and (3) specific components of the program such as training, technical assistance, and management.

BOOKS

412. Better Schools, Better People: How Schools Can Help to Prevent Drug and Alcohol Abuse. California State Department of Education, Sacramento, CA: The Department, 1979, 44p.

This publication is not a step-by-step manual; rather it contains descriptions of school-based drug-abuse prevention programs and resources for program planning and implementation. It is based on first-hand documentation of 25 different California programs. It also considers the role of state and local agencies in drug education and makes suggestions for ensuring program survival.

413. The Complete Handbook of Peer Counseling. An Authoritative Guide for the Organization, Training, Implementation and Evaluation of a Peer Counseling Program. Samuels, Don; Samuels, Mimi. Miami, FL: Fiesta Publishing Corp., 1975, 191p.

This handbook describes the merits of peer counseling within a drug education and prevention program, especially its effectiveness as compared to traditional approaches to drug-abuse prevention. The means and methods to developing, organizing, and implementing a peer counselor program are described in detail. Implementation is presented on a day-by-day basis for the 15-day training cycle. The authors also provide methods and instruments for evaluating the programs as a whole, and the individuals within the program: the teacher, the peer counselor, and the student.

414. Drug Education: Goals, Approaches, Evaluation, ERS Report. Bushey, Julia A. Arlington, VA: Educational Research Service, 1975, 33p.

An examination of the extensive drug education literature as well as of specific school drug education programs indicates that the present confusion over drug education results from confusion over definitions, goals, approaches, and evaluation. This report, based on an examination of recent literature and on information and printed materials on specific 1974–75 school drug education programs, contains descriptions and examples of the goals, teaching methods, and evaluation techniques used in drug education programs. Pertinent definitions are presented within each area. The seven major goals of drug education, each or any number of which could be the goal of a program, are to increase an individual's knowledge about drugs, to affect an individual's attitudes toward the personal consumption of drugs, to alter an individual's drug-use behavior, to increase an individual's participation in alternatives, to enhance an individual's ability to clarify his/her values, to improve an individual's decision-making skills, and to improve an individual's self-concept. The major approaches used are the cognitive and affective and a combination of the two. Outlines of drug education programs used in 13 school systems and an extensive bibliography are included.

415. Drug Education: Results and Recommendations. Blum, Richard H. et al. Lexington, MA: Lexington Books, 1976, 217p.

This book describes a four-year California study on the effects of drug education and offers strategies for educators to apply in their communities. It begins with three overview chapters on children's drug use, educational approaches, and the evaluation of drug education. The rest of the chapters report the study itself, with a special chapter devoted to inhalant users. Results indicated that successful drug education is associated with information giving and classroom discussion of values, but more strikingly with the former. But, in interaction with student age and community type, any single method of drug education may prove productive, nonproductive, or even counterproductive in decreasing student drug use.

Drug Education: Instructional Materials

JOURNAL ARTICLES

416. Alcohol Education Materials 1978–1979: An Annotated Bibliography. Milgram, Gail Gleason; Page, Penny Booth. *Journal of Alcohol and Drug Education.* v24, n4, p1–94, Sum 1979.

This annotated bibliography cites 218 books, curriculum guides, paperbacks, pamphlets, leaflets, periodicals, and miscellaneous items related to alcohol education. Publications were drawn from the library of the Rutgers Center of Alcohol Studies and from contacts with approximately 600 public and private publishers and health, education, and liquor agencies in the United States and Canada. Each citation is indexed for publication type, intended audience, and major content. A title index is included. Annotations run 100–300 words.

417. An Alternative Source of Information on a Popular Topic: A Course on Drinking. Leavy, Richard L. *Teaching of Psychology.* v6, n2, p97–100, Apr 1979 (EJ 200 431; Reprint: UMI).

Describes and evaluates a university psychology course which provides an academic and personal look at drinking and problem drinking. The structure of the course encompasses three phases: lecture, seminar, and student presentation.

418. Chem I Supplement: Effects of Ethanol on Nutrition. Shorey, RoseAnn L. *Journal of Chemical Education.* v56, n8, p532–34, Aug 1979 (EJ 210 043; Reprint: UMI).

In this article for high school science, malnutrition due to alcoholism is discussed. It includes energy from the metabolism of ethanol as it contributes to obesity, the replacement of nutritious foods by sources of ethanol, inhibition of vitamins being activated, the increase in excretion of valuable minerals, and toxicity to cells of organ systems.

419. Chem I Supplement: Some Biochemistry of Sedatives. *Journal of Chemical Education.* v56, n6, p402–04, Jun 1979 (EJ 208 487; Reprint: UMI).

In this article for high school science classes, antianxiety agents are discussed in terms of their effects on the brain and central nervous system. Formulas for some substances, commonly prescribed as sedatives, are given. Includes a discussion on the toxicity and side effects of the drugs.

420. The Growing Alcohol Problem among Teens: What Needs to Be Done in the Classroom? Von Holdt, Barbara. *Illinois Teacher of Home Economics.* v21, n1, p41–47, Sep–Oct 1977.

Discusses the need for alcohol education programs within schools, the common approaches used by teachers for alcohol education, some new teaching approaches, and several ideas for student projects in an alcohol education class. A pretest on facts about alcohol with the answers and suggested references for teachers are included.

421. Health and Fitness. *Curriculum Review.* v19, n2, p133–42, Apr 1980.

This review of recent health curriculum materials includes evaluations of eight kits and texts for drug, alcohol, and smoking education: *Marijuana Bulletin: A Research Update* (kit, grades 9–12); *Pot—What Is It, What It Does* (text, grades 2–4); *Marijuana* (text, grades 4–12); *Drug Use and Abuse* (text, grades 5–12); *The Center: From a Troubled Past to a New Life* (novel, grades 7–12); *Cancer: What Is It, How to Beat It* (kit, grades 9–12); *Alcohol and Teenagers: Four Case Studies* (kit, grades 9–12); and *Decisions about Drinking* (professional reference kit, grades 3–12). All of these materials are 1979 publications.

422. How to Get Dead Drunk and Survive. Cook, John. *Calculators/Computers Magazine.* v2, n6, p66–68, Sep–Oct 1978.

A BASIC computer program is given that simulates the effects of alcohol. A student enters his/her weight, the number of hours of drinking, the kind of alcoholic beverage consumed, and the number of drinks consumed. The program also prints the resulting effect on behavior.

423. Marijuana: Assessing the Cost. *Science Teacher.* v47, n4, p29–32, Apr 1980.

The author reviews recent studies of drug use by high school seniors and of the health impact of marihuana smoking. He presents teaching concepts on marihuana and health which a science teacher may use in class discussion.

424. A Practical Approach to Drug Education. Chunko, John A. *Journal of Drug Education.* v6, n4, p343–60, 1976.

This article outlines drug education teaching concepts for the different grade levels, correlated to a list of recommended teaching aids, and discusses developmental and cultural factors.

425. Senator Hogwash. Young, Michael. *Health Education.* v10, n3, p36, May–Jun 1979.

Presents the details of a simulation game especially designed for smoking education, "Senator Hogwash and His Tobacco Advisory Committee." It is intended to bring out not only the health hazards of smoking but also to show that there are many economic, social, and political forces that make quick elimination of cigarette smoking unlikely.

426. Smoking and Cigarette Smoke: An Innovative, Interdisciplinary, Chemically-Oriented Curriculum. Zoller, Uri. *Journal of Chemical Education.* v56, n8, p518–19, Aug 1979 (EJ210 037; Reprint: UMI).

A description is given of a chemically oriented curriculum on "Smoking and Cigarette Smoke" for science and nonscience oriented high school students. Laboratory activity is emphasized.

427. The Smoking Classroom. Barnes, S. Eugene. *Health Education.* v7, n2, p37–38, Mar–Apr 1976.

Offered are suggestions for educating elementary school children to the effects of smoking on health.

428. Teen-Age Drinking and Driving: What Can a Parent Do? Garretson, Kim. *Better Homes and Gardens.* v57, p13–14,18–19,24, Jul 1979.

This article reviews basic facts of teenage drinking and driving and suggests ways parents can help their teenagers learn to avoid the hazard of driving after drinking or riding with someone under the influence of alcohol.

MICROFICHE

429. Albert's Coloring Book about Alcohol. Wayne County Intermediate School District, Detroit, MI, 1978, 19p. Sponsoring agency: Michigan State Department of Education, Lansing (ED159 524; Reprint: EDRS).

This "consumable" coloring book is intended to encourage discussion about alcohol with elementary school students, and it can be used alone or within another unit of study such as a health unit dealing with the body or within a unit on science. It is part of the DARTE Project (Wayne, MI, ISD).

430. Alcohol: Pleasures and Problems. Finn, Peter; Lawson, Jane, Abt Associates, Inc., Cambridge, MA, 1975, 25p; for related documents see entries 445, 453, 461–62. Sponsoring agency: National Institute on Alcohol Abuse and Alcoholism (DHEW/PHS), Rockville, MD; Office of Education (DHEW), Washington, DC, Division of Educational Technology (ED 145 343; Reprint: EDRS).

This student booklet is to be used in conjunction with the Teacher Manual and films of the DIAL A-L-C-O-H-O-L series. It presents facts and illustrations on the use of alcohol and is intended to aid young people in deciding whether or not to drink. This booklet is divided into the following parts: (1) introduction, (2) the enjoyment of drinking, (3) alcohol's effects on the mind and body, (4) drinking and driving, (5) problem drinking and alcoholism, and (6) glossary.

431. Alcohol and Drug Education Guidelines. Wright, David; Hays, Mary, Iowa State Department of Public Instruction, Des Moines, Jun 1977, 295p (ED 145 361; Reprint: EDRS).

The purpose of this guide is to assist school districts and teachers to define what alcohol and drug education is intended to do (establish curriculum goals and objectives) and to develop an instructional framework to serve this purpose. The guide is divided into four chapters: (1) introduction; (2) definition and approaches to alcohol and drug education including correlation and/or integration with other subjects; (3) instructional framework (four grade level programs, K–3, 4–6, 7–9, 10–12); and (4) teacher resources.

432. Alcohol and You. Hargraves, Ruth et al., United Methodist Church, New York, 1976, 58p (ED 174 920; Reprint: EDRS).

Prepared in response to a request from members of the United Methodist Church, this guide can be used with high school students generally, if the theological orientation is recognized. The guide provides opportunities, in four lesson outlines, to share experiences concerning alcohol use, to present information regarding the effect of alcohol on mind and body, and to explore guidance offered by Christian theology and Methodist tradition in use and abuse of alcohol. Appendices include a precourse and postcourse questionnaire with instructions for use, and a section in judging and selecting teaching media and resources. Resources used in the curriculum, as well as supplemental resources, are fully cited.

433. Alcohol Education: A Teacher's Curriculum Guide for Grades K–6. New York State Education Department, Albany, 1976, 98p; for related documents see entries 434–36. Sponsoring agency: New York State Education Department, Albany, Division of Drug and Health Education Services (ED 143 959; Reprint: EDRS).

This guide is one of a series of three units which include guides for K–6, 7–12, and adult education. This one which focuses on K–6 discusses the following topics: (1) why alcohol education is important, (2) what should be taught about alcohol, and (3) how alcohol education should be taught. The guide also includes supplementary content information for the teacher as well as a resource list for potential use by the teacher.

434. Alcohol Education: A Teacher's Curriculum Guide for Grades 7–12. New York State Education Department, Albany, Bureau of Drug Education, 1976, 120p; for related documents see entries 433, 435–36 (ED 141 648; Reprint: EDRS).

This teacher's curriculum guide is designed as an interdisciplinary resource on alcohol education for teachers of grades 7–12. The guide is divided into the following parts: (1) Why should we teach about alcohol? (2) What should we teach about alcohol? (3) How should we teach about alcohol? (4) Suggested content information for the teacher (alcohol in history, current attitudes toward drinking, reasons for drinking and abstinence, alcoholism, alcohol and driving); and (5) teaching resources.

435. Alcohol Education: Curriculum Guide for Grades K-6. New York State Education Department, Albany, Bureau of Drug Education, 1976, 135p; for related documents see entries 433–34, 436 (ED 163 367; Reprint: EDRS—HC not available).

This alcohol curriculum guide was designed to assist school personnel to more effectively combat the alcohol problem through education as a primary prevention vehicle. "Practice experiences" comprise the most important components of the elementary health education curriculum for decision making. There are units with separate sections at each grade level which identify the topics and the objectives and list the suggested learning experiences. These sections serve as guidelines to school districts in developing their own programs designed to meet their own special interests and needs. At the K–3 level topics include health habits, body care, chemical and nutritional values of food. At grade levels 4–6, topics focus on the nature of alcohol, factors influencing its use, alcohol effects, responsibility, and treatment. Also included are topic outlines for the two levels.

436. Alcohol Education: Curriculum Guide for Grades 7–12. New York State Education Department, Albany, Bureau of Drug Education, 1976, 144p; for related documents see entries 433–35 (ED 140 180; Reprint: EDRS).

This curriculum guide is designed as an interdisciplinary resource on alcohol education for teachers of grades 7–12. Developmental traits are discussed, and objectives and learning experiences are presented. The following topics are covered: (1) the nature of alcohol, (2) factors influencing the use of alcoholic beverages, (3) alcohol effects on people, (4) social responsibility for the control of the use of beverage, and (5) the social responsibility for the treatment of individuals. A division is made between grades 7–9 and 10–12, with each set of three grades considered separately.

437. All in the Family: Understanding How We Teach and Influence Children about Alcohol. Participant's Workbook and Chairman's Guide. United States Jaycees, Tulsa, OK, 1975, 67p. Sponsoring agency: National Institute on Alcohol Abuse and Alcoholism (DHEW/PHS), Rockville, MD (ED 116 063; Reprint: EDRS; also available from Products Division, US Jaycees, Box 7, Tulsa, OK 74120).

These two booklets comprise a new program by the Jaycees called Operation THRESHOLD. Patterned after the US Jaycees Family Life Development Program, these booklets focus primarily on prevention. They employ a group discussion format to elicit responses from people on how we influence and teach children. The responsible use and nonuse of alcohol is given a special emphasis in this respect. "All in the Family" can be read alone, can be used by parent and child, or employed as a participant's workbook in a relaxed, informal group discussion setting.

438. Annotated Resource Guide for Alcohol, Tobacco and Other Drug Abuse/Misuse Prevention Education Programs. Elementary Level. New York State Education Department, Albany, Bureau of Drug Education, 1978, 86p (ED 165 032; Reprint: EDRS).

This booklet is intended to provide teachers with a selective list of instructional aids and resources for use in drug education programs. It provides some guidance in choosing, from the items listed, those to use at the local level. Items listed are: printed materials for children; audiovisuals for children; printed materials for teachers and parents; audiovisuals for teachers and parents; basic sources of information; and regional offices for community agencies.

439. Communicating with Our Sons and Daughters. Multicultural Drug Abuse Prevention Resource Center, Arlington, VA, 1978, 18p. Sponsoring agency: National Institute on Drug Abuse (DHEW/ PHS), Rockville, MD, Division of Resource Development (ED 176 171; Reprint: EDRS; also available from Superintendent of Documents, US Government Printing Office, Washington, DC 20402, stock no. 017-024-00772-2).

This booklet examines the role of Mexican American parents in the educational lives of their children. Information is also included to help parents understand the reasons behind drug and alcohol abuse and to help them lessen the chances of their children becoming victims. Using pictorial representations as illustrations, this booklet explains what parents can actively do to help children develop into responsible adults; becoming involved in the schools, instilling values and attitudes, and providing love and encouragement. Chicano parents should help their children develop a positive self-image.

440. Communication and Parenting Skills: Leader Guide and Parent Workbook. D'Augelli, Judith Frankel, System Development Corporation, Falls Church, VA, 1979, 293p. Sponsoring agency: Governor's Council on Drug and Alcohol Abuse, Harrisburg, PA; National Institute on Drug Abuse (DHEW/PHS), Rockville, MD, Division of Resource Development (ED 176 153; Reprint: EDRS; also available from Superintendent of Documents, US Government Printing Office, Washington, DC 20402).

This workbook has been designed to educate parents in skills for the effective communication of acceptance and the constructive management of power in relation to their children. Included is an overview of the Communication and Parenting Skills Program

(CAPS), a discussion of the skills, guidelines for group leadership, home activities, and an outline of the CAPS program. The program involves goal setting, communication in the family, problem solving in the family setting, drug education, and an assessment of goal attainment. The program is designed for a class of 10–12 parents meeting once a week for a two-hour session.

441. DANE Teen Leader Manual. Blankenship, Betty, San Diego City School District, CA, 1975, 139p; for related document see entry 406 (CM 000 981; Reprint: SMERC—HC not available).

This manual has been developed to assist secondary students in their training as teen leaders and to serve as a resource for materials. The teen leader's purpose is to work with sixth graders to help them relate better to school; build their self-concepts; develop better peer relationships; improve academically; and deal with drug issues.

442. Deciding: Student Oriented Activities for Exploring Information about Alcohol. Alameda County School Department, CA, 1975, 42p (CM 001 207; Reprint: SMERC—HC not available).

"Deciding" is a unique and creative tool for helping students explore information, attitudes, and pressures regarding the use of alcoholic beverages. It is anticipated that the activities herein will enable students to make informed decisions about their own behavior. This guide contains information on the effects of alcohol on the body, on the percent of alcohol in various alcoholic beverages, and statistics on the frequency of the use of alcohol compared to other beverages.

443. Decisions and Drinking: A National Prevention Education Strategy. Proceedings of a Workshop. Davis, Carolyn, National Center for Alcohol Education, Arlington, VA, Jan 1978, 102p; Sponsored in part by the Western Area Alcohol Education and Training Program; for related documents see entries 475, 477–78. Sponsoring agency: National Institute on Alcohol Abuse and Alcoholism (DHEW/PHS), Rockville, MD (ED 173 741; Reprint: EDRS).

This set of training materials was developed for a nationwide prevention education program designed to develop new citizen awareness of the importance of making sound, personal decisions leading to the reduction of drinking problems and alcoholism. There are three packages of prevention education materials presented: Reflections in a Glass, for women; The Power of Positive Parenting, for parents of young children; and An Ounce of Prevention, for Black Americans. The workshop materials are designed so that participants can develop individual plans to be used in their own states. These proceedings also describe a new strategy designed to reach into local communities through the use of community people as group leaders.

444. Development of a Junior High School Module in Alcohol Education and Traffic Safety. Columbia University, New York, Teachers College, 1977, 307p; several charts and tables may not reproduce clearly due to small print type of numbers throughout original document. Sponsoring agency: AAA Foundation for Traffic Safety, Falls Church, VA (ED 177 053; Reprint: EDRS).

Five 45-minutes teaching units for junior high school students on alcohol education and traffic safety are presented. Lesson I examines alcohol as a drug. Activities include a question/answer survey, a film, and a game. Assignments are a "find the word" game and an evaluation of an advertisement for an alcoholic beverage. Lesson II considers alcohol and behavior. Students identify comparative amounts of alcohol in commonly used beverages. Activities include a mini-lecture, interviewing people who do or do not drink, and completing a crossword puzzle. Lesson III explores the nature of beverage alcohol by examining the relationship between the oxidation rate and time. Students list risks and rewards connected with a decision to drink. Assignments are answering questions and listing places where a person could get help for problem drinking. Lesson IV considers drinking and driving behavior. Activities include role playing and group discussions of interviews. Students write a paragraph describing a drinking and/or driving situation in which they could become involved. Lesson V discusses dealing with drinking and driving situations. Activities are the same as for Lesson IV. Objectives, an overview of the content, materials needed, homework assignments, and instructional aids are provided for each unit. Appendices include a rationale for combining alcohol education and traffic safety, explanations of participatory teaching techniques, professional references, and test battery forms with instructions for administering, scoring, and analyzing results.

445. Dial A-L-C-O-H-O-L and Jackson Junior High: Adult Group Leader Guide. Finn, Peter et al., Abt Associates, Inc., Cambridge, MA, 1977, 53p; films not included; for related documents see entries 430, 453, 461–62. Sponsoring agency: National Institute on Alcohol Abuse and Alcoholism (DHEW/PHS), Rockville, MD; Office of Education (DHEW), Washington, DC, Division of Educational Technology (ED 170 655; Reprint: EDRS; also available from Superintendent of Documents, US Government Printing Office, Washington, DC 20402, stock no. 017-080-01773-3).

This guide is designed to assist those helping professionals who work with adults in the area of alcohol education. Although originally developed for use with junior and senior high school students, the materials presented contain pertinent information about alcohol use, deal with significant issues related to alcohol abuse, and provide examples of behavior associated with drinking. Although the films which accompany this guide are not included, synopses of the films are provided together with sufficient information to make this guide a useful educational tool by itself. The content of the guide is organized in the following manner: (1) learning activities with foci on previews, highlights, and follow-up procedures; (2) information about alcohol and alcohol education; and (3) resources for obtaining further information about alcohol and alcohol education.

446. Drug Abuse Prevention Films: A Multicultural Film Catalog. Development Associates, Inc., Arlington, VA, 1978, 58p. Sponsoring agency: National Institute on Drug Abuse (DHEW/PHS), Rockville, MD, Division of Resource Development (ED 168 584; Reprint: EDRS).

This multicultural annotated filmography lists films reviewed and recommended by the Center for Multicultural Awareness. Films included not only deal with drugs or drug use, but also with the cultural and personal conflicts that can lead to problems with drugs. Each film is listed under one or more of nine categories—drugs, cultural values, personal values, life skills, alternatives, cross-cultural awareness, parent education, films in Spanish, and staff training. Included in each citation are title, distributor, length, configuration, purchase or rental price, intended audience, and a brief summary. A list of other film sources, the distributors and their addresses, other films reviewed, and a user comment form are appended.

447. Drug Education Program. Department of Defense, Washington, DC, Feb 1978, 9p (ED 172 086; Reprint: EDRS).

Although designed specifically for schools on overseas military bases, this brief guide for the development of drug education programs for elementary and secondary school students can be used as an outline for any school-related drug education program. The materials in the handbook address the following areas of concern: (1) suggestions of topics to be included in health education curricula, (2) techniques for integrating drug-related topics into other classes, (3) school referral procedures for students exhibiting inappropriate behavior in school, and (4) ideas representing the perceptions of many students about American schools in general.

448. Drugs and Drug Abuse: Alcohol, Tobacco, and Controlled Dangerous Substances (A Supplement to the Course of Study for Science, Grade 7). Bulletin No. 278; and Bibliography and Teacher Packet, Bulletin No. 278-A. Montgomery County Public Schools, Rockville, MD, 1975, 127p (ED 114 758; Reprint: EDRS).

The primary bulletin outlines a teaching program for seventh-grade students on drugs and drug abuse and is designed to supplement the school science curriculum. The program is directed towards providing factual information about various drugs and appropriate techniques that the teacher needs. It also provides appropriate learning experiences for the student. Stress is placed on the physical nature of the drugs and their physiological effects on the human body. It is hoped that this approach will ensure that students will become aware of the effects of drug abuse on the individual, his family, his community, and society as a whole. Suggestions are offered as to potential community resources that could be utilized as consultants and guest speakers. The guide is organized into two sections for each drug: a teacher information section and a teaching unit. The supplementary bulletin contains a bibliography of drug literature, tests for students, drug-abuse symptoms, and Maryland laws on drug abuse.

449. A Family Response to the Drug Problem; A Family Program for the Prevention of Chemical Dependence with Group Facilitator Guidelines. 1976, 181p; publication is based on work done by the Christian Family Movement. Sponsoring agency: National Institute on Drug Abuse (DHEW/PHS), Rockville, MD (ED 153 097; Reprint: EDRS; also available from Superintendent of Documents, US Government Printing Office, Washington, DC 20402, stock no. 017-024-00537-1).

This manual, with accompanying facilitator's guide, presents a program for drug education designed for use by groups of families led by volunteer facilitators. The program offers an approach toward building better communications and understanding among family members. The program consists of six group sessions based on learning experiences emphasizing communication skills. For each session the participant's manual includes readings, exercises, assignments, discussion questions, and suggestions for role playing. The appendix provides necessary background information: a brief history of drugs and drug use, a brief pharmacology of selected drugs, and a glossary of medical/scientific terms. The facilitator's guide includes instructions for each session, specific suggestions for group discussion techniques, and a number of role-playing situations. Audiovisual materials are available and the appendix includes a list of NIMH lending libraries.

450. Guide to Alcohol and Drug Abuse Audio-Visual and Print Sources about the Spanish Speaking—In Spanish, English, or Bi-Lingual. Partansky, Joseph V. A. Do It Now Foundation, Phoenix, AZ, Nov 1977, 65p; International Action Conference on Substance Abuse (Phoenix, AZ, November 8–13, 1977); best copy available (ED 150 990; Reprint: EDRS).

Materials on the topics of alcohol and drug abuse which are in Spanish, English, or both languages are included in this resource guide. The first section lists and describes international and Pan American organizations interested in alcohol and drug abuse. This is followed by lists of audiovisual materials; pamphlets, posters, and specialist publishers; periodicals related to mental health, alcoholism, or drug abuse; books, proceedings, journal symposia, and scientific reports; reference works, bibliographies, and information sources; and works in progress/forthcoming products.

451. Human Behavior and Drug Education. Amador County Schools, CA, 1976, 198p (CM 001 069; Reprint: SMERC—HC not available).

Eleven aspects of human behavior are treated in this guide; self-esteem, friendship, decision making, peer influence, needs, communication, stress, and sharing are included. Learning activities, procedures, and materials are specified. Section two contains ungraded activities related to drugs and the effects of substances on the human mind and body. Part three provides information on resource materials for the teacher which give an unbiased and factual presentation about drugs.

452. Is Beer a Four Letter Word? National Institute on Alcohol Abuse and Alcoholism (DHEW/PHS), Rockville, MD, 1978, 62p. Sponsoring agency: Public Health Service (DHEW), Arlington, VA (ED 174 868; Reprint: EDRS; also available from Superintendent of Documents, US Government Printing Office, Washington, DC 20402, stock no. 017-024-00800-1).

This guide is designed to assist teenagers as well as those who work and live with them in examining issues, attitudes, and feelings about drinking. Numerous action plans are provided to help the user focus on various aspects of drinking and its potential effect on individuals, their families, and their relationships with others. The objectives in the action plans address the following areas of concern: (1) family drinking behavior; (2) alternatives to drinking; (3) school and community projects for alcohol education; (4) legal rights of teenagers; (5) peer pressure; and (6) physical, mental, and emotional effects of drinking.

453. Kids and Alcohol: Facts and Ideas about Drinking and Not Drinking. Finn, Peter et al., Abt Associates, Inc., Cambridge, MA, 1975, 24p; for related documents see entries 430, 445, 461–62. Sponsoring agency: Office of Education (DHEW), Washington, DC, Division of Educational Technology (ED 146 481; Reprint: EDRS).

This student booklet is to be used in conjunction with the teacher manual and films of the Jackson Junior High series. It presents facts and illustrations on the use of alcohol and is intended to aid young people in deciding whether or not to drink. The booklet is divided into the following parts: (1) introduction; (2) alcohol's effects; (3) kids and drinking; (4) drinking problems; (5) alcohol crossword puzzle; (6) for more information about alcohol; and (7) glossary.

454. Making Decisions; Guidelines for the Development of a Drug Education Program. Kentucky State Department of Education, Frankfort, Division of Program Development, 1977, 247p. Sponsoring agency: Kentucky State Department of Education, Frankfort (ED 174 910; Reprint: EDRS).

This guide is designed to provide teachers with concepts and instructional experiences for use in classroom drug education. Teachers are encouraged to develop additional student activities, audiovisuals, and evaluation tools. Activities have been developed to enable students to: (1) increase their knowledge of drugs; (2) develop skills in making decisions about drugs; and (3) clarify their values regarding drug use. There is also a reference section which includes pharmacological information about most drugs of abuse, and a primer on alcoholism. Treatment programs in Kentucky and additional state and national sources of information are listed.

455. Miss Heroin. Riley, Bernice. 1977, 52p (ED 179 910; Reprint: EDRS).

This script, with music, lyrics, and dialog, was written especially for youngsters to inform them of the potential dangers of various drugs. The author, who teachers in an elementary school in Harlem, New York, offers Miss Heroin as her answer to the expressed opinion that most drug and alcohol information available is either too simplified and boring or too complicated and dry. Miss Heroin is a musical play that youngsters can participate in, produce, and present themselves and, as such, should be of interest to teachers, guidance personnel, youth group sponsors, and church groups.

456. Pennsylvania Alcohol Highway Safety Program (Curriculum Guide, Judicial, Law Enforcement, Counseling & Rehabilitation, and Local Officials Manuals). International Alcohol and Mental Associates, Inc., Philadelphia, PA, 1976, 234p. Sponsoring agency: National Highway Traffic Safety Administration (DOT), Washington, DC (ED 151 645; Reprint: EDRS).

This material is for the use of educators involved in the Pennsylvania Alcohol-Highway Safety Program. The 16-hour course of instruction has been prepared to inform both teachers and students of the Commonwealth of Pennsylvania's DUI (Driving under the Influence) Safe Driving School. It concentrates on the development of knowledge, and the changing of attitudes for all DUI offenders arrested in the commonwealth. A curriculum guide, as well as judicial, law enforcement, counseling and rehabilitation, and local officials' manuals, are included.

457. Smoking and Health Experiments, Demonstrations, and Exhibits. Center for Disease Control (DHEW/PHS), Atlanta, GA, 1977, 25p (ED 154 285; Reprint: EDRS; also available from Superintendent of Documents, US Government Printing Office, Washington, DC 20402, HEW publication no. CDC 77-8318).

This booklet of experiments was compiled from various teachers' guides in response to the many requests from students for help in preparing smoking demonstrations and exhibits. The booklet is divided into three sections. Part 1 illustrates a number of experiments, most of which require some laboratory equipment. Part 2 includes a number of demonstrations which can be performed by one or two persons. Part 3 contains suggestions for exhibits. Teachers and students will find this a helpful resource for demonstrating the effects of smoking.

458. Sociological Health Problems: Individualized Incentive Program Modules for Physically Disabled Students for Grades Kindergarten through Twelve. Teacher's Edition. Reggio, Kathryn D. et al., Human Resources Center, Albertson, NY, 1977, 111p. Sponsoring agency: Office of Education (DHEW), Washington, DC (ED 148 044; Reprint: EDRS—HC not available; also available from Human Resources School, Albertson, NY 11507).

Presented is the second in a series of modules from a project to adapt the New York State Health Education curriculum for physically disabled students (grades K–12). An introductory section to the volume on sociological health problems provides definitions and summarizes about nine physically disabling conditions and briefly considers activities at the Human Resources School (Albertson, New York) related to sociological health problems. Modules are described for grades 4–9 (developing a positive self-concept and smoking and the health of the disabled student); grades 7–9 (developing alternatives to the use of drugs and developing self-confidence through assertiveness); and grades 10–12 (sharing and service to others through a combined drug education project). Each module contains background information specific to the topic for nine physically disabling conditions. Also included are listings of concepts, student activities, and student self-evaluations. Among four appendixes are lists of additional resources and an annotated bibliography for specific disabilities.

459. Students: You . . . Alcohol and Driving. Department of Transportation, Washington, DC, Feb 1977, 73p; for related document see entry 463 (ED 147 679; Reprint: EDRS).

The purpose of this manual is to provide accurate information about alcohol and about drinking and driving, so that the student may make responsible decisions about both. It covers youth drinking, drinking and driving, and the individual's responsibility to others in drinking situations. The booklet consists of eight readings, as well as activities for study and for class use. The first two readings examine drinking behavior and what the body does with alcohol. The third deals with how alcohol affects the individual and points out that the same person may react differently to alcohol at different times. The fourth and fifth readings provide information to help students deal with the problem of drinking and driving. The sixth is about drugs and driving, and the last two are about what to do when other people drink and drive. Designed for classroom use with a separate teacher guide, the booklet helps the student devise plans for how to handle future drinking and driving situations involving others.

460. **Teacher Activity Package; Drug Information. Grades 2–6.** Cooperative Educational Service Agency 8, Appleton, WI, Oct 1977, 73p.

This drug information package contains factual materials for the teacher to use with primary and intermediate students. But the total program emphasizes using the factual materials in conjunction with having students learn more about themselves, their values, and how to make decisions. The activities are geared toward several essential areas of drug prevention education: making the child understand what constitutes a drug and how drug abuse is defined; classifying household medicines; and understanding the different effects of major drugs. Charts on different drugs, their uses and effects, are provided for the teacher. Several activities are designed to help the student understand the influence that advertising and the media have on public drug consumption. The overall design of the activities, however, is to promote the proper use of drugs by the students and to help them consider for themselves the propriety of using or abusing drugs.

461. **A Teacher Manual for Use with DIAL A-L-C-O-H-O-L: A Film Series for Grades Nine through Twelve on Alcohol Education.** Finn, Peter; Lawson, Jane, Abt Associates, Inc., Cambridge MA, 1976, 45p; for related documents see entries 430, 445, 453, 462. Sponsoring agency: Office of Education (DHEW), Washington, DC, Division of Educational Technology (ED 145 345; Reprint: EDRS).

This manual is designed to enable teachers to use the four DIAL A-L-C-O-H-O-L films with maximum effect. While students will learn a great deal just by viewing them, it is essential to involve students in preparatory and follow-up activities using the issues and facts presented in the films. The manual provides the following materials to help use the films effectively: (1) learning activities which preview important points the films make, highlight easily missed points, and reinforce and expand on points which the films make; (2) information about alcohol and alcohol education; (3) resources for obtaining additional information about alcohol and alcohol education; and (4) spirit masters for student handouts to accompany selected activities.

462. **A Teacher Manual for Use with Jackson Junior High: A Film Series for Grades Five through Eight on Alcohol Education.** Finn, Peter et al. Abt Associates, Inc., Cambridge, MA, 1975, 44p; for related documents see entries 430, 445, 453, 461. Sponsoring agency: Office of Education (DHEW), Washington, DC, Division of Educational Technology (ED 145 342; Reprint: EDRS).

This manual is designed to help the teacher use the four films with maximum effect. While students will learn a great deal just by viewing them, it is essential to involve students in preparatory and follow-up activities using the facts and issues presented in the films. The manual provides the following materials to help use the films effectively: (1) learning activities which preview important points the films make, highlight easily missed points, and reinforced and expand on points which the films make; (2) information about alcohol and alcohol education; (3) resources for obtaining additional information about alcohol and alcohol education; and (4) spirit masters for student handouts to accompany selected activities.

463. **Teacher's Guide: You . . . Alcohol and Driving.** Department of Transportation, Washington, DC, Feb 1977, 114p; for related document see entry 459 (ED 147 680; Reprint: EDRS).

This instructional program, developed by the National Public Services Research Institute, is designed for the implementation in secondary schools. It employs a student-centered approach in order to simulate the kind of interactions youth experience when making decisions to drink or not to drink. The teacher guide provides background and administration information on the program, as well as guidance on requirements, strategies, and procedures for conducting instructional activities. The guide is presented through a set of administrative guidelines and instructional guidelines. It is to be used with a student manual.

464. **Teenage Self Test: Cigarette Smoking. Discussion Leader's Guide. How Do You Score?** Public Health Service (DHEW), Rockville, MD, National Clearinghouse for Smoking and Health, 1975, 16p; colored print may reproduce poorly (ED 157 928; Reprint: EDRS; also available from Superintendent of Documents, US Government Printing Office, Washington, DC 20402, stock no. 646-388).

This self-scoring questionnaire on attitudes related to smoking includes norms based upon the responses of 7,000 teenagers and a discussion of the meaning of eight subscores. The subscores are: (1) effect of smoking on health; (2) nonsmoker's rights; (3) positive effects of smoking; (4) manufactured reasons for smoking; (5) reasons for starting; (6) are teenage smokers "bad"?; (7) feeling toward authority; and (8) can I control my future? The booklet begins with a list of questions which teenagers can answer about themselves on the basis of the questionnaire results.

465. **This Side Up: Making Decisions about Drugs.**
Cook, Maureen H.; Newman, Carol, Research for
Better Schools, Inc., Philadelphia, PA, 1978, 66p;
marginal legibility of some pages due to color of paper.
Sponsoring agency: National Institute on Drug Abuse
(DHEW/PHS), Rockville, MD (ED 179 854; Reprint:
EDRS; also available from Superintendent of
Documents, US Government Printing Office,
Washington, DC 20402, stock no. 017-024-0076-5).

This guide was developed as a source of information for
young people who are faced with making decisions about drugs.
Written in a "catchy" yet informative style, the materials presented
address the following areas of concern: (1) definitions and effects of
various drugs, including alcohol, tobacco, and narcotics; (2)
physical and psychological effects of drugs; and (3) exercises
designed to facilitate self-knowledge, awareness, and attitudes
toward drug use. The format of this guide is self-instructional in
nature, permitting individual users to explore drug-use issues at their
own pace.

466. **Trainer Catalog of Alcohol and Drug Training
Materials from the National Center for Alcohol
Education and the National Drug Abuse Center.**
National Center for Alcohol Education, Arlington,
VA; University Research Corporation, Washington,
DC, Sep 1978, 347p. Sponsoring agency: National
Institute on Alcohol Abuse and Alcoholism (DHEW/
PHS), Rockville, MD (ED 176 142; Reprint: EDRS;
also available from Superintendent of Documents, US
Government Printing Office, Washington, DC 20402,
stock no. 017-024-00889-3).

This catalog apprises trainers and course developers in fields
of alcohol and drug abuse of existing materials developed by the
National Center for Alcohol Education and the National Drug Abuse
Center. Course overviews and a topical index help the user identify
complete training packages or portions which can be used in meeting
training objectives. Course overviews include package source,
publication date, components, trainer requirements, intended
audience, and instructional setting. A list of course contents
provides a brief description of training methods and indicates time
required. Specific goals and objectives for the overall course and for
each section are delineated. The index serves as a reference to all
major topics treated in the courses.

467. **Viewpoints: Health Education—Drug Use, Misuse,
and Abuse.** 1977, 26p. Sponsoring agency: Georgia
State Department of Education, Atlanta, Office of
Instructional Services (ED 153 121; Reprint: EDRS).

This publication is primarily an information resource with
some suggestions for teaching. It provides guidance and materials
for instruction in elementary and secondary schools. These sources
describe a variety of modern drugs, their significance to mankind,
the respect required when using them, and finally the nature and
consequences of their abuse. It will enable those who develop school
policies and programs to be fully informed about the nature of drugs.
The content of this publication is planned for the teacher as a
resource from which information may be infused into the present
curriculum, particularly in health, science, and the social studies. It
is not intended for student use.

468. **Where the Drug Films Are: A Guide to Evaluation
Services and Distributors.** National Institute on Drug
Abuse (DHEW/PHS), Rockville, MD, 1977, 25p
(ED 155 514; Reprint: EDRS; also available from
Superintendent of Documents, US Government
Printing Office, Washington, DC 20402, stock no.
017-024-00607-6).

This guide to evaluation services and distributors of drug
audiovisuals is intended to aid in the location and selection of drug
films, slides, and recordings. Evaluators of drug-abuse
audiovisuals, film libraries, sources for federal materials, and
commercial and nonprofit distributors are listed.

469. **Youth Alcohol Safety Education Curriculum for
the Secondary Shool.** † McPherson, Kenard et al.
National Public Services Research Institute,
Alexandria, VA; National Highway Traffic Safety
Administration, Washington, DC, Sep 1976, 130p
(PB-258 307/8ST; Reprint: NTIS).

The objective of the project described in this report was to
develop an alcohol safety instructional program for use at the
secondary school level. An instructional program that emphasized
youths' responsible use of alcohol and problems from drinking and
driving resulted from the project. The program consisted of a student
manual and teacher guide. The instructional program was designed
to counter youth information deficiencies about drinking, and
drinking and driving. The ultimate objective set forth for the
instructional program was to reduce alcohol-related crashes among
young drivers. The program was developed as a self-contained
package to reduce noninstructional task requirements imposed on
students and teachers.

BOOKS

470. **Alcohol Education.** Sheppard, Margaret A. et al.
Toronto: Alcoholism and Drug Addiction Research
Foundation, 1978, 2 vols: "Grades 7 and 8" (58p) and
"Grades 9 and 10" (83p).

Each of these volumes contains 10 lesson plans on aspects of
alcohol use, which were developed and field-tested in cooperation
with the Toronto Board of Education. Five of the lessons are
recommended as a minimum subset to cover the more essential
aspects of alcohol education. Each lesson includes objectives,
activities, teacher background, explanations of special teaching
processes, and suggestions for supplemental materials.

471. **Alcohol Education Materials; An Annotated
Bibliography.** Milgram, Gail Gleason. New
Brunswick, NJ: Rutgers Center of Alcohol Studies,
1975, 303p.

This 873-item annotated bibliography cites books,
pamphlets, leaflets, and other materials produced for education
about alcohol from 1950 to May 1973. The major part of each
annotation is a brief summary of the contents. The annotation also
contains a statement of orientation or type of presentation and
evaluative comments. Each item is classified by its main concepts.
Subjects include the following: (1) general source material, (2)

nature and history of alcohol, (3) effects of alcohol on the human body, (4) sociology of drinking habits, (5) alcohol and life, (6) teenage drinking, (7) individual controls, (8) social controls, (9) intoxication, (10) alcohol and highway safety, (11) alcoholism: disease, (12) alcoholism: alcoholics, (13) alcoholism: treatment, (14) alcoholism: industry, (15) alcoholism: Alcoholics Anonymous, and (16) alcohol education. Indexes of publication titles, grade levels, publication types, and major content of texts are also included.

472. Alcohol, Tobacco, and Drugs: Their Use and Abuse. Worick, W. Wayne; Schaller, Warren E. Englewood Cliffs, NJ: Prentice-Hall, Inc., 1977, 170p.

This text examines some of the problems and concerns surrounding drug use and abuse in society. The central theme is that alcohol, tobacco, and drugs are a part of our society and that our failure to deal with the resultant problems represents a betrayal to society. Education and prevention are stressed as the ultimate answer, but it is recognized that rehabilitation and enforcement programs must be expanded, upgraded, and utilized. Specific areas of consideration include: (1) social implications of the use and abuse of alcohol, tobacco, and drugs; (2) theories of drug dependence; (3) alcohol; (4) smoking and health; (5) drug use and abuse; and (6) countermeasures against alcohol, tobacco, and drug use. This text is designed primarily for use in college-level courses.

473. Alcoholism. Silverstein, Alvin; Silverstein, Virginia B. Philadelphia, PA: Lippincott, 1975, 128p.

This text for secondary school alcohol education covers the major aspects of alcohol use, as well as its abuse. Intended for the teenage reader, it considers pertinent problems of drinking and driving, teenage drinking, and living with an alcoholic parent.

474. In Focus: Alcohol and Alcoholism Media. Rockville, MD: National Clearinghouse for Alcohol Information, 1977, 73p. (Also available from Superintendent of Documents, US Government Printing Office, Washington, DC 20402, stock no. 017-024-00573-8.)

This guide lists a selection of media created since 1960 on alcohol. Each citation includes product information, grade level, sale and rental cost, clearance for television, distributor, and a synopsis of content. A subject index is provided.

475. An Ounce of Prevention: A Course for Blacks. Facilitator's Handbook. Arlington, VA: National Center for Alcohol Education, 1977, 36p; for related documents see entries 443, 447–78.

This kit was developed as part of a series called ''Decisions and Drinking,'' which focuses on intelligent decision making about alcohol use based on knowledge and freedom of choice. Each kit in the series contains a facilitator handbook, session outline cards, a set of transparencies, participant work sheets, and ''take-home'' summaries for each group session. Instructions are very specific, thus enabling the facilitator to use the materials ''as is.'' Included are provisions for the use of films designed to be shown with particular sessions, as well as feedback forms to be completed by both facilitator and participants. This kit is targeted to Blacks in the

belief that an exploration of drinking decisions by Blacks must take place within the context of the fundamental importance of Black self-image in making any kind of life decision.

476. Parents, Peers and Pot. Manatt, Marsha. Rockville, MD: National Institute on Drug Abuse, 1979, 106p. (Also available from Superintendent of Documents, US Government Printing Office, Washington, DC 20402, stock no. 017-024-00941-5.)

Presents to parents a strategy they might employ to prevent their children from using marihuana.

477. The Power of Positive Parenting: A Course for Parents of Young Children. Facilitator's Handbook. Arlington, VA: National Center for Alcohol Education, 1977, 35p. For related documents see entries 443, 475, 478.

This kit was developed as part of a series called ''Decisions and Drinking,'' which focuses on intelligent decision making about alcohol use based on knowledge and freedom of choice. Each kit in the series contains a facilitator handbook, session outline cards, a set of transparencies, participant work sheets, and ''take-home'' summaries for each group session. Instructions are very specific, thus enabling the facilitator to use the materials ''as is.'' Included are provisions for the use of films designed to be shown with particular sessions, as well as feedback forms to be completed by both facilitator and participants. This kit is designed for use with parents in their role as models for their children's behavior.

478. Reflections in a Glass: A Course for Women. Facilitator's Handbook. Arlington, VA: National Center for Alcohol Education, 1977, 34p. For related documents see entries 443, 475, 477.

This kit was developed as part of a series called ''Decisions and Drinking,'' which focuses on intelligent decision making about alcohol use based on knowledge and freedom of choice. Each kit in the series contains a facilitator's handbook, session outline cards, a set of transparencies, participant work sheets and ''take-home'' summaries for each group session. Instructions are very specific, thus enabling the facilitator to use the materials ''as is.'' Included are provisions for the use of films designed to be shown with particular sessions, as well as feedback forms to be completed by both facilitator and participants. This kit is targeted toward women with the expectation that an exploration of their historical role in society and the role alcohol had played will enable them to make intelligent decisions regarding alcohol use.

479. Taking Risks: Activities and Materials for Teaching about Alcohol, Other Drugs, and Traffic Safety. California State Department of Education. Sacramento, CA: The Department, 1979, 2 vols: ''Elementary Education'' (grades 3 and 5, 68p) and ''Secondary Education'' (grades 7 and 10, 76p).

''Taking Risks'' involves an unusual approach to classroom activities focusing on alcohol, other drugs, and traffic safety. Although many materials in this field include techniques emphasizing affective learning, ''Taking Risks'' differs from most materials that are currently available in that its primary emphasis is on risk taking as a normal aspect of everyday living with which students must learn to deal. Thus, all the learning activities in ''Taking Risks'' are aimed at enhancing the students' awareness of when they are taking risks and how to make decisions about the risks they take. Throughout, the teacher and the students are encouraged to share in a mutual process of insight and discovery. This course is designed to require a minimum of preparation and training, and teachers may use these materials in many different ways. Some teachers may choose to follow the explicit, step-by-step instructions for each lesson and activity. Others may wish to use parts of various ''Taking Risks'' units, to modify materials for use at different grade levels, or to develop entirely new activities based on the themes and concepts they find in these pages.

480. Teaching Tools for Primary Prevention: A Guide to Classroom Curricula. Knowles, Charmain Duce. Walnut Creek, CA: PYRAMID, no date, 64p.

This guide was developed to offer school personnel, youth group leaders, and others who work with youth (elementary through post-high school) an overview of some of the best curricula available relevant to the primary prevention of substance abuse. The 15 materials included were selected for their focus on living skills, freedom from obvious bias, and usefulness. Each abstract includes materials description, target group and setting, goals, a sample exercise, materials and time needed, training requirements for teachers, cost, and ordering address. Topic and grade level indexes are provided.

481. Teenage Alcoholism. Haskins, James. New York: Hawthorn Books, 1976, 156p.

This book explores many aspects of teenage drinking—motives for drinking, immediate and long-range effects, possible solutions—and offers young people and adults a guide to recognizing alcohol addiction in themselves and others, understanding its causes, and finding out what to do about it.

Index

For the purpose of this index, "drug" is used as a generic term. For example, "Attitudes toward Drugs" includes attitudes toward narcotics, alcohol, cigarettes, etc. When a specific drug, such as alcohol, marihuana, or angel dust, is the focus of a document, it is so highlighted in this index.